Items should be returned on or before the last date shown below. Items not already requested by other borrowers may be renewed in person, in writing or by telephone. To renew, please quote the number on the barcode label. To renew online a PIN is required. This can be requested at your local library.
Renew online @ **www.dublincitypubliclibraries.ie**
Fines charged for overdue items will include postage incurred in recovery. Damage to or loss of items will be charged to the borrower.

**Leabharlanna Poiblí Chathair Bhaile Átha Cliath
Dublin City Public Libraries**

Baile Átha Cliath
Dublin City

SANTRY BOOKSTORE
DUBLIN CITY PUBLIC LIBRARIES

Date Due	Date Due	Date Due

D1357593

Flaubert and Postmodernism

Drawing by Roland Gerards

Flaubert and Postmodernism

Edited by Naomi Schor and Henry F. Majewski

University of Nebraska Press

Lincoln and London

Publication of this book
was aided by a grant
from the National Endowment
for the Humanities.

The paper in this book meets
the guidelines for
permanence and durability
of the Committee on
Production Guidelines for
Book Longevity of the
Council on Library Resources.

Library of Congress
Cataloging in Publication Data

main entry under title:

Flaubert and postmodernism.

Papers presented at the
Brown University Flaubert
Symposium, Nov. 6–8, 1980.
Includes index.
1. Flaubert, Gustave,
1821-1880 – Criticism and inter-
pretation – Congresses.
2. Postmodernism – Congresses.
I. Schor, Naomi.
II. Majewski, Henry F.
III. Brown University
Flaubert Symposium (1980)
PQ2249.F54   1984
843'.8   83-12541
ISBN 0-8032-4143-7 (alk. paper)

In Memoriam Reinhard Kuhn

6 September 1930 – 6 November 1980

The Brown University Flaubert
Symposium was dedicated
to the memory of our colleague
and friend Reinhard Kuhn,
whose untimely death occurred
on the opening day of the
conference. Professor Kuhn had
taken great interest in
the project and was to preside
over the inaugural session.

Contents

Acknowledgments, viii

Naomi Schor   Introduction, ix

Jonathan Culler   The Uses of *Madame Bovary*, 1

Raymonde Debray-Genette   Profane, Sacred: Disorder of Utterance in *Trois Contes*, 13

Eugenio Donato   The Crypt of Flaubert, 30

Shoshana Felman   Flaubert's Signature: *The Legend of Saint Julian the Hospitable*, 46

Fredric Jameson   Flaubert's Libidinal Historicism: *Trois Contes*, 76

Françoise Gaillard   A Little Story about the *bras de fer*; or, How History Is Made, 84

Victor Brombert   Flaubert and the Status of the Subject, 100

Dennis Porter   *Madame Bovary* and the Question of Pleasure, 116

Leyla Perrone-Moisés   *Quidquid volueris:* The Scriptural Education, 139

Charles Bernheimer   Fetishism and Allegory in *Bouvard et Pécuchet*, 160

Michael Riffaterre   Flaubert's Presuppositions, 177

Gérard Genette   Demotivation in *Hérodias*, 192

A Bibliography of 1980–81 Conference Proceedings, 203

Notes on the Contributors, 205

Index, 209

Acknowledgments

The editors wish to thank the following for permission to use previously copyrighted material:

Diacritics, for permission to reprint "Flaubert's Presuppositions," by Michael Riffaterre; and "The Uses of *Madame Bovary*," by Jonathan Culler.

Yale University Press, for permission to reprint "Fetishism and Allegory in *Bouvard et Pécuchet*," which appeared originally in different form in *Flaubert and Kafka: Studies in Psychopoetic Structure*, by Charles Bernheimer.

Revue des Sciences Humaines for permission to reprint "A Little Story about the *bras de fer*; or, How History Is Made," by Françoise Gaillard; and "Flaubert's Signature: *The Legend of Saint Julian the Hospitable*, which originally appeared in different form, by Shoshana Felman—excerpts from special issue of *Revue des Sciences Humaines* on Gustave Flaubert (*R.S.H.*, no. 181).

Nineteenth-Century French Studies for permission to reprint "Flaubert and the Status of the Subject," by Victor Brombert.

Poétique for permission to reprint "*Quidquid volueris*: The Scriptural Education," by Leyla Perrone-Moisés.

Introduction

Naomi Schor

The facts of literary history provided the original impetus for the Brown University Flaubert Symposium, 6–8 November 1980: Gustave Flaubert died on 8 May 1880, and throughout 1980 the centenary of his death was commemorated by an impressive array of symposia and other cultural events in France, the United States, Great Britain, and elsewhere in the world. As we began to plan for the symposium, however, it became apparent that there existed other, less contingent but more intellectually compelling reasons than the purely commemorative to hold this conference in 1980.

In the past decade there were two major Flaubert colloquia which published their proceedings, the Colloque de London, held in 1973 at the University of Western Ontario in London, Canada, and the Colloque de Cerisy, held in 1974 at the Centre Culturel International de Cerisy in France.[1] While both these conferences brought together distinguished Flaubert scholars representing varied critical approaches—indeed, several of them are among the contributors to this volume—it would, I think, be fair to say that these gatherings took place at a time when structuralism was in what might be called its imperialist phase and thus all-pervasive. Since 1974 significant developments have taken place in the field of literary criticism; structuralism has entered the mainstream of academic discourse, and we are now in a period of what has been termed poststructuralism or, in a broader cultural context, postmodernism.

The question arises: if Flaubert was the nineteenth-century novelist most highly esteemed by both the French "new novelists" and the adherents of "la nouvelle critique" who held sway in France in the third quarter of this century, what does he represent for the postmodernist generation now at the forefront of contemporary thought? Or in the words of Germaine Brée:

As far as we are concerned, our "modernity" is by now pretty well spent. The terms "modern," "modernism," "modernity" are dangerous, mined not only by polysemy (there are so many definitions of these terms!) but also by the vagueness and obsolescence of their signifier, unfocused though it may be. Already a new generation hastens to define its "post-modernity." . . . Will this generation find a contemporary in Flaubert?[2]

Before addressing the question raised explicitly by Brée and implicitly by the title of the symposium, a few remarks about postmodernism are called for. If indeed the terms *modern, modernism,* and *modernity* are treacherous, what can one say about *postmodernism,* a term which, according to Ihab Hassan, the literary critic responsible for giving it wide currency, "is not merely awkward" but "conceptually troublesome"?[3] This is not the appropriate place to undertake a survey of all that has been written about this slippery notion; I would focus here on one aspect of the ongoing debate on postmodernism which is particularly germane to *Flaubert and Postmodernism:* however much theoreticians may disagree about the proper definition of postmodernism—and disagree they do; as John Barth observes: "A principal activity of postmodernist critics . . . consists in disagreeing about what postmodernism is or ought to be"[4]—almost all concur in stressing the mutual implication of modernism and postmodernism. Contrary to what the prefix *post-* would suggest, postmodernism in all its multiple manifestations—deconstruction, parody, performance, ornamentation, and so forth, depending on the field one considers—is not the name of a belated movement that follows modernism as Romanticism follows Neo-classicism, or as modernism itself follows Victorianism; rather, it is a moment *in* and *of* modernism.[5] Beyond the shared recognition that modernism and postmodernism are somehow yoked together, accounts of their relationship vary. According to one ritual genealogy, postmodernism is an extension of modernism, an exacerbation of its most radical impulses. This understanding of the modernism / postmodernism relationship we might call Postmodernism 1. *Flaubert and Postmodernism*, for reasons which will become clear in a moment, is placed under the sign of Postmodernism 2, a position clearly articulated by Barth in his previously cited "Literature of Replenishment":

The proper program for postmodernism is neither a mere extension of the modernist program . . . nor a mere intensification of certain aspects of modernism, nor on the contrary a wholesale subversion or repudiation of either modernism or what I'm calling premodernism. . . . A worthy program for postmodernist fiction . . . is the synthesis or transcension of these two antitheses, which may be summed up as premodernist and postmodernist modes of writing.[6]

Unlike modernism then, which is characterized by a gesture of rupture, a rejection of the old and an embracing of the new in the name of progress, Postmodernism 2 is marked by a less spectacular return of the repressed of modernism, a sense of recovery of the usable past unencumbered by nostalgia.

Now the return of the repressed of modernism, what Barth and others call premodernism, has important consequences for our reading of Flaubert, as it may not, for example, for our reading of Balzac or Zola, whose modernist credentials are of very recent vintage. Flaubert, on the other hand, has at least for a generation been canonized—perhaps paradoxically in view of his own rejection of modernity—as the patron saint of modernity: "Flaubert the precursor," in Nathalie Sarraute's epoch-making phrase. The question of postmodernism *concerns* Flaubert studies as it does not concern the study of any other major nineteenth-century French novelist, though that might be debated. What is indisputable, however, on the evidence of work already carried out in a postmodernist perspective,[7] is the capacity of this or, rather, these approaches to shed light on aspects of Flaubert's work which traditional scholarly readings as well as orthodox structuralist methods have left in the dark.

The essays in this volume are notable for the diversity of approaches represented, and this very diversity, otherwise known as pluralism, is one of the hallmarks of the postmodernist era. There is no *dominant* discourse; philosophical, ideological, psychoanalytic, and rhetorical analyses share an ecumenical critical forum, free of polemical posturing and terrorist intimidation. And yet, despite their heterogeneous methodological assumptions, these essays are all informed to a greater or lesser degree by the concerns of the critical age we live in: the status of the referent, the performative aspect of language, the revaluation of the marginal, the production of undecidability, and the pleasure in the text.

The question of the referent is raised explicitly in two essays which address the topic of Flaubert and postmodernism frontally and thus constitute the central axis of the symposium: Jonathan Culler's "The Uses of *Madame Bovary*" and Victor Brombert's "Flaubert and the Status of the Subject." Both Culler and Brombert raise an issue whose repression enabled the modernistic approach to Flaubert: they point to the coexisting in Flaubert's aesthetics of two contradictory but equally strong positions. Motivated or blinded by their own theoretical agenda, modernists chose to emphasize Flaubert's antimimetic pronouncements to the exclusion of his statements in favor of the representational vocation of art. Postmodernists, on the other hand, recognize, in Culler's felicitous phrasing, "the collision and collusion of the representational and antirepresentational" bodied forth in Flaubert's writings. This recognition does not, of course, signify a return *to* the repressed, a regression to a premodernistic view of Flaubert. What it does signify is a taking into and turning to account of the productive tensions between the traditional and the antitraditional aspects of Flaubert's aesthetics and novelistic practice.

The essays by Raymonde Debray-Genette, Shoshana Felman, and Françoise Gaillard all testify to the impact on Flaubert studies of a major development in linguistic theory: the displacement of a Saussurean linguistic model by an Austinian one, the shift away from the stasis of binary oppositions to the dynamics of performance.

This development has led to a new interest in the workings of direct discourse in Flaubert, marking a radical break with a history of extensive and exclusive concern with Flaubert's idiosyncratic use of free indirect discourse. What is emphasized in this Austinian conceptual framework is the force of words, the efficaciousness of utterance. Speech, whether sacred or profane, has, as both Felman and Debray-Genette demonstrate in their convergent readings of *La Légende de saint Julien l'hospitalier*, the power to shape a man's destiny. Similarly, taking issue with Sartre and Barthes, Gaillard argues that, far from being inert and harmless, *la bêtise* is a highly effective and pernicious use of language, which draws its power from what she shows to be its radical decontextualization of speech-acts.

The shift away from Saussurean linguistics, or rather away from one of its aspects, has precipitated another change in contemporary readings of Flaubert: a waning concern with the "production of meaning"—the title of the Cerisy conference—and a growing preoccupation with the production of undecidability. The insight—derived from Derrida's deconstruction of Saussure in *Of Grammatology*—that the play of difference can undo as well as make meaning constitutes a common thread running through several articles in the volume, notably those by Charles Bernheimer, Gérard Genette, and Fredric Jameson. Confronted with the subversion of Bouvard and Pécuchet's quest for a "systematic code of differences" by the workings of allegory (Bernheimer), or the collapse of interpretation written into the endlessly spinning tripartite structure of *Trois Contes* (Jameson), or the unintelligibility resulting from the disparity between *hypertext* (*Hérodias*) and *hypotext* (the Bible) featured by Genette, the reader comes to view Flaubert's texts as a sort of hermeneutic quicksand where origins and stable meanings vanish, covered up by the shifting sands of difference.

Postmodernist valorization of the marginal—in this instance all those Flaubertian texts the modernists chose to ignore—is prominent in the texts of both Eugenio Donato and Leyla Perrone-Moisés. In what cannot be a mere coincidence, the image of the crypt haunts these texts; Donato delves into Flaubert's crypt, while Perrone-Moisés unravels the bands of the "mummy" of literature, suggesting that revaluation is bound up with archeology. Donato's speculations about the uncanny relationship between death and the (lost) origins are grounded in a reading of two celebrated but "unduly neglected" letters in Flaubert's *Correspondance*, while Perrone-Moisés enlists an equally neglected short story in her call for a "nonevolutionist" approach to his juvenilia (the pun is intended: the hero of the story, *Quidquid volueris*, is an ape).

The promotion of the marginal is, of course, inseparable from the demotion of the central, in this instance those masterpieces whose hegemony has prevailed for a century: *Madame Bovary* and *L'Éducation sentimentale*. Indeed, perhaps the most authentically new trend in Flaubert studies to have emerged in the course of the Brown Flaubert Symposium is the pride of place accorded *Trois Contes*. The temptation to speculate on the timeliness of *Trois Contes* is great but risky. This much can be said: the evident affinity of the postmodernist sensibility for this late text represents the final step in a process which began with the modernists' raising of *Bouvard et Pécuchet* to the canonic supremacy previously reserved for *Madame Bovary*.

This is not to say that *Madame Bovary* has become useless, a critical cast-off. A new tone is, however, discernible in the three essays that do focus on *Madame Bovary*: the high seriousness of earlier commentaries has been replaced by a playfulness which, as Jonathan Culler cheerfully acknowledges, owes as much to the boulevard postmodernism of a Woody Allen as to Roland Barthes. The texts by Culler, Dennis Porter, and Michael Riffaterre are all shot through with a kind of irreverence that may either shock or delight the reader but that cannot leave him or her indifferent. All three call upon us to abandon ourselves to the play of the signifier, in the form of outrageous puns (Culler), comestible phonemes (Porter), or titillating kernel words (Riffaterre). The reader is invited to enjoy *Madame Bovary* as a "pleasure-text," to derive oral gratification from mouthing its words (Porter) and voyeuristic satisfaction from lifting its metaphorical and metonymic skirts (Riffaterre).

The eroticization of the reader's response points up what is from my point of view the most significant and surprising lack in this volume: a reading or readings informed by the recognition of the conventions of sexist representation and interpretation.[8] Riffaterre,

xv   Introduction

for example, skirts, as it were, the issue: retracing the fatal sequence
of the adulteress's plot, he demonstrates the mechanisms of presupposition, while stopping short of exposing the workings of ideology in
the service of sexual stereotypes. It remains then for some future
Flaubert symposium to produce what *Flaubert and Postmodernism*
did not: a feminist critique of Flaubert and his critics.

In closing, we gratefully acknowledge the generous support of the
National Endowment for the Humanities, which made *Flaubert
and Postmodernism* possible. Special thanks are also due to two
members of the Brown Modern Language secretarial staff: Betty Lou
Reid, administrative secretary of French Studies, who saw us
through the planning stages of the conference with her customary
efficiency, and Yvonne Morin, our Modern Language secretary,
who helped us prepare the manuscript of the proceedings with un-
failing patience.

Notes

1. Colloque de London: Michael Issacharoff, ed., *Langages de Flaubert*
(Paris: Nizet, 1976); Colloque de Cerisy: Claudine Gothot-Mersch, ed., *La
Production du sens chez Flaubert* (Paris: Union Générale d'Editions, 1975).
A supplementary bibliography listing the published proceedings of the 1980
Flaubert conferences is provided at the end of this volume.

2. Germaine Brée, "Flaubert et la critique récente," in *Essais sur
Flaubert: En l'honneur du professeur Don Demorest*, ed. Charles Carlut
(Paris: Nizet, 1979), p. 35.

3. Ihab Hassan, "Culture, Indeterminacy, and Immanence: Margins of
the (Postmodern) Age," *Humanities in Society* 1 (Winter 1978): 68.

4. John Barth, "The Literature of Replenishment: Postmodernist Fiction," *Atlantic Monthly*, January 1980, p. 65.

5. In a recent article on poststructuralism—"The Poststructuralist Condition," *Diacritics* 12 (Spring 1982): 2–24—with important implications for
our understanding of postmodernism, Philip Lewis writes that poststructuralism is "structuralism's auto-critical moment" (p. 5). In addition to the
previously cited articles, I have found the following works particularly useful
in arriving at an understanding of postmodernism: Ihab Hassan,

"POSTmodernISM," *New Literary History* 4 (Fall 1971): 5–30; Charles Jencks, *The Language of Post-Modern Architecture* (London: Academy Editions, 1977); Gerald Graff, *Literature against Itself* (Chicago: University of Chicago Press, 1979); Jean-François Lyotard, *La Condition postmoderne: Rapport sur le savoir* (Paris: Minuit, 1979); and David Lodge, *Working with Structuralism: Essays and Reviews on Nineteenth- and Twentieth-Century Literature* (London: Routledge and Kegan Paul, 1982).

A notable exception to the conventional yoking together of modernism and postmodernism is William Spanos. In a provocative text entitled "Postmodernism and Its Occasion: Towards a Definition" (forthcoming), Spanos carries the deperiodization of the term to its logical conclusion, claiming that postmodernism is "an errancy that has manifested itself . . . throughout the literary history of the West," and further, "that the postmodern impulse is . . . a permanent mode of human understanding." According to this radical extension of the term, postmodernism is at work in the fictions of Petronius, Cervantes, Rabelais, Swift, Sterne, and Melville, just as it is in those of John Barth, Samuel Beckett, Jorge Luis Borges, Robert Coover, and Thomas Pynchon. In some sense, for Spanos modernism is a moment in and of postmodernism, and not the other way around.

6. Barth, "Literature of Replenishment," pp. 69–70.

7. In addition to works by the symposium participants (see Notes on the Contributors), at least two other references are in order: Tony Tanner, *Adultery in the Novel: Contract and Transgression* (Baltimore, Md.: Johns Hopkins University Press, 1979); and Jeanne Bem, *Désir et savoir dans l'oeuvre de Flaubert: Étude de la Tentation de saint Antoine* (Neuchatel: À la Baconnière, 1979).

8. This assessment reflects, of course, my own critical concerns; see my "Pour une thématique restreinte: Écriture, parole et différence dans *Madame Bovary*," *Littérature* 22 (May 1976): 30–46 ("For a Restricted Thematics: Writing, Speech, and Difference in *Madame Bovary*," trans. Harriet Stone, with a Postscript, in *The Future of Differences*, ed. Hester Eisenstein and Alice Jardine [Boston: G. K. Hall and Co., 1980], pp. 167–192); and "Salammbô enchaînée; ou, Femme et ville dans *Salammbô*," in *Flaubert: La Femme, la ville*, ed. Marie-Claire Bancquart (Paris: Presses Universitaires de France, 1982), pp. 89–104. Both Culler and Porter, it should be noted, do pay homage to feminist criticism, but feminism cannot be said to inform their critical approaches.

The Uses of *Madame Bovary*

Jonathan Culler

It seems appropriate to begin a celebration of Flaubert with the work for which he has been most celebrated. Percy Lubbock declared in *The Craft of Fiction* that *Madame Bovary* "remains perpetually the novel of all novels which the criticism of fiction cannot overlook," and the reasons he cites would make it a particularly appropriate point of departure for a critical conference. "There is no mistaking or mis-reading it," he continues:

> He is not one of those who present many aspects, offering the support of one or other to different critical doctrines; Flaubert has only one word to say, and it is impossible to find more than a single meaning in it. He establishes accordingly a point in the sphere of criticism, a point which is convenient to us all; we can refer to it at any time, in the full assurance that its position is the same in everybody's view; he provides the critic with a motionless pole. [1]

Lubbock, like other critics before and since, uses *Madame Bovary* as the defining example of the novel. It establishes a powerfully convenient point in the sphere of criticism because it is "a book in which the subject is absolutely fixed and determined, so that it may be possible to consider the matter of its treatment with undivided attention." To use *Madame Bovary* as the supreme example of the craft of fiction thus depends on the fact that its subject may be taken for granted as absolutely fixed and determined, and the subject, of course, is Emma Bovary: "The book is the portrait of a foolish woman, romantically inclined, in small and prosaic conditions," or again, "a foolish woman in narrow circumstances." This might seem unexceptionable, but it is clearly not absolute. What Lubbock calls foolishness can be described in other ways. Naomi Schor, for example, in an article on "Écriture, parole et différence dans *Madame Bovary*" identifies Emma as "the portrait of the artist, but of the artist as young woman," of whom she claims that "what she needs in order to write are not the words nor the pen but the phallus."[2]

Emma can also be read in terms of what Freud calls "the difficult development to femininity." Attempting to follow Freud's third road, the road to "normal feminine sexuality," Emma accepts marriage and motherhood. "The feminine situation is only established," writes Freud, "if the wish for a penis is replaced by one for a baby, if that is, a baby takes the place of a penis. . . . Her happiness is great if later on this wish for a baby finds fulfillment in reality—quite especially so if the baby is a little boy who brings the longed-for penis with him."[3] Flaubert presents Emma's thoughts about her child: "She hoped for a son; he would be strong and dark: she would call him George; and this idea of having a male child was like an expected revenge for all her impotence in the past."[4] The passage goes on to contrast the conditions of men and women, and when Charles announces, "It's a girl! . . . She turned her head away and fainted." "The difference in a mother's reaction to the birth of a son or a daughter," writes Freud, "shows that the old factor of lack of a penis has even now not lost its strength."[5] Schor concludes, "What Flaubert understood very well, long before Freud, is that for motherhood fully to appease penis-envy, the child must be male (a condition which would condemn the majority of women to certain neurosis)."[6] But Flaubert also knows, and says, that what is envied is a social role and condition.

Thus the subject of *Madame Bovary* need not be absolutely fixed and determined as a foolish woman, or even, in another phrase of

Lubbock's, as "a woman of her sort, rather meanly ambitious, rather fatuously romantic."[7] Moreover, we could see Emma not as a person with a given character but as the product of a role and position defined by the title of the novel and by its other occupants. The first Madame Bovary, Charles's mother, is presented in a paragraph that follows a long description of the ineffective, self-indulgent, wastrel father:

His wife had adored him once on a time; she had loved him with a thousand servilities that had only estranged him the more. Lively once, expansive and affectionate, in growing older she had become (after the fashion of wine that, exposed to air, turns to vinegar) ill-tempered, grumbling, irritable. She had suffered so much without complaint at first, when she had seen him going after all the village harlots, and when a score of bad houses sent him back to her at night, weary, stinking drunk. Then her pride revolted. After that she was silent, burying her anger in a dumb stoicism that she maintained till her death. She was constantly going about looking after business matters. She called on the lawyers, the judges, remembered when notes fell due, got them renewed, and at home ironed, sewed, washed, looked after the workmen, paid the accounts, while he, troubling himself about nothing, eternally besotted in a sleepy sulkiness from which he only roused himself to say nasty things to her, sat smoking by the fire and spitting into the cinders. [P. 576]

In the case of the first Madame Bovary, also trapped by marriage, what might be regarded as her character is explicitly described as the product of a situation which offers only restricted alternatives. Emma's predicament may be viewed in the same way, but in the critical tradition and beyond, considerable pressures are exerted in the other direction. Madame Bovary is used to define a psychological type, a cultural essence, a basic stereotype. The most extreme example is Jules de Gaultier's Le Bovarysme, which grants that the novel presents Emma as partly determined by circumstance but argues that we must nevertheless assume that the internal necessity ruling her chooses these circumstances and that her "need to see herself as other than she is constitutes her true personality; it attains in her an incomparable violence and manifests itself by a refusal to accept or content herself with any reality whatsoever."[8] One could cite dozens of less extreme critical reactions which perform the same conversion of existence into essence and of culture into nature. Claudine Gothot-Mersch in her introduction to the standard edition of the novel declares that "Emma considers herself superior to her fate."[9] Circumstance is converted into destiny, while her reactions are distilled into her nature, which is then made a cultural type, a major feminine stereotype.

Criticism, says Roland Barthes in *Essais critiques*, is not "a homage to the truth of the past or to the truth of the other, but construction of the intelligibility of our time."[10] The celebration of *Madame Bovary* as the novel of novels is closely connected with the celebration of Emma as a model of human nature. For Lubbock, it is the fixity of the subject that enables *Madame Bovary* to be analyzed as the supreme example of the craft of fiction, and fixity means essence. The events of Emma's story, he argues, are not part of the subject; they illustrate it. Her situation and behavior are themselves of no interest: "There was not the stuff in Emma, more especially, that could make her the main figure of the drama; she is small and futile, she could not well uphold an interest that would depend directly upon her behaviour. But for a picture, where the interest depends only on what she is—that is quite different. Her futility is then a real value."[11] Futility is a real value, it seems, when it can be made an essence, a model of feminine nature. Doubtless we are close here to the famous image that celebrates the masterful masculine surgeon dissecting and explaining the feminine organism.

Madame Bovary has been used and will continue to be used to "construct the intelligibility of our time." Contemporary readings which question what others have taken as given, and which explore the numerous and powerful elements in the text that contest or undo these traditional hypostatizations, are more than new or alternative interpretations. They are attempts to transform the cultural concepts that *Madame Bovary* has been used to establish.

There are, of course, other interests at work in the use of *Madame Bovary* as the supreme example of the novelist's art. Zola, who took it as the code of a new novelistic practice—"the code of the new art had been written"—saw it as a rejection of prior novelistic convention ("the absence of any novelistic element") in favor of what he calls "the exact reproduction of life" but which we have learned to

ROMAN RÉALISTE.

identify as "l'effet de réel"—a reality-effect.[12] By more recent accounts, *Madame Bovary* yields the code, not of naturalism, but of modernism—I'm thinking particularly of the criticism focused on point of view—and, most recently, the code of postmodernism. If Nathalie Sarraute's famous claim that Flaubert's novels were devoid of subject, rid of character, plots, and all the old accessories seems undiscriminating, we nevertheless have in other contemporary readings of Flaubert accounts of how he subverts in postmodern fashion the modernist techniques that he also inaugurates. Thus, if, as Raymonde Debray-Genette has suggested, Flaubert's scattered description of Emma is modernist (because of its rejection of Balzacian setpiece descriptions which introduce characters), one can also argue that Flaubert breaks with this modernist practice by reintroducing achronic, set-piece descriptions—of Charles's cap, of the wedding cake, of Yonville—that are constructed in such a way as to disrupt the attribution of meaning and foreground themselves as writing.[13] Or, to take a second case, *Madame Bovary* is sometimes cited as a splendid example of modernist narrative technique, with subtle distinctions of perspective and frequent shifts in point of view; but it has also been possible to reveal here ironic disruptions of point of view and, indeed, its radical indeterminacy.[14] "Working with an irony impregnated with uncertainty," writes Barthes, Flaubert "achieves a salutary discomfort of writing: he does not stop the play of codes (or stops it only partially), so that (and this is doubtless the *proof* of writing) *one never knows if he is responsible for what he writes* (if there is a subject *behind* his language); for the very being of writing (the meaning of the labor that constitutes it) is to keep the question *who is speaking?* from ever being answered."[15] It is as if Barthes were saying: with Flaubert "the code of postmodernism had been written."

I want, however, to focus on another use of *Madame Bovary* as model of the postmodern. In a paper delivered at the Colloque de Cerisy on Flaubert and later expanded in his book *Nouveaux Problèmes du roman*, Jean Ricardou developed a provocative argument concerning this motionless pole. Distinguishing under the labels "progressiste" and "révolutionnaire" what in a conference on postmodernism should be called the modern and the postmodern, he claims that the test of the *révolutionnaire* is whether it contributes to or undermines representation. He cites as a revolutionary technique in *Madame Bovary* what he calls "Roussellian activity," in which "it is the words that select or determine the descriptions and narratives."[16] At the beginning of the novel, he argues, action and description are directed by the name Charles Bovary. Words beginning in C and B are prominent in the description of the *casquette*, which is presented as an emblem of Charles himself. "Charbovari," the form in which the *nouveau* shouts his name, gives us a *char* and a bovine root, a *ri* that determines *rire* and *ridiculus sum*, which he is charged with conjugating twenty times; but above all "Charbovari" gives us the *charivari* which follows hard upon the enunciation of the name: "Le nouveau . . . lança ce mot: Charbovari. Ce fut un vacarme qui s'élança d'un bond" (p. 575). ("The new boy . . . shouted . . . the word 'Charbovari.' A hubbub broke out, rose in crescendo.") A *charivari* is a vacarme.

Ricardou opts for a genetic hypothesis: the name comes first and directs description and event; as would be confirmed by Maxime Du Camp's famous story of Flaubert in Nubia suddenly crying, "J'ai trouvé, Eûreka, Eûreka, je l'appellerai Emma Bovary" ("Eureka, Eureka, I've got it! I'll call her Emma Bovary"), which gives us not only the name but also the setting, the department of the Eure, from Eureka, and the village of Ry, destined to be transformed into Yonville.[17] However, it is striking that the textual evidence one can accumulate seems equally compatible with an expressive or representational perspective, in which names do not direct action or description but express themes that are developed at these levels. Names in *Madame Bovary* are surprisingly meaningful: Homais is *homo*, Emma is *Femina* or *femme*; at another level, Emma Bovary is *celle qui aima Bovary*. This highly allegorical procedure extends to the names of minor characters, which continue the bovine motif: the mayor of Yonville, as Roger Bismut points out, is M. Tuvache, and Leon eventually marries a Mademoiselle Leboeuf.[18] This sort of detail seems to be recuperating for thematic representation proper names, which usually denote without representing. Can this possibly be, as Ricardou claims, a revolutionary, antirepresentational procedure?

It seems to me there would be two ways of making such an argu-

ment. The first would be to show that this almost comically allegorical procedure violates conventions about names in modernist fiction, in an apparent reversion to earlier modes of signification. The
claim would be that the postmodern Flaubert is invested in procedures that look regressive in relation to modernist techniques. Just
as his elaborate and absurd set-piece descriptions resist the perspec-
tival functionality of modernism and hearken back to the excess and
display of premodern novels striving to be epical, so the significance
of names in *Madame Bovary* is allegorical rather than synecdochic.

The second argument would be based on the claim that the proliferation of bovine elements undermines their representational
quality, making them elements which refer to one another and to the
mechanical process that produces them rather than to a theme.
Shoshana Felman makes an analogous argument a propos of "Un
Coeur simple" and of parrots rather than cows: "As repetitive elements multiply, the referential 'foundation' is dislocated: as repetition is repeated, the linguistic sign detaches itself both from its
meaning and its referent."[19] Once we are watching for it, we can see
the bovine species proliferate. The story commences with bovine
Bovary, still young, a *jeune veau, le nouveau* at school. The novel
opens, "Nous étions à l'étude," and in the opening scene, *Nous*
meets *veau* (later, of course, *le jeune veau* meets *la jeune Rouault*).
There are further manifestations of *veau*. Each week Charles's mother sends him "un morceau de veau," on which he lunches every
day. The ball, the great event in the life of the Bovarys, takes place at
Vaubyessard, and when they return home they eat "veau à l'oseille."
Finally, the artist who helps Charles choose a monument for Emma
is called Vaufrylard, which, according to Ernest Feydeau, was one of
Flaubert's own names.[20] In each of these cases we have a minor,
insignificant detail, apparently working, through its very triviality, to
connote the real; yet where we expect the real, we get more veal.

When such strata of *Madame Bovary* seem to be under the direction of these two names with the same vowels, Vaufrylard and Bovary, we might conclude that it is not a realist novel so much as a
vealist novel. But the question is whether this puzzling proliferation
of veal is, as Ricardou would have it, *révolutionnaire*. One might
argue that this procedure of placing veal in the proper names where

it shouldn't be and mocking the serving dishes where it should be exploits representation and plays between the representational and the nonrepresentational in a move that is, not an attack on representation, but a parodic use of it. If we ask about the relation of such a procedure to revolution, the answer must be that it reveals the *veau* in *révolution: révolution* is a turn of the veal.

What indicates most surely that we should not read this pattern simply as a revolutionary attack on representation is the fact that if we were tempted to reject this vealism as a decadent critical invention, the most decisive evidence we could cite to show its genuine presence in the text would be two thematic representations. If we set out to question the pertinence of puns—*veau / nous / nouveau, charbovari / charivari*—we would be brought up short by the behavior of Dr. Larivière, whose authoritative position in the novel every critic asserts. When called to Emma's deathbed, the doglike, decisive, efficacious surgeon finds that there is "plus rien à faire," nothing more to do, but he does perform one act as he leaves Yonville. Madame Homais, like the other villagers, has been pestering him with questions about health. Homais, she thinks, has a problem with his *sang*. "Oh! ce n'est pas le *sens* qui le gène," replies Larivière. "Et, souriant un peu de ce calembour inaperçu, le docteur ouvrit la porte" (p. 683). ("'Oh! Sense [blood] isn't his problem.' And smiling a little at his unnoticed pun the doctor opened the door.")

That his only act and moment of pleasure should be a *calembour inaperçu* at the expense of a Yonvillais would seem to establish the status of *calembours* in the novel, and this is confirmed by the only information given about Vaufrylard, the artist who bears Flaubert's name. Charles and Homais go to Rouen to look at funeral monuments, "accompagnés d'un artiste peintre, un nommé Vaufrylard, ami de Bridoux, et qui, tout le temps, débita des calembours" (p. 691) ("accompanied by an artist, one Vaufrylard, a friend of Bridoux's, who never ceased to make puns"). The convergence of these two figures on this point is a powerful thematic representation of the artistic and satirical function of *calembours*. So what would confirm the revolutionary, antirepresentational technique of the novel is a convergent pair of thematic representations.

We thus have a complicated situation with several interacting possibilities: (1) the insertion of representation in proper names might be postmodern in its deviation from modernism, (2) repetition of apparently representational elements might undermine representation, and (3) representations of the value of *calembours* substantiate the importance of an antirepresentational technique of repetition. Certainly the phenomena are not postmodern or revolutionary in the sense that they leave behind what they challenge. This general predicament is noted by Blanchot in a comment on Flaubert as revolutionary:

Let us not forget that if Flaubert was assuredly at a turning point, we too are ourselves given over to the requirements of "turnings," this movement of turning oneself in turning away which we do not yet have the theoretical means required to elucidate, sometimes conceiving of it as a movement of historical evolution, at other times becoming aware of it in structural terms and recognizing in it the enigma of any relation—that is to say in the end, of all language. [21]

The *révolution* of *Madame Bovary*'s vealism is a turn of or in that text but also a relation to us as we turn, turn away, or turn it in a revolution that can be seen as a turning back on modernism as well as a turn beyond it. Flaubert's vealism puts us in the position of trying to interpret—without adequate means—the collision and collusion of the representational and antirepresentational: a postmodern situation.

In his account in *La Condition post-moderne*, Jean-François Lyotard speaks of an "incredulity concerning *meta-récits*" or meta-statements which means that a *méta-récit* will be taken as a *récit* about which further *méta-récits* will be attempted; and he stresses the importance in the postmodern society of the present and future, of information circuits whose positions can be interchangeably occupied. [22] In effect expanding Andy Warhol's claim that in the future everyone will be famous for ten minutes, he argues that the postmodern condition involves a greater interchangeability in language games of the positions of sender, receiver, and referent.

We can see here an extension of familiar postmodern *méta-récits* such as Barthes's argument that "the goal of literary work (of literature as work) is to make the reader no longer a consumer but a producer of the text" or the demonstrations of psychoanalytic and deconstructive readings that the reader comes, through a transferential process, to be entrapped by the text in the very act of mastering it. [23] The postmodern *méta-récits* are literalized as *récits* in a recent use of *Madame Bovary* that falls outside the regular critical canon but which is nevertheless pertinent here: a text entitled "The Kugelmass Episode," by that master of the postmodern, Woody Allen.

Kugelmass is a professor of humanities at City College, unhappily married for the second time, up to his neck in alimony and child support, and longing for romance and adventure. In the most intense version of reader-response criticism so far invented, Kugelmass achieves an affair with Madame Bovary (he has exchanged his analyst for a magician who can help to enter the text). This reader becomes an active participant in the text, as long as he can get into the right chapter—before Emma meets Rodolphe, who would be too much competition. Not only has this reader become a producer of the text, he has also become a referent: "What he didn't realize was that at this very moment students in various classrooms across the country were saying to their teachers, 'Who is this character on page 100? A bald jew is kissing Madame Bovary?'"[24]

To explore further permutations of textual positions—possibilities not envisaged in *Le Plaisir du texte*—one should consult Allen's volume, *Side Effects*. Kugelmass occupies all the roles, even writing a new script for Emma in Manhattan. After this unhappy experience he attempts to renounce changes of textual position, but the system of possibilities exerts a powerful force, and as the story closes, he is drawn into a final attempt to enter a text. This time, however, something goes wrong. There is an explosion; Kugelmass "had not been thrust into *Portnoy's Complaint*, or into any other novel, for that matter. He had been projected into an old textbook, *Remedial Spanish*, and was running for his life over a barren, rocky terrain as the word *tener* ("to have")—a large and hairy irregular verb—raced after him on spindly legs."[25] This is a scene where words have the initiative ("l'intiative aux mots") as Ricardou puts it in his chapter on *Madame Bovary*: a chapter which he calls, in a title that would apply better to "The Kugelmass Episode," "Problèmes de la belligérance textuelle à partir de *Madame Bovary*." Allen's episode, which ends with textual belligerence on the barren rocky terrain of postmodernism, makes clear, however, that the pleasures of *Madame Bovary*—described here as postmodern pleasures involving a polymorphous interchangeability of textual positions—depend upon representation, even as they parody and displace it. And when Kugelmass finds himself, not in Flaubert's novel with its seductive and exploitable representations, but in what Allen specifically calls a *text*book, where aggressive words are in charge, this is an experience vividly experienced, if not understood, by the postmodern reader Kugelmass represents.

Notes

1. Percy Lubbock, *The Craft of Fiction* (London: Jonathan Cape, 1965), p. 60.

2. Naomi Schor, "Pour une thématique restreinte: Écriture, parole et différence dans *Madame Bovary*," *Littérature* 22 (May 1976): 30–46.

3. "Femininity," in *The Standard Edition of the Complete Psychological Works of Sigmund Freud*, ed. and trans. James Strachey, vol. 22. (London: Hogarth, 1964), p. 128.

4. Gustave Flaubert, *Madame Bovary*, in *Oeuvres complètes*, ed. Bernard Masson, 2 vols. (Paris: Seuil, 1964), 1: 604. Subsequent references to *Madame Bovary* are to volume 1 of this edition and will be given parenthetically in the text. Translations are mine.

5. Freud, "Femininity," p. 133.

6. Schor, "Pour une thématique restreinte," p. 42.

7. Lubbock, *Craft of Fiction*, p. 79. If, as Michael Riffaterre argues in his paper in this volume, *Madame Bovary* presupposes, and is an expansion of, sexist nineteenth-century clichés concerning *la femme adultère*, then the novel's indication of alternative interpretations of Emma's condition is all the more striking.

8. Jules de Gaultier, *Bovarysm*, trans. G. M. Spring (New York: Philosophical Library, 1970), pp. 13–14.

9. Claudine Gothot-Mersch, introduction, *Madame Bovary* (Paris: Garnier, 1971), p. xxii.

10. Roland Barthes, *Essais critiques* (Paris: Seuil, 1964), p. 27.

11. Lubbock, *Craft of Fiction*, p. 83.

12. Émile Zola, *Les Romanciers naturalistes* (Paris: Charpentier, 1881), pp. 125–26.

13. Jonathan Culler, *Flaubert: The Uses of Uncertainty* (Ithaca, N.Y.: Cornell University Press, 1974), pp. 91–109. See Claudine Gothot-Mersch, ed., *La Production du sens chez Flaubert* (Paris: Union Générale d'Éditions, 1975), pp. 75, 117.

14. See R. J. Sherington, *Three Novels by Flaubert* (Oxford: Oxford University Press, 1970) and discussion in Culler, *Flaubert*.

15. Barthes, *S / Z*, trans. Richard Miller (New York: Hill and Wang, 1974), p. 140.

16. Jean Ricardou, *Nouveaux Problèmes du roman* (Paris: Seuil, 1978), p. 37.

17. Ibid., p. 87.

18. Gothot-Mersch, *La Production du sens*, pp. 113–14.

19. Shoshana Felman, *La Folie et la chose littéraire* (Paris: Seuil, 1978), p. 165. Proper names work somewhat differently in "Un Coeur simple." As Felman shows, they are clichés and citations whose representational inappropriateness works to undermine referentiality. In *Madame Bovary* the very appropriateness of the proper names produces, through repetition, a parody of the proper.

20. See Gothot-Mersch's edition of *Madame Bovary*, p. 465 n. 116.

21. Maurice Blanchot, *L'Entretien infini* (Paris: Gallimard, 1969), p. 487.

22. Jean-François Lyotard, *La Condition post-moderne* (Paris: Minuit, 1980), p. 46.

23. Barthes, *S/Z*, p. 4.

24. Woody Allen, *Side Effects* (New York: Random House, 1980), p. 46.

25. Ibid., p. 55.

Profane, Sacred: Disorder of Utterance in *Trois Contes*

Raymonde Debray-Genette

Critics have never tired of demonstrating the fact that Flaubert, whether seen as a writer or a storyteller, is always at odds with language. *Trois Contes* constitutes a perfect example of this, as it is a condensation of many forms of this confrontation. But in comparing the short stories to Flaubert's other fictional pieces, we find that the religious reflection running through *Trois Contes* calls into question the relationship between language and the sacred more specifically than it does in the other works. It should be noted in this regard that the status of utterance differs from one story to the next in *Trois Contes*, although the narrative and discursive modes are often identical. It is the frequency and the context in which it is used that change its functional value. Though all three of the *Contes* are written with the same kind of technical virtuosity, their aesthetic and philosophic yield differs for this reason. Utterance in *Trois Contes*, from its most infrequent to its most omnipresent manifestation, is always characterized by a specific kind of disorder, which in turn is either the product or the cause of a more general disintegration of the relationship of the individual to the world.[1] For lack of space here, however, one panel will be missing from my analysis: the primary diverting of sexuality toward religion, or rather the sacred, will not be spoken of in this paper. Many thematic and psychoanalytic critics have already dealt with this aspect of the problem. As I am more concerned with forms of narrative discourse, I have chosen to sketch out the lines of confrontation between sacred utterance and its profane counterpart.

In referring to utterance in the narrative, I am thinking not only of speech in its literary sense, as in the monologue, the dialogue, or the quotation (in general, quoted discourse); but I am also thinking of all narrated forms of elocution, be they physical or mental, the responsibility for which is adopted to a greater or lesser extent by the narration. These range from, on the one hand, the naming of an act, which implies that one speaks or speaks to oneself, to, on the other hand, indirect discourse, free indirect discourse, and italicized discourse. I will be following Dorrit Cohn's categories of interiority in this discussion (psycho-narration, quoted monologue, narrated monologue), applying them to narratives which propose a global representation of life.[2] In particular, the psycho-narration is an accounting of utterance in the form of narrative event. As is also the case with silence, utterance—at times hidden, but more frequently mentioned in Flaubert as figure of its own absence or failure—is one of the primary event-centered forms of narrative. From a methodological standpoint, it is not feasible to limit oneself to a linguistically based analysis of all of these forms, unless it be to point out, as Ann Banfield has done, the irreducible nature of literary discourse.[3] On the other hand, what is being studied here will not be revealed by pure thematic analysis that bypasses formal literary aspects either. Narratively speaking, that which is divine and prophetic manifests itself in specific aspects of the language, like direct discourse, figurative expression, or the proleptic mode. Consequently, the theoretical path I have chosen may seem narrow and paved with thin narrative detail. In the end, however, the narrative speaks for itself: nourished with language, it produces among other things a fiction that can be called utterance.

This discussion will be organized in accordance with the order in which the stories were written, for one may well conceive of the group in terms of the repetition and contrast that result from the compositional genesis of the work, with *Hérodias* constituting the most difficult of the three. I will, therefore, return to an interpretation respectful of the order of publication. Consequently, we shall begin with *Saint Julian*, or *sacrificial utterance*. It would seem here that human utterance is sacrificed in favor of a sacrificial Voice. By Voice (*voix*), we mean the utterance of sacred origin (the Voice of God, of Jesus, of the Holy Spirit, or of the prophets and diviners), while by *parole* we are referring to the *utterance* which is human in origin. From a linguistic point of view, this distinction would appear to be without basis. Whereas pragmatically, Voice pertains to the performative domain, utterance is affiliated with the constative— though reversals in these functions are of course possible. From a narrative standpoint, however, this distinction corresponds to several clear-cut narrative techniques that appear in *Saint Julian*.

Saint Julian is the least prolix of the three stories, but this is due to the fact that it belongs to the strict, even restrictive generic category of the legend. Insomuch as the legend is or pretends to be an oral phenomenon, it does not contain many utterances that are attributable to its characters. Instead, the narrator-speaker tends to control the enunciation as much as possible. Interventions are rapid though incisive because they occur in the first person singular or plural and are addressed to an overall community of listener-narratees. "Our father Adam," "Our Saviour Jesus Christ," and the celebrated ending "And this is the story of Saint Julian Hospitator, more or less as it is depicted in a stained-glass window in a church in my part of the world"[4] all function this way. Another, even more devious way that the narrator has of depriving the hero of access to utterance is through the process of exaggeration. Carried away by a kind of ardent enthusiasm that recalls that of Don Quixote, the narrator insists upon the truth of his own words: "It was he, and no other, who slew the viper of Milan and the Dragon of Oberbirbach!" (p. 70). The entire first section of chapter 2 ("He enlisted in a troup of soldiers of fortune which were passing by" [p. 69]) is in fact a marvelous pastiche of the chivalric novel. This doubling of the narrator has the effect of further obscuring the enunciation and causes a kind of fading of the fundamental line of the legend to take place.

What then is left for the characters? In general, we find an efficacious utterance geared toward action rather than representation. There are nineteen instances of direct discourse in this story, though most of these are attributable to beings with supernatural qualities. The hermit, the bohemian, and the deer form a prophetic trilogy: you shall be a saint, you shall be an emperor, you shall be a parricide. And along with them stands the leper, the relentless beggar, before he is transformed into Christ. The main characters, on the other hand, intervene very rarely: Julian's wife speaks three times briefly, and Julian himself only five times—four of which are actually inner thoughts. I will not elaborate on these instances in detail, but I will make a few general statements about them. Two comments are in order: all literary sources of Saint Julian—be they Latin or Romantic—contain a great deal of direct discourse.[5] In Flaubert's version, however, this form of narration is not only reduced; it is also frequently invented. This does not mean that utterance is unimportant, but rather that its role is extremely well defined and limited. As for the Voice, its role is quite obviously to announce various stages of the legend and their contradictory outcomes as well. Curiously, in the 1856 draft of Flaubert's text, Julian's own utterance incorporates the Voice as well: "Mother, I have been told that I would kill you." The final text isolates the Voice and attributes a more subtle role to utterance.

It is worth mentioning that each of the three stories, even in their earliest forms, grows out of a central event that is verbal, without the occurrence of which nothing would come to pass. We have already seen this in Saint Julian. In the earliest version of Un Coeur simple, entitled Perroquet, possibly also dating from 1856, the structure of the story is based on a fully deployed dialogue between Félicité and the priest which serves as a starting point for the confusion between the sacred and the profane ("It seemed to me that the small chains of the censers made the sound of his chain—is this a sin, my father?— no, my child"). In Hérodias it is the myth, or mythos, that we will be examining. In each case, narrative developments should be read as corollaries growing out of the key utterances in question. The outward expansion is literal in the case of Saint Julian: what was predicted comes to pass. In Un Coeur simple, it was metonymic at first, metaphoric afterwards: the confusion is carried through to its final metaphoric resolution. The expansion in *Hérodias* verges on the allegoric, though this tendency is never fully actualized: instead, realization of the figurative utterance transforms it into a consumable myth.

It is the narration, of course, that dominates in the overall design of *Saint Julian*, and, to a lesser extent, description rather than dialogue. What Flaubert refers to as "analysis" does not occur until the third chapter, after the murder has already been accomplished. At this point, all communication, human and animal, is blocked. The forms most frequently used to translate interior life are, first, verbs expressing opinions or sentiments, and second, indirect constructions. Flaubert's celebrated free indirect discourse ("indirect libre"— I′ as it shall be referred to here) is in fact relatively infrequent. It is set off grammatically and appears most predominantly in chapter 2 in the discreet debate between the influence of Julian's wife and the renewed attractions of the hunt. Here it constitutes a résumé of the conversations, reflections, and orders that Julian gives before becoming a mendicant. One example among others seems to me to illustrate the role of utterance particularly well by means of a triple opposition. Julian "told [his wife] of his dreadful fear" (p. 73). This résumé of utterances is apotropaic. Even more perverse is the response of his wife, which appears in a sequence of I′: "She fought against it [this thought] reasoning very soundly: his father and mother were probably dead, but if he were ever to see them again, what chance or purpose could possibly lead him to commit such a horrible crime? His fear was completely groundless, and he ought to take up hunting again" (p. 73). The use of I′ partially shifts responsibility from the wife to the transcribing narrator. Direct discourse would on the other hand shift the burden of guilt in her direction. It is not surprising then that the only case in which Julian addresses himself directly to his wife permits him to succumb to the temptation of the hunt: "I am obeying your orders," he said; "I shall be back at sunrise" (p. 73). The subtlety of the three-part usage of the various modes of representation of utterance is visible here: they avoid the expression of the murderous desire, exonerating Julian, and all the same trap him by the very fact of this circumlocution.

Among the many deceptive forms of utterance, one might well expect to encounter the irresponsible italics, a discursive form which does not carry the mark of its source. There is, however, not a single instance of this in *Saint Julian*. Perhaps, this is because there is no real social discourse at work here—there is only that discourse which the narrator needs to affirm the existence of a communal spirit among the readers. The narrator speaks of the "Good Lord," of "charming paintings," and of Julian as a child "who looked like an Infant Jesus" (p. 60). Such mental quotations are not set off by quotation marks; they represent a fictional and heroic vox populi. On the other hand, we will see further on how important citations set off by quotation marks are in *Un Coeur simple*. Julian, for his part, is actually alone and settling a personal score. Granted, he is born within a social context. His father, for example, speaks of or has read or recited the exploits of former warriors and the adventures of pilgrims to him. Julian listens to them. Even as a young child, he already knows by heart "all there was to be known about the chase" (p. 62).

As for Julian's mother, she speaks a different, more secret language that is at the same time more lyrical than the father's: there are prayers, and the crowing of the cocks, the voices of the angels, and the singing of the church bells become audible. The mother teaches Julian to sing. But the silence, which is even stronger than these sounds, takes over the protagonist very early in his life—and it is a guilty silence: "About the murder of the little mouse, he said nothing to anyone" (p. 61). The silence comes along with the padded, dampening effect of the château belonging to Julian's wife; it is also the result of that wife's choosing not to speak. She does not reveal the reasons for Julian's departure to his parents.

Everything changes, however, when the murder occurs. Julian howls while committing the act, and it is with a voice wholly different from his normal voice, according to the text, that he takes leave of his wife and the world. The latter takes fitting revenge on Julian by preventing him from confessing his deed. It will be recalled how, as a beggar, Julian tries to deliver himself by utterance, to tell his story: people listen to him in horror and drive him away with shouts and threats. He silences himself in turn, but wishes at least to listen:

"The triviality of their conversation froze his heart" (p. 81). Even worse than this is the fact that while Julian agrees to accept absolute solitude, he is unable to attain total silence for himself. Evil noises resound in him: death-rattles, the dripping of his blood, sobs come forth. At last, all that is heard in the final moments of this dispossession is the Voice which cries out in the tempest, which moans and supplicates in the hovel, and reaches its goal without drawing a response. This is a tyrannical voice, and Julian carries out its instructions quite literally and automatically without grasping its significance. In the end, he becomes absorbed by the Voice, though he no longer has recourse to the utterance he has misused. The fact that ultimately Julian is carried off to heaven is a sublimation of his loss of power over utterance and over its receptacle. As much as the ending tries to appear optimistic, this new version of the Oedipus story tells us above all the lethal power of utterance, be it silent or pronounced.

Contrary to what one might expect, there is no real sacrifice of utterance by the charitable Félicité. All of those who have written about her have noted it: Félicité has little gift in this area, or at least few such gifts are allowed here, and those that are seem poor in quality. Yet she does express herself more than is usually indicated, and hardly can be said to have recourse alone to the kind of psittacism (whose inverse is violence) which has already been so excellently commented upon by others that I would hardly want to begin to parrot it here.[6] I would, however, like to elaborate. First, Félicité speaks far more than one realizes: sixteen direct responses, though only from one to twelve words in length, are to be found here. This means that Félicité speaks as much by herself as all the other characters of *Saint Julian* put together. Her interventions range from the modest "Ah" expressed in the company of Théodore to the tender "Is he all right?" (p. 55) directed toward Loulou by Félicité *in articulo mortis*, and includes the accusatory challenge: "It doesn't matter a bit, not to them it doesn't!" (p. 28). This particular remark concerns the death of Victor, but it could as well refer to the entire life of Félicité, as it has been lived up to this point. Félicité's mistress speaks almost as much.

These utterances, in addition to those of the minor characters and the parrot's four interventions, total thirty-six instances of direct discourse (if my calculations are correct). Thus there is a lifelike presence here testifying to the existence of the linguistic universe. But a majority of the conversations are truncated, generally being absorbed by descriptive passages that follow or precede them. For example, the narrator describes at length Félicité's sister and her two children, one of whom is a young cabin boy. Yet the next paragraph reads: "Madame Aubain sent her off after a quarter of an hour" (p. 28). This is representative of the status of social discourse in general in this story: we are given only a small hint of reality. Also, in marked contrast to what we shall see in *Hérodias*, direct discourse contributes little information—with the exception of the announcement of the nephew's death, where a kind of reticence predominates: "'They have some bad news for you . . . your nephew . . .' He was dead. Nothing more was said" (p. 36). What are such passages expressive of? Are they indicative of a stylistic trait or a personality at least? It would seem not, for there appears to be nothing individual or revealing about them—we find just one popular expression ("Poor little lad!" [p. 36]) and orders having come in particular from others, spread here and there like cartoon captions. The actual substance of the story is not vehicled by these instances of utterance, but rather by other narrative techniques.

Nonetheless, brief occurrences of direct quotation, interspersed in the narrative proper, do prolong the dialogue with the world, do maintain the effect of direct discourse, at least until the death of the parrot. This type of rapid intervention allows some of Félicité's idiolect to appear: "To use her own words, she was 'eaten up inside'" (p. 32), and in another example, "To 'occupy her mind,' she asked if her nephew Victor might come and see her" (p. 32). This emphasizes Félicité's naïveté: "Was it possible, she wondered, 'in case of need' to come back by land?" (p. 36) (note the insertion of direct discourse in the sequence of I´). Finally, this technique allows Félicité to adopt the role of respectful servant: "'Madame's bedroom'" (p. 18), "a portrait of 'Monsieur'" (p. 18), "the style of the house" (p. 21), "in remembrance of 'her' [Virginie]" (p. 40). The more typical Flaubertian cliché of politeness, such as we find spoken by Mère Liébard, can be left aside, as well as the unctuous euphemisms of the nun and the gossip about Bourais. It would seem that Flaubert focuses more on the speech act itself than on the cliché. This undoubtedly explains why there is only one italicized expression repeated: "*those* Rochefeuille girls" (p. 44). Thus one is dealing here less with social discourse per se than with the bits of speech which refer to the presence of characters, of Félicité especially, in fragmentary fashion.

Even the I´ type of discourse underlines this citational forcefulness. It occurs more frequently than is usually recognized, though it is scattered and often very brief. Also, at least five such instances, and not the least important of them at that, render the thoughts of Félicité herself. Note that I do not intend to reinstitute the more than fifty years of grammatical, stylistic, and now even psychoanalytic debate concerning the basis and effects of free indirect discourse. [7] As the use of this style is purely literary, we should be attentive here above all to the question of its effects. Paradoxically, when utilized to reveal in part Félicité's thoughts, the I´ is indicative of an attempt to establish an autonomy of the utterance that direct discourse either cannot or does not want to accomplish. Will Félicité manage to elucidate her way of thinking? That part of the story where she receives instruction in the catechism and reflects upon it is of primary importance in this respect. Beginning with a singulative narrative ("The priest began with a brief outline of sacred history"), the narration then shifts to the discourse of Félicité herself, making use of the all-important verb to gain access to an interiority, without actually entering on this inward path: "Félicité saw in imagination" (p. 29). The I´ form of discourse in the following sentence allows Félicité to interpret the life of Jesus as emanating from the life of the fields.

At this point in the text, there are three voices intertwined; Félicité's voice of course is one: "Why had they crucified Him, when He loved children, fed the multitudes, healed the blind?" (p. 29). There is also the voice of the narrator, which carries out the substitutions of the profane for the sacred. Finally, there is the voice of the Gospels, whose traces we find here and there, seeming so natural in the mouth of Félicité: "Seeds," "harvest," "pressing of the grapes," "lambs," "doves" (pp. 29–30). These words seem to fall upon her ear and sanctify her heart as if the Host were being offered to her.

They constitute such an intimate part of Félicité that her reflections about the Holy Ghost are expressed through a present-tense monologue. Except for the fact that there is no direct manifestation of the first person, the technique here resembles that of the most modern of novels: "She wondered whether that was its light she had seen flitting about the edge of the marshes at night, whether that was its breath she had felt driving the clouds across the sky, whether that was its voice she had heard in the sweet music of the bells" (p. 30). Here Félicité speaks, or rather speaks to herself of abundance. Naturally, she is no more capable of aiming for the purity and property of her discourse than are any other Flaubertian characters. *Breaths, clouds, bells* are all words coming from Romantic discourse and grafted onto peasant superstitions. In this respect, Félicité resembles Emma Bovary. Thus we find a qualitative rather than a quantitative insufficiency in her: a lack of expressivity, along with fragmented quotations, and a diverting of her discourse in its sincerest, most intimate forms.

Félicité's salvation in the end will come from her being deaf, which in turn is the outgrowth of Loulou's pranks. Sheltered from the words of the world ("Every living thing moved about in a ghostly silence" [p. 46]), Félicité first takes great joy in listening to the parrot. Critics have already explored not only the type of words, but also the sounds this voice reproduces. The next step comes when—"They held conversations with each other" (p. 47)—Félicité begins to discover a language of her own: "words which were just as disconnected, but which came from the heart" (ibid). Though deaf, Félicité does not always remain silent, as the first chapter would have us believe. Admittedly, during her mourning work for the dead Loulou, Félicité sanctifies the bird, and an iconic form of identification is established. But the most telling passage, written in I′, is doubly related to language: "God the Father could not have chosen a dove as a means of expressing Himself, since doves cannot talk, but rather one of Loulou's ancestors" (p. 50). If "it is language which makes Félicité vulnerable," as Shoshana Felman has so convincingly demonstrated,[8] if it is by means of language that she is exploited, it should nonetheless be recognized that once this point has been reached, Félicité—in the midst of her tears and mourning—has only simple words to speak. Yet it is because of this very simplicity that these words are sublime. Being sick, she suffers "like Madame," she forgives Fabu, she devotes all that she thinks and says to Loulou. As for the parrot, having lost or rather returned the borrowed gift of language, he is transformed from mere voice to the voiceless Verb. The parrot's silence consequently offers Félicité access to a Holy Ghost that is "intelligible," incarnate. Yet he is also seen to be stuffed, a deteriorated and thoroughly destroyed form. Félicité dies adoring an image of the Word [*Verbe*], a sheaf of utterance; but in the end, what we hear is the gentle sound of her heart—the most profound thing she has to say.

Thus Félicité's liberation from utterance comes about through a progressive muting of the Word. In *Hérodias*, much to the contrary, it is a noisy combat between utterance and the Word, between utterances and the Voice, that takes place. Narratively speaking, this story is based on the expansive development and necessary realization of what Flaubert called "myth," this as early on as the scenarios. The myth in this case, it should be said, is a figurative phrase that makes reference to a sacred event: "In order for him to grow, I must be diminished." In the Book of John (3:30), this expression is pronounced by John the Baptist as he tries to explain the humility of his role to his disciples. Flaubert's Iaokanaan repeats the formula in the darkness of his prison. He does not seem to be the originator of these words and needs to justify them to himself. Nonetheless, he experiences them as a parable. In contrast to this, when the same words are spoken by Mannaëi, they remain enigmatic and empty for him, as they do for Antipas. Also, the use of such words is in marked contrast to those at work within the prophetic system in *Saint Julian*. Iaokanann is not alone in his preoccupation with this utterance, for he serves as vehicle for an Other. An intervention from outside is needed in order for the utterance to be filled. Thus the prophet is neither author nor master of his fate. It is most likely for this reason that he is represented only by a voice—a voice that is skillfully modulated. First, it is a voice in the silence. Then, in chapter 2, it is a "diabolical machine," a thundering that transmits the prophecies of doom "like mighty blows," one after the other. And at another moment, it is instead an enchanted voice bringing the news of future happiness. In the third act, contrary to all indications in the first scenarios, Iaokanaan no longer has the right to participate. Not only does this character constitute a voice because of his physical power but also because of the fact that he is incapable of speaking in his own name.

The narrative here, all of which is rendered in direct discourse (for were Iaokanaan to speak in I', the entire face of the heavens would be transformed), is a tissue of biblical quotations, generally taken from the Books of the Prophets and chosen for their violence and vivid character. The intertextuality is very powerful here and so well executed that the reader retains only the excess, as if it were a caricature of the Old Testament. The prophet too is reduced to a voice, for he soliloquizes; no one responds; he resembles the coryphacus more closely than he does a character. "The voice grew louder and stronger, rolling and roaring like thunder, and as the mountains sent it back, it broke over Machaerus in repeated echoes" (p. 109). There is a bit of Loulou in Iaokanaan. The Syrian interpreter, a kind of parrot in his own right, even indicates this: "The Tetrarch and Herodias were forced to endure them twice over" (p. 108). Thus Iaokanaan constitutes the Voice of God before the incarnation of the Word becomes known.

Interposed between this voice and Antipas, we find Phanuel—a mediator of sorts. Phanuel is a mediator first of all in that he attempts to reconcile the interests of the prisoner with those of Antipas. He plays a mediatory role even more so because he is situated at a midway point—not between the sacred and the profane—but between the pagan sacred and the Christian sacred, which he communicates without understanding even though his ideas and actions seem to grow out of it. He is thus an oracle of sorts. We do not know what it is that inspires him when he says at the end of chapter 1: "If you ill-treat him, you will be punished," or "He will go among the Arabs, the Gauls, the Scythians. His work must extend to the ends of the earth!" (p. 98). He is always very near the other truth; he burns; he is only mistaken as to the person. At the same time, he has difficulty in delivering his own astronomical-astrological message, which is put off from the end of chapter 1 to the end of chapter 2. And for the one and only time in *Trois Contes*, the oracular utterance is rendered in I': "From all this he augured the death of an important man that very night in Machaerous" (p. 111). The I' type

of discourse implies interiority: Phanuel no longer constitutes a single voice, but rather a character which is the human, more engaging
double for the intractable Iaokanaan. As the indefinite article ("a
man") indicates, he is not sheltered from doubts by his purity. Of
course, Antipas will try to take advantage of his hesitation, thinking it
possible to change destiny. Having failed to understand the proph-
ecy, he turns to the oracle. Phanuel, on the other hand, will be the
only one, along with his two disciples, to be enlightened by the end
of the story. For there is one utterance never to be spoken in the
course of the tale, which is nonetheless ever present: "At the very
moment that the sun rose, two men who had been sent out by
Iokanaan sometime before returned with the long-awaited reply.
They confided it to Phanuel, who received it with transports of
delight" (p. 124). The response that Matthew gave (11:4–6) appears
nowhere directly: "John is Elijah and Jesus the Messiah." The story
retains this last bit of mystery. Caught midway between the human
and the divine interpretations, it finds its ultimate resolution in
myth. Although it goes beyond the purely historic, it is never transformed into the allegoric mode. The messages of the Voices, among
others, are not directly figured.

Antipas, receiving these words directly or indirectly, is traversed by
them, but understands neither their sense nor their character. He
cuts short their impact. For example, all that he retains of them is a
threat of death. The rest remains a fog of sorts, which seems to
dissipate like Arab tents at sunrise. In one sense we might say that the
semiotics of a character such as Antipas are the opposite of the
semiotics of Félicité. Whereas Félicité understood what were merely
spoken or written signs to be icons, Antipas takes all that is meant as
symbol to be sign and utterance. At other moments, however, superstition reverses his interpretive system and refers back to Félicité's.
No sooner has the name Iaokanaan been pronounced than he falls
backward "as if he had been struck full in the chest" (p. 116). He
obstructs the free circulation of these symbolic messages as much as
possible. As for the crowd, although it repeats them, it has an equally
distorted grasp of the meaning of these messages. To name Elie is to
unleash all kinds of visions in the crowd. This complex of semiotic
confusion is paralleled by linguistic confusion.

Flaubert presents all this in a kind of theater of words (*théâtre de paroles*). He is once again tempted to create a dramatic form of discourse, just as Mallarmé with his "Hérodiade." Far removed from the realist dramatic form, this work looks toward symbolic theater as its model; and contrary to what we might expect, the historicity of this writing does not inhibit its theatricality in the least. The need to amplify the use of direct response, already indicated in the preliminary drafts, and the existence of a widely spaced mise-en-scène, made up of paragraphs that have been broken apart into fragmented incidents, are characteristic of this story. The traditional style of ancient history provides much liberty of discourse. I am referring here to the Latins, to Tacitus and Suetonius primarily, but also to Livy, whose style is recalled most of all by the I' type of discourse, and this at times to the point of pastiche. The marriage of the two models—the historic and the dramatic—is in fact what gives the story its greatest originality.[9]

Flaubert has constructed a modern drama upon the foundation of ancient phrasing, a drama where utterance is protean. The following is one of many examples of this. Hérodias greets Vitellius, and she speaks to him of her brother Agrippa, who has just been imprisoned in Rome: "She added: 'It is because he wanted Caïus to be Emperor!' While living on their charity, Agrippa had been trying to obtain the title of king, which they coveted just as much as he did. But in future they would have no cause for fear! 'The dungeons of Tiberius are hard to open,' said Herodias, 'and life inside them is sometimes far from safe!'" (p. 93). In this passage, we move successively from a verb of speech to a segment of truncated direct discourse, then to the narrator's explanation of the state of affairs, next to a second instance of direct discourse (with neither dashes nor quotation marks, but only an exclamation mark), and finally to a genuine direct reply. All of this appears in the absence of any manifestation of the first person, which accounts for the exemplary character of utterance. It is because of this kind of well-controlled variation from one form of discourse to the next that history seems to reinstate discourse and vice-versa. But all of the techniques of reinstatement originate in the writing process itself and are designed to cloud the sources of enunciation. The movements of the crowds, for example, provoke uproars, vociferations, and sometimes even laughter that would seem unattributable: "Murmurs of disapproval interrupted him [Jacob]. It was generally believed that Elias had only disappeared" (p. 116). I will not take up a discussion of the banquet here that Victor Brombert has already so astutely analyzed elsewhere.[10] It is useful to retain, however, the idea that one cannot attribute a clear-cut position to Flaubert in this matter. Although there is sufficient distance at work in the text for us to experience utterance as a kind of cacophony, there is at the same time enough presence for that utterance to function in a wholly efficacious way. There is a fundamental sense of frustration that remains with the reader as well as the characters. No one is responsible, though each word stands as a fragment of the drama as a whole. Except for the descriptions, which are of prime importance, all else—the summary and analysis—disappears, merges into the fabric of the generalized discourse, of this verbal anomaly.

There is indeed a current passing from the sacred utterance (myth, Voice, or oracle) to the human, disordered utterance, but through a catastrophically faulty circuit. The manner in which human utterance comes into contact with the sacred texts and *verba* provokes all kinds of sacrileges, the most extreme of which is the murder of Iokanaan. What we find here is a struggle between two distinct powers: utterance always reveals a bit too much, the Word apparently not quite enough. Hérodias thinks it possible to benefit from this conflict—first by creating a zone of reticence and secrecy around Salomé and then by allowing her a seemingly inoffensive power of speech. Salomé forgets, rediscovers, and lisps. Nonetheless, thanks to her delicate speech, she charms words out of Antipas, draws the Voice out of the prophet. In this way, she permits the realization of the myth to come about, which in turn allows the Word to rediscover a means of expression—an expression whose murderous power we have already seen in the case of Julian, whose pathetic nature was evident in the story of Félicité. From this point on, the Christian myth takes on the role which Lévi-Strauss has spoken of: "to legitimate a social order and a world view by means of an original vision of things, to explain what things are on the basis of what they were, to find a justification for their present state in their past and conceive of the future as a function of the present and the past."[11]

This hardly means that Flaubert adheres to the contents of this myth, but that he draws attention to its use, and, in a pessimistic vein, to the necessity of its effects as well. This at least is as one particular reading of *Trois Contes*—one that respects the order in which the stories were published—would have it. Man is constantly delegating his power of speech, his very being, to one form of divinity or another, and this in an ever more degraded way. All that he worships diminishes him, with the exception perhaps of art, which as Flaubert would say, attempts to counter this loss with the power of man's own utterance.

[Translated by Susan Huston]

Notes

1. Throughout the text *parole* will be translated as "utterance." "Utterance" would seem to be a more accurate translation of *parole* than either "speech" or "word," since it is used here to convey nonvocal or nonvoiced as well as voiced types of communication.—TRANS.

2. Dorrit Cohn, *Transparent Minds* (Princeton, N.J.: Princeton University Press, 1978).

3. Ann Banfield "Le Style narratif et la grammaire du discours direct et indirect," *Change* 16–17 (September 1973): 188–226; and "Où l'épistémologie, le style et la grammaire rencontrent l'histoire littéraire: Le Développement de la parole et de la pensée représentées," *Langue française* 44 (December 1979): 9–26.

4. Gustave Flaubert, *Three Tales*, trans. Robert Baldick (Harmondsworth: Penguin Books, 1975), p. 87. All page references cited in the text are to this edition. Texts quoted other than those of Flaubert are translated by the translator.—EDS.

5. See Benjamin F. Bart and Robert F. Cook, *The Legendary Sources of Flaubert's Saint Julian*, (Toronto: University of Toronto Press, 1977).

6. Marc Bertrand, "Parole et silence dans les *Trois Contes* de Flaubert," *Stanford French Review* 1 (1977): 191–203.

7. Claude Perruchot, "Le Style indirect libre et la question du sujet dans *Madame Bovary*," in *La Production du sens chez Flaubert*, ed. Claudine

Gothot-Mersch (Paris: Union Générale d'Éditions, 1975); and D. G. Laporte, "Le Lieu commun" *Ornicar*, nos. 20–21 (1980), pp. 281–306.

8. Shoshana Felman, *La Folie et la chose littéraire* (Paris: Seuil, 1978), pp. 159–169.

9. See Michael Issacharoff, "Hérodias et la symbolique combinatoire des *Trois Contes*," and "Trois Contes et le problème de la non-linéarité," in *L'Espace et la nouvelle* (Paris: Corti, 1976), pp. 21–59.

10. Victor Brombert, *The Novels of Flaubert* (Princeton, N.J.: Princeton University Press, 1966).

11. Claude Lévi-Strauss, *Le Nouvel Observateur*, no. 818, (15 July 1980).

The Crypt of Flaubert

Yes, we are bound to
disaster, but when failure
returns, we must understand
that failure as precisely
that return. The "begin-
ning again," as a power
anterior to beginning, that
is the error of our death.

Maurice Blanchot

Eugenio Donato

The statement of Flaubert regarding the fact that "a book is not made like a child, but like the pyramids, with a premeditated design, by laying large blocks one upon the other, by dint of toil, time and sweat, and it's good for nothing, and it remains in the desert!" has often been considered a privileged genetic emblem of Flaubert's art. [1] The metaphor of the pyramid, after all, offers a perfect illustration of the belated prose writer's plight—"When one is unable to build the Parthenon, one must accumulate pyramids" (CC, 3:31)—who, incapable of having an immediate access to a principle of unity which would guarantee the privileged nature of the literary work, has to attempt, at the expense of great labor, by the patching up of fragments, to give the illusion—"I believe in the eternity of only one thing, and that one thing is illusion, which is the real truth" (CC, 3:429), or "The first quality and the end of Art is illusion" (CC, 3:344)—of a perfectly harmonious entity.

The aesthetic principle that governs the unity of the belated work is not organic but constructed—"What a heavy machine a book is to build" (CC, 3:20)—and the author has no genealogical privilege over his production. In fact, the belated modern writer not only does not engender his work but has to face the task of producing a work in spite of his generative impotence:

We take notes, we travel, misery, misery. We become scholars, archaeologists, historians, physicians, jokers [gnaffes], and men of taste. What does all this matter? Where is the heart? The verve? The sap? From whence should we start, and where should we go? We're good at sucking, we tongue each other a lot, we pet for hours [nous gamahuchons bien, nous langottons beaucoup, nous pelotons lentement]: but—the real thing! Can we ejaculate [décharger], can we engender a child!²

This Flaubertian phantasmagorical, theoretical scenario is too well known to warrant an extensive elaboration.

I have suggested elsewhere that the Flaubertian statement "A book is not made like a child, but like the pyramids" could also be read in a related yet different key.³ Since Hegel—and we might recall that Flaubert had read Hegel's Aesthetics—the pyramid is a privileged symbol for symbolical art. Like the sphinx, the pyramid can be said to be, in Hegel's words, "the symbol of the symbolic itself."⁴ In this sense, Flaubert's statement about books' being built like pyramids becomes one episode in the great nineteenth-century debate about the representational status of the work of art. In that sense, Flaubert's statement radicalizes Hegel's quarrel with an earlier Romantic view which held the symbol to be a privileged epistemological tool in art's attempt to produce an essential apprehension of the object in spite of the representational machinery of perception and language. The context of the statement of Flaubert is in this respect significant. The statement comes from a letter dated the end of November or beginning of December 1857, while Flaubert was writing Salammbô and in which he discusses some of the problems he is encountering in attempting a reconstruction of Carthage. Specifically, a few lines before the passage concerning pyramids, Flaubert writes:

The difficulty is in finding the right note. This is achieved by an excessive condensation of the idea, either naturally or willfully, but it is not easy to imagine a constant truth, that is, a series of striking and probable details in a place that is two thousand years away. Moreover, to be understood, one must undertake a kind of permanent translation, and what an abyss that creates between the absolute and the work. [CC, 4:238]

The work of art, thus, will not only be made up by a series of "striking details," but the author will be forced into a "permanent translation." That is to say, into an open-ended chain of metaphorical displacements, and the representational mechanism of this chain of metaphorical displacements will create an unbridgeable abyss between the work and any transcendental principle which might legitimate the former. And it is in this space between subject and representation that we might locate the origin of Flaubert's figuration.

It is this disjunction between representation and an ultimately privileged reality that makes Flaubert's statement relevant to Hegel's treatment of the pyramid. For Hegel, a symbol is defined by the inadequacy of a content with its formal representation; yet, if pyramids are exemplary of symbolical art, it is because in them something dies and what they signify, in relationship to the nature of the symbol, is death itself:

In this way the pyramids put before our eyes the simple prototype of symbolical art itself; they are prodigious crystals which conceal in themselves an inner meaning and, as external shapes produced by art, they so envelop that meaning that it is obvious that they are there for this inner meaning separated from pure nature and only in relation to this meaning. But this realm of death and the invisible, which here constitutes the meaning, possesses only one side, and that a formal one, of the true content of art, namely, that of being removed from immediate existence, and so this realm is primarily only Hades. [5]

If the pyramids signify, then they signify death; inscribing the latter, so to speak, within themselves, they appear as crystals (Hegel's symbolic order is more organic than Flaubert's), but what these crystals at the same time signify and hide is death itself. Death, however, is already elevated by Hegel to signifying ideality. What Hegel's theory sublates is a corpse which is significantly absent from his pyramid. If the pyramid is a figuration, this figuration, no matter in how inadequate a fashion, signifies death. The pyramid can only become a figure—the figure of the inadequacy of form and content—by postulating an absent corpse.

Maurice Blanchot is, without a doubt, the most lucid reader of the problem of the relationship of figuration to death and the problem of the corpse. For Blanchot "not only is the *image* of an object not the *sense* of this object, and not only is it of no avail in understanding the object, it tends to withdraw the object from understanding by maintaining it in the immobility of a resemblance which has nothing to resemble."[6] Figuration reflexively constitutes the image of an object, yet this image of an object resembles no object, since the object which stands at the "beginning"—as opposed to the origin, to use Edward Said's distinction—of figuration is nothing but a corpse: "But the cadaver's strangeness is perhaps also that of the image."[7] But then the corpse undoes the temporal and spatial properties of representation to transform the latter into figuration.

The corpse, a necessary condition for the logic of any representational system, will itself always remain in a relationship of absolute Otherness to it. Using the syntactical facility of French, all we can say is "Il y a du cadavre" or, to use Blanchot's expression, "On meurt." What we cannot say is "A corpse is," or "A corpse is there and then," for we would then have to ask the questions, "There where?" and "Then when?", "Is where?" and "Is when?"; but, as we have seen, what the corpse does is to cleave spatial and temporal identities so as to make the questions of where and when highly problematic.

Death suspends the relation to place, even though the deceased rests heavily in his spot as if upon the only basis that is left him. To be precise, this basis lacks, the place is missing, the corpse is not in its place. Where is it? It is not here, and yet it is not anywhere else. Nowhere? But then nowhere is here. The cadaverous presence establishes a relation between here and nowhere. . . . The corpse is here, but here in its turn becomes a corpse.

. . . .

No matter how calmly the corpse has been laid out upon its bed for final viewing, it is also everywhere in the room, all over the house. At every instant it can be elsewhere than where it is. It is where we are apart from it, where there is nothing; it is an invading presence, an obscure and vain abundance.[8]

The corpse, then, is not an idealized, recollected, nostalgic evocation or conceptual idealization, but problematizes the temporal and spatial markers of representation. The relationship of death to representation is, strictly speaking, dialectical, whereas, within the relationship of corpse to representation, the corpse destabilizes all the oppositions necessary to maintain the economy of the dialectical operation, namely that of negated object and sublated idealized representation or that between object and sign, the function of the latter being to restore the object to an idealized conceptual entity. At least since Hegel we know that death partakes of dialectics; Blanchot's remark, on the other hand, underscores the subversive role of the corpse in relation to any operation that aims at recapturing the lost object in a belated rememoration.

The corpse cleaves the here and now which constitutes the space of visibility and presence. By never being in its proper place and by never having a proper place to be in, as Blanchot would have it, the corpse establishes a relationship between a "here" and an elsewhere which is a nowhere. The corpse inhabits this uncanny space which assumes the properties of the corpse which inhabits it. Blanchot's meditation on the corpse is in fact a meditation on the poetical image and the peculiar representational space it generates and inhabits.

Images are woven in the web of a representational system, yet, if images give us the mirage of the presence of the object and if images can be read or allegorized to evoke nostalgically the absence of the Object—or, in Blanchot's Heideggerian vocabulary, of the Thing— it is only because the very possibility of the image depends upon the Thing / Corpse. The Thing, having yielded an image

instantly . . . has become that which no one can grasp, the unreal, the impossible. It is not the same thing at a distance but the same thing as distance, present in its absence, graspable because ungraspable, appearing as disappeared. It is the return of what does not come back, the strange heart of remoteness as the life and the sole heart of the thing.[9]

Whether we try to read in the image the plenitude of the Object or whether we see in it a nostalgic evocation of the loss or the absence of the Object, speculation always follows figuration. What "precedes" figuration, the corpse of the object which conditions and pervades the image, remains invisible, unattainable. Any attempt to speculate on the corpse of the Thing / Object which subtends figuration can have the only status of a mythopoeic speculation on the absent Origin of representation.

Paul de Man, in his brilliant analysis of Shelley's "The Triumph of Life," referring in part to the illustrations and graphic figurations on the blank pages that follow the unfinished manuscript, writes:

The poem is sheltered from the performance of disfiguration by the power of its negative knowledge. But this knowledge is powerless to prevent what now functions as the decisive textual articulation: its reduction to the status of a fragment brought about by the actual death and subsequent disfigurement of Shelley's body, burned after his boat capsized and he drowned off the coast of Lerici. This defaced body is present in the margin of the last manuscript page and has become an inseparable part of the poem. At this point, figuration and cognition are actually interrupted by an event which shapes the text but which is not present in its represented or articulated meaning. It may seem a freak of chance to have a text thus molded by an actual occurrence, yet the reading of *The Triumph of Life* establishes that this mutilated textual model exposes the wound of a fracture that lies hidden in all texts. [10]

For de Man, then, Shelley's text is doubly emblematic. On the one hand it constitutes itself by representationally staging its "negative knowledge." In this particular configuration, the poem is "readable" even if the critic's task will eventually reveal the impossibility of constituting an ultimate meaning and if the poem's textual function is to undo the possibility of a "meaningful reading." On the other hand, the poem is framed by a margin that is inhabited but also constituted by a corpse which cannot be represented in or by the text but which ultimately conditions the ontological status of the text.

With all the necessary qualifications implicit in the preceding remarks regarding the possibility of a "Theory" that could account for the status of the Corpse / Thing in relation to representation, I should like to refer to one such theory if for no other reason than that it has been the pretext for an important development by Jacques Derrida to which I shall refer in a moment. Nicholas Abraham and Maria Torok, in a number of studies now collected under the title of *L'Écorce et le noyau,* have attempted to reinstate the concept of introjection as originally introduced by Sandor Ferenczi, arguing the necessity of distinguishing the notion of introjection from the notion of incorporation—and hence from the latter's closely related notion of interiorization.

Ferenczi's definition of introjection—namely, "a mechanism

which allows primitive auto-erotic interests to extend to the exterior world by taking into the Ego as large as possible a part of the outside world, making it the object of unconscious phantasies"—differs little, as Jean Laplanche and J.-B. Pontalis have pointed out, from the Freudian notion of incorporation, defined by them as a "process by which the subject, in a more or less fantasmatic fashion, introduces and keeps an object in the interior of his body."[11]

Rather than attempt to summarize Nicholas Abraham and Maria Torok's argument as to the difference between the two notions, with all the necessary distortions implied by such a way of proceeding, I shall simply attempt to subordinate the distinction to my interests and ask the question, what does one do faced with a corpse?

Within a psychoanalytical framework, the simplest and normal answer is, of course, that one considers the corpse as dead and goes through the work of mourning, which consists of detaching one's libidinal investments for the lost object. In one sense, a normal mourning consists in forgetting the dead, or as Daniel Lagache, barely paraphrasing Freud, puts it, the normal mourner "kills the dead."[12] (Psychoanalysis does not say it, but it is not too difficult to infer that at the end of a normal work of mourning one should be left with, at the most, a nostalgic memory of the lost object.)

The work of mourning might, of course, fail and take on a pathological aspect. The failure of a normal mourning is a failure to "kill the dead" and, instead, to incorporate it. In Freud's words: "The ego wants to incorporate this object into itself, and, in accordance with the oral or cannibalistic phase of libidinal development in which it is, it wants to do so by devouring it."[13] The inevitable complications of narcissistic identification that accompany incorporation need not concern us here. Let us simply note that if as Laplanche and Pontalis would have it—"Three significations are in fact present in incorporation, to give oneself pleasure by having an object penetrate into oneself, to destroy this object, and to assimilate the qualities of the object by conserving it within oneself"[14]—these three meanings, far from being contradictory, taken together constitute a coherent dialectical mechanism not unrelated to that of Hegelian sublation. The object is destroyed to allow it to remain ideally present inseparably from the subject through whom the operation takes place. The process of incorporation leads thus to a representational idealization of the object. As such, the dead object is eliminated yet maintained within a representational scheme. The incorporated object will eventually allow a further secondary elaboration in a psychoanalytic context which in turn will exorcise it and speculatively transform it into a theoretical object. Psychoanalysis thus buries the corpse and "reads" the dead not unlike the way in which, according to de Man, we read the dead in romantic literature:

For what we have done with the dead Shelley, and with all the other dead bodies that appear in romantic literature . . . is simply to bury them, to bury them in their own texts made into epitaphs and monumental graves. They have been made into statues for the benefit of future archaeologists. [15]

Following Abraham and Torok, the third alternative, regarding our question as to what to do with a corpse, would be that of introjecting it, maintaining it intact as a living dead, enshrining it in a mausoleum, allowing it to maintain its words, its utterances, its language, allowing it to hide its name in a foreign crypt that inhabits the Ego. The incorporated corpse becomes thus an Otherness absolutely close yet absolutely distant from the representational veil that surrounds it. Yet this operation of introjection is enormously fragile. The name, the body, and the text of the introjected corpse have to remain occult and should resist any form of analytical or theoretical elaboration. Abraham and Torok insist on the difficulty of analyzing patients who have introjected the corpse of an object, desire, or person. Clinically they claim to have accidentally stumbled upon that which is enshrined rather than brought forth through the patient work of an analytical working through. Without questioning their clinical good faith, we may, nevertheless, question their undertaking in the name of their own theoretical suggestions. In other words, we may legitimately ask the question, what is the relationship of an introjected object to an incorporated object or of a corpse to the representational machine of reading?

To illustrate the problem, let me turn to some unduly neglected letters by Flaubert in which he describes the wake of the body of his sister Caroline and the wake of his close friend, Alfred Le Poittevin. Flaubert's sister Caroline died on the 21 January 1846. A year later, in a letter to his mistress, Louise Colet, Flaubert reminisces:

When my sister died, I stood vigil over her at night; I was on the edge of her bed; I was looking at her lying on her back in her wedding dress with a white bouquet.—I was reading Montaigne and my eyes were going from the book to her corpse; her husband was sleeping and breathing heavily; the priest was snoring; and I was saying to myself, in contemplating all this, that forms pass and that only the idea remains, and I had shivers of enthusiasm from the way in which the author worded some of his sentences. Then I thought that he too would pass; it was freezing, the window was open because of the odor, and from time to time I got up to see the stars, calm, caressing, sparkling, eternal; and I told myself that when, in turn, they should become pale, when they should send, like the eyes of those in agony, lights full of anguish, all will be said and everything will be even more beautiful. [CB, p. 431]

What can one deduce from this extraordinary scene? Nothing much perhaps, except that Flaubert, at the wake of his sister, read Montaigne and in reading Montaigne came to savor an extraordinary kind of pleasure. Yet it is this "nothing much" which is interesting, for we can already suspect that the paradox of the "nothing much" is the very paradox of the corpse. It is in the presence of his sister's corpse that Flaubert realizes the noncongruity between form and content. That realization leads him to read and obtain a libidinal satisfaction, not from the act of writing, but from the act of reading. In other words, Flaubert discovers himself a critical writer and thus comes to realize the unique nature of his aesthetics.

Flaubert himself is conscious of the necessary relationship between writing and corpses; in the first *Éducation sentimentale* he writes:

Women do not like death. That profound love for nothingness that the poets of our age carry in the very depths of their being frightens them; a being that gives birth to life is angered by the thought that life is not eternal. Do not tell them that you like the empty sockets of yellowed skulls and the greenish walls of tombs; do not tell them that you have an enormous aspiration to return to the unknown, to the infinite, like the drop of water that evaporates in order to fall back into the ocean; and certainly do not ask them, O pale-faced thinkers, to accompany you on your journey or to scale the mountain at your side, for their eyes are not steady enough to contemplate the precipices of thought, nor their lungs deep enough to breathe the air of the upper regions.[16]

We could, in fact, complicate the scenario and point out the extraordinary libidinal investment on the part of Flaubert on the corpse of his dead sister. In an earlier letter to Maxime Du Camp, describing the same scene of his sister's wake, Flaubert wrote:

She [Caroline] seemed taller and much more beautiful than when she was alive, with the long white veil that went down to her feet. In the morning, when everything was done, I gave her a long and last farewell kiss in her coffin. I leaned over her, I put my head into the coffin and I felt the lead fold under my hands. [*CB*, p. 258]

This necrophiliac scene will be echoed in the first version of the *Tentation de saint Antoine* when Anthony admits having desired a young dead girl:

By dint of letting your eyes wander from above, it seemed to you at times that the pall was trembling from one end of its length to the other, and you took three steps to see the figure; with a hand slower than that of a mother opening a cradle, you raised the veil and you uncovered her head:

A funeral wreath with closely tied knots surrounded her ivory forehead, her blue pupils paled in the milky tint of her sunken eyes, she seemed to be sleeping with her mouth open, for her tongue passed over the edge of her teeth. . . .

Then you imagined her husband, you thought that you might be able to be him, that you had been him; you felt her girdle tremble under your fingers and her mouth moved upward towards your lips. You looked at her: on her neck, on the left side, you saw a rose-colored blemish; desire, like a thunderbolt, ran through your vertebrae, you extended your hand a second time. [17]

Let us return to Flaubert's letter to Louise Colet. Just before recollecting the scene of the wake, Flaubert writes: "Perhaps I am only a violin. A violin sometimes so much resembles a voice that it is said that it has a soul" (*CB*, p. 431).

If he is the violin, we may well ask, who plays the violin, and what melody is being played? The melody is perhaps Montaigne's—or that of any of the innumerable texts which constitute the backbone of Flaubert's belated literary enterprise. Still, the name of the virtuoso remains absent and perhaps has to remain so. The temptation is, of course, to name the player, to say that in fact Flaubert has introjected his sister's body, that it is the corpse that plays the instrument, that the content is separated from the form because the content belongs to the corpse; yet that is a step we cannot take.

Precisely because we suspect that the corpse manipulates this scene of the birth of a certain type of literary representation, we must allow for that very corpse to determine the limits and nature of our discourse as well as those of the text that we call Flaubert.

Not surprisingly, Flaubert constructs a similar scenario when his friend Alfred Le Poittevin dies. Flaubert's unique affection and attachment to Alfred Le Poittevin is well known, as is the fact that the friend acted as a literary and philosophical mentor to the budding writer. In a letter to Maxime Du Camp describing the wake of his friend, Flaubert writes:

Alfred died on Monday night at midnight. I buried him yesterday, and I am now back. I buried him in his shroud, I gave him the kiss of farewell, and I saw his coffin being sealed. I spent two very full days there. While watching over him, I read Creuzer's *Les Religions de l'antiquité*. The window was open, the night was superb, one could hear the cock crow, and a night-butterfly was fluttering around the torches. I shall never forget all that, neither the look on Alfred's face nor the first night at midnight, the distant sound of a hunting horn that came to me through the woods. . . . The last night I read the *Feuilles d'automne*. I kept coming across pieces that he liked best or that for me had some relation to the present situation. From time to time I got up and went to lift the veil that they had placed on his face, and looked at him. I was myself bundled up in a coat that belonged to my father and that he had worn only once, the day of Caroline's wedding. . . . There, my dear friend, you have what I have lived through since Tuesday night. I have had unheard-of perceptions and flashes of untranslatable ideas. Many things have been coming back to me with choirs of music and whiffs of perfume. . . . I feel the need to say incomprehensible things. [B, p. 493]

Again, we are faced with a scenario that stages the presumed origin of literary representation. Flaubert himself gives us a clue as to the relationship between this scene and that of his sister's wake, remembering that he was wearing the coat that his father wore at Caroline's wedding, that is to say, on the day on which she wore the dress that was to become her shroud. Alfred Le Poittevin is also covered with a shroud—like a Christ about to be entombed, not to be resurrected in body but as a vision, text, music, and perfume, that is to say, as representation.

Flaubert again reads; the choice of texts, however, is not his. "Accidentally" he comes across either passages that the dead liked or that bear some relation to the scene that the corpse inhabits; more importantly, however, the narrator reads the French translation of Georg Friedrich Creuzer's *Symbolik und Mythologie*, translated in French under the title of *Les Religions de l'antiquité*. The choice of this text is again far from innocent, for Creuzer's book is the foundation of Flaubert's *La Tentation de saint Antoine*, which he was to qualify as "the work of all my life." *La Tentation de saint Antoine* is in a sense a reading of *Les Religions de l'antiquité*, but such a reading does not reveal the content or the adequation of form to content of the text but translates it into pure form, "music," "perfume," "incomprehensible things," detached from any ordinary content.

More importantly, however, Flaubert will problematize the representational machine triggered by Alfred Le Poittevin's corpse. What he sees, hears, and understands is strictly speaking unrepresentable, and the statements describing the unrepresentable will be "meaningless" oxymorons—"unheard of perceptions," "flashes of untranslatable ideas." His final wish will be to say "incomprehensible things," and yet it is the need to utter "incomprehensible things" which will be the foundation of his literary career. In the last analysis, Flaubert's literary output will necessarily refer to another text which by definition will remain as unreadable as it is unalterable.

As I suggested, Flaubert provides us with a mythopoeic staging for the generation of a representational system. Unlike earlier romantics like Keats and Shelley, however, the corpse that governs the scene is the corpse of another—another corpse—and the representational quest, rather than being one of writing, is one of reading. If such a discrimination is important in characterizing Flaubert's text—or any text for that matter, witness de Man's reading of Shelley's "The Triumph of Life"—and if such a distinction is only a practical one, nevertheless, it may serve the purpose of reminding us that the critic and the analyst are in no way privileged. Neither the critic nor the analyst will ever succeed in grounding a theory of the relation of the corpse to representation and in their reading will never know who reads. The knowledge of the dead which we, perhaps, carry in us will have to remain every bit as occult as the corpses that lie hidden in the texts which we read, for can we be so certain that Abraham and

Torok's theory is, in fact, a theory which allows them to exorcise the corpses hidden in the crypts of their patients?

We might never have felt the need to ask that question had it not been for Derrida's *Fors*. On the surface, *Fors* is not a problematic text; assuming the role of an introduction to the collected works of Abraham and Torok and particularly their own reading of the Wolf-man, it pretends to underscore their most important contribution to psychoanalytical theory, namely their elaboration of the notions of introjection, of a dead / live body maintained within a Crypt itself within the Ego, where it stands in relative independence from the latter.

Let us briefly attempt to characterize Derrida's elaboration of the notion of the crypt. A crypt is the phantasmatic, hermetically sealed space which surrounds, encloses, hides, yet maintains, a corpse introjected by the Ego. The inhabitant of the crypt is always "a living-dead, a dead entity we are perfectly willing to keep alive, but *as* dead, one we are willing to keep, as long as we keep it, within us, intact in any way save as living."[18]

The phantasmatic space of the crypt is a linguistic space as well; as such it encloses and maintains a hidden name through the elaboration of a cryptic code whose function is to dissolve or mislead a symbol or sign which attempts to penetrate it or to read the name that it hides.

Since the crypt escapes its inscription in any representational system, perceptual or verbal, a crypt "does not present itself. The grounds [*lieux*] are so disposed as to disguise and to hide: something, always a body in some way. But also to disguise the act of hiding and to hide the disguise: the crypt hides as it holds" (*F*, p. 67). And hence cannot, strictly speaking, be temporally or spatially located: "The crypt keeps an undiscoverable place" (*F*, p. 65).

Following Derrida's argument, one might be tempted to say that a crypt is by its singular nature undecipherable, its language untranslatable, and the name it conceals unreadable, that any attempt to read a crypt not only reduces an introjection to an incorporation, the crypt to a funerary monument, and the noun to a metaphor, but that such a reading, or more precisely—and literally—such a translation is itself an *effect* of the Crypt.

Derrida himself suggests that Abraham and Torok's attempt to read the crypt of the wolf-man is, on the one hand, such a reduction: "What happens here—I speak of both an *event* and a *monument*—will at first be analogous to an archaeological decipherment."[19] But on the other hand such an attempt reads "like a novel, a poem, a myth, a drama, the whole thing in a plural translation" (*F*, p. 82). That is to say, reads as literature, and hence Abraham and Torok's theoretical undertaking is itself, like Flaubert's, a scenario for the birth of literature.

One suspects, however, that the ultimate aim of Derrida is not simply to provide a sympathetic, even though problematical, introduction to the work of Abraham and Torok. In a gesture that is strictly his, Derrida, in an obvious reference to Heidegger, relates the crypt with the Thing: "What, originally, is a Thing? What is called Thinking . . . indicates that the Thing is to be thought out *starting from* the Crypt, the Thing as a 'crypt-effect'" (*F*, p. 66).

The elaboration of this Heideggerian reference is better left to Derrida. Let us simply note that it is in this context that Derrida reveals the ultimate aim of his essay. After elaborating on the literary forms to which Abraham and Torok have to resort in their attempt to uncrypt the wolf-man, Derrida points to the insufficiency of these very forms to recuperate the Thing which lies buried in the crypt and concludes:

But if this description is still insufficient, it is because it does not explain the necessity of this recourse to all these "forms." That necessity, it seems to me, springs in the final analysis from the *cryptic* structure of the ultimate "referent." The referent is constructed in such a way as never to present itself "in person," not even as the object of a theoretical discourse within the traditional norms. The Thing is encrypted. Not *within* the crypt (the Self's safe) but *by* the crypt and *in* the Unconscious. The "narrated" event, reconstituted by a novelistic, mytho-dramatico-poetic genesis, never appears. [*F*, p. 33]

Representation, then, and hence literature, is the effect of the occultation of the "ultimate referent" which can only be evoked as "The Thing" which lies buried in the crypt. Ultimately, the thrust of Derrida's textual operation points to Hegel, for the postulation of the inevitably cryptic nature of the Thing establishes, in fact, the breakdown, at the origin, of the Hegelian dialectic, the original incapacity for dialectics to recuperate the Thing, and states dialectics as an after-effect of the originally cryptic nature of the Thing. As Derrida would have it, the crypt maintains and suppresses without any possible synthesis. What the crypt commemorates is not "the object itself, but its exclusion" (F, p. 72).

Derrida's Fors acts then as a generative scenario for both writing and reading and stands in a reading relation to the earlier statements of Derrida regarding death and representation, pointing to the necessary Hegelian complicity of his earlier formulation. But if Fors reads, it reads by pointing to the limits of reading, inserting itself as a theoretical crypt within Derrida's philosophical corpus and infinitely problematizing his signature.

To conclude—the critic, like the writer and analyst, reads, writes, translates, and in the accomplishment of his task manipulates a number of representational systems, contemplates images without body, speculatively generates abstract and transparent idealities. Nevertheless, ultimately the bodies, names, or things which generate these representations are occulted by them. We may all share a necrophiliac desire to "track down the path to the tomb, then to violate a sepulchre" (F, p. 97), yet we must also recognize the impossibility of the task and the necessary failure of our undertaking—pun intended.

If, as readers and critics—after Flaubert from the standpoint of our repeated belatedness—we name and we sign, we may have to resign ourselves to the fact that we may never know to whom the signature properly belongs, for, to quote Flaubert one last time, "one dies almost always in the uncertainty of one's own proper name, unless one is an imbecile" (CB, p. 114).

Notes

1. Gustave Flaubert, *Correspondance*, 9 vols. (Paris: Louis Conard, 1926–33), 4:239–240. Hereafter, this edition will be referred to parenthetically within the text as CC. Throughout this essay, all translations are my own unless otherwise noted.

2. Flaubert, *Correspondance*, *1830–1851*, ed. Jean Bruneau, vol. 1 (Paris: Pléiade, 1973), p. 628. Further references to this edition and volume will be referred to parenthetically within the text as *CB*.

3. See my "The Idioms of the *Text*: Notes on the Language of Philosophy and the Fictions of Literature," in *Glyph 2* (Baltimore, Md.: Johns Hopkins University Press, 1977), pp. 8–9.

4. Georg Wilhelm Friedrich Hegel, *Aesthetics*, trans. T. M. Knox, 2 vols. (Oxford: Oxford University Press, Clarendon Press, 1975), 1:360.

5. Ibid., p. 356.

6. Maurice Blanchot, *L'Espace littéraire*, (Paris: Gallimard, 1962); trans. Ann Smock, *The Space of Literature* (Lincoln: University of Nebraska Press, 1982), p. 260.

7. Ibid., p. 256.

8. Ibid., pp. 256, 259.

9. Ibid., pp. 255–56.

10. Paul de Man, "Shelley Disfigured," in *Deconstruction and Criticism*, by Harold Bloom et al. (New York: Continuum, 1979), pp. 66–67.

11. Sandor Ferenczi's *First Contribution*, 1909, p. 40; in *Vocabulaire de la psychanalyse*, by Jean Laplanche and J.-B. Pontalis (Paris: Presses Universitaires de France, 1967); Laplanche and Pontalis, *Vocabulaire*, pp. 200, 209.

12. Daniel Lagache, "Le Travail de deuil," *Revue française de psychanalyse* 10, no. 4, (1938): 695, quoted in Laplanche and Pontalis, article: "Travail du deuil," p. 504.

13. "Mourning and Melancholia," in *The Standard Edition of the Complete Psychological Works of Sigmund Freud*, ed. and trans. James Strachey, vol. 14 (London: Hogarth Press, 1957), pp. 249–50.

14. Laplanche et Pontalis, *Vocabulaire*, p. 200.

15. De Man, "Shelley Disfigured," p. 67.

16. Flaubert, *L'Education sentimentale*; *Version de 1845*, in *Oeuvres complètes*, 2 vols. (Paris: Seuil, 1964), 1:323.

17. Gustave Flaubert, *La Tentation de saint Antoine: Version de 1849*, in *Oeuvres complètes*, 2 vols. (Paris: Seuil, 1964), 1:379–80.

18. Jacques Derrida, "Fors," trans. Barbara Johnson, *Georgia Review* 31 (1977): 78. Hereafter cited parenthetically within the text as *F*.

19. Quoted from a leaflet inserted in *Le Verbier de l'homme aux loups*, by Nicholas Abraham and Maria Torok (Paris: Aubier-Flammarion, 1976).

Flaubert's Signature:
The Legend of Saint Julian the Hospitable

Shoshana Felman

An uncanny superimposition of the myths of Oedipus and of Christ, *The Legend of Saint Julian the Hospitable* is the strange story of Christ the murderer and / or of Oedipus the saint: the story of a child who kills his parents only to be sainted by this very deed, which turns out to be at once his fated cross and his redeeming Calvary.

The tale, divided into three parts strictly calculated in conception and composition, does not articulate a simple chronology or succession of events, but a veritable narrative logic, a *structural necessity* that links, through the central murder of the parents (chapter 2), the initial story of the child (chapter 1) and the final legend of the saint (chapter 3). The parents' murder, by its mediate position, would appear, then, as the paradoxical transition, as the unexpected necessary juncture between the *birth of a child* and the *birth of a legend*. Through the mediating gap thus structurally produced by the murder, two underlying questions seem to be concurrently inscribed in—and articulated by—Flaubert's text:

What is a child?

What is a legend?

I

Julian's Destiny

What is a child? A child, the text seems to suggest, is first of all a dream: the combined dream of his two parents.

Rejoice, oh mother! Your son will be a saint![1]

says the apparition of a hermit to the mother; and to the father, a beggar looming up from the mist predicts:

Ah! Ah! Your son! . . . Much blood! . . . Much glory! . . . Always happy! An emperor's family. [P. 178]

What is the meaning of these two prophecies regarding Julian's destiny? In what way do the oracles reveal the origin, at once of the child's fate and of the legend's meaning?

_We may note, to begin with, the way in which the oracle of Julian's destiny significantly differs from the oracle concerning Oedipus. In the Oedipus myth, the parents receive—by way of a divine *curse*—a *single* oracular message warning them of the *misfortune* their son will bring them. Here, the parents receive two separate messages—*two* oracles—which they perceive, not as a curse, but on the contrary as a *blessing*. Their son appears in the oracular message, not as an agent of misfortune, but as a promise of good fortune:

He was dazzled by the splendors destined for his son, even though the *promise* of these splendors was not clear. [P. 179]

The underlying Flaubertian question, *What is a child?*, here translates textually into the following question: Why does the promise of good fortune the child embodies prove to be, as such, incapable of fulfillment? Why can't Julian keep the promise he is supposed to be except by transforming its good fortune into bad? How—and why—is the blessing changed into a curse?[2]

If the destiny of Oedipus—the fatal curse uttered to the parents—is here ironically believed to be a blessing, and if the divine message concerning Julian divides itself into two distinct predictions separately given to the mother and the father, it is because Flaubertian oracle in reality only returns to each parent *his own* unconscious message, his own *desire* for the child.

In both cases, in effect, the text discreetly puts in question the objective reality of the oracle: no one but the father and the mother sees the respective apparitions.

The next day, all the servants questioned said that they had seen no hermit. [P. 178]

The good nobleman looked right and left, called out as loudly as he could. No one! The wind was whistling, and the morning mists were clearing away. [P. 179]

The ambiguous status of the oracle—real or fantasized—does not, moreover, escape the notice of the parents themselves, who very much suspect, each in his turn, the hallucinated, dreamlike nature of the message that so gratifies them. "Dream or reality," the mother tells herself, "it must have been a message from heaven" (p. 178). As for the father, "He attributed the vision to his mental fatigue from having slept too little" (p. 179).

Thus not only are the oracles themselves of different substance for the mother and the father, but the two parental *readings* of the oracles are in turn diametrically opposed: while the mother chooses to interpret what could be her symptom as no less than a supernatural sign, the father, for his part, chooses to interpret what could be a supernatural sign as nothing but a symptom; while the mother chooses to reduce the very ambiguity of the vision to a single, mystical meaning (religious or transcendental), the father chooses to reduce the ambiguity of the vision to a single, realistic meaning (psychological or pathological). On one side, an absolute passion for mysticism; on the other, an absolute passion for realism; on one hand, a fantastic reading, and on the other, a phantasmic reading of the legendary element of the oracle: two antithetical interpretations, mutually exclusive, and yet whose destiny it is to coexist, to coincide thoughout the tale—two schemes of meaning whose contradictory dynamic fights over the text, two schemes of meaning whose dynamic contradiction fights over—and within—Julian himself.

This is, in Flaubert, the fateful secret of the oracle: the two distinct fates prophesied for Julian correspond to the two ambitions that the father and the mother secretly nurture for their son.[3] The father, a veteran of war who regularly and nostalgically takes pleasure in "regaling . . . his old battle companions" (p. 179), wishes for his son heroic distinction and military fame ("Much blood! . . . Much glory!"); the mother, religiously ascetic, and whose household is "governed like the inside of a monastery" (p. 178), hopes her son will be "a saint": two heterogeneous ambitions, two irreconcilable parental desires whose difference is determined not just by two scales of value, by two different *ethics*, but, above all, by two distinct *self-images*, two narcissistic constellations radically foreign to each other. Each parent, in effect, projects onto the son his own idealized self-image. On both sides, the child is imagined, dreamed, desired as a double—as a narcissistic reflection.

Torn, from before his birth, between two narcissistic programmings, caught between two laws, between two unconscious minds, between two projects for his future, Julian will be called upon to satisfy two radically contradictory parental wishes. "What is a child?" asks the text. The answer, ironically outlined by the very silence of the narrator, arises out of that which can be articulated, not by words, but only by events: a child is, paradoxically enough, nothing other than the embodiment of the *contradiction between his parents*.

The Blank, The Silence, The Gap

The problem for Julian—the model child, "a little Jesus" (p. 179)— is thus the following: how can he *live* the contradiction that has begotten him? How can he conform to the double, contradictory model ordained by his two parents?

Often, the nobleman would regale his old battle companions. As they drank, they would recall their wars, the assaults on fortresses with the clash of armor and the prodigious wounds. Julian, listening to them, would let out cries at this; then his father had no doubt that he would later be a conqueror. But in the evening, as the Angelus drew to a close, when he would pass between the bowing poor, he would dip into his purse with such modesty, with such noble air, that his mother was convinced she would eventually see him an archbishop.

His place in the chapel was at his parents' side. [P. 179]

The silence of the narrator (of the story) is audible only in the blank that separates and links the two indented paragraphs so as to situate— to mark—Julian's "place." It is important to note that this paragraph immediately precedes Julian's first act of violence: the murder of the mouse. The succession of the paragraphs suggests that, in some way, the murder—as dissonant as it may be—comes out of Julian's place: Julian's place, precisely, in the chapel. But what is, strictly speaking, this place beside his parents, one of whom envisions him as an archbishop and the other—as a conqueror? It is a middle place, but a place—an *in-between space*—that is totally contradictory, impossible: a place which, like the blank of the indented paragraph that introduces it, is the silent locus of *discontinuity*, the very place of a division, of a gap. Julian's problem, his tragic dilemma, is, precisely, *how to assume the lapse* of that location, the hiatus of that place? How can he respond to the *division* between the two demands addressed to him? How can he take on, how can he realize the gap between his parents?

Two parents that the text, from its first words, simultaneously *juxtaposes* and *opposes:*

The *father* and the *mother* of Julian lived in a castle. [P. 178]

Two parents that the text, once again, carefully juxtaposes and opposes in the two contiguous paragraphs that describe them for the first time. The contrast between the father and the mother is not spelled out: the opposition comes out of a concerted technique of juxtaposition. As always with Flaubert, it is the last sentence of the paragraph that *punctuates* the latter (gives it a *point*), while also making it ambiguous. That is, it at the same time gives the paragraph all its meaning and suspends the meaning: it makes the meaning veer toward the silence of the blank space, which it overloads with the unsaid. Now the parallel structure of the two paragraphs describing the parents is punctuated by two concluding sentences between which a dissonance begins ironically to resonate from one paragraph to the other:

Always wrapped up in a fox fur, he would walk about his house, give justice to his vassals, arbitrate his neighbors' quarrels. . . . *After many adventures, he had taken as his wife a maiden* of high birth.

She was very white, somewhat proud and serious. . . . Her household was governed like the inside of a monastery. . . . *By dint of praying to God, a son came unto her.* [P. 178]

What is striking is the *nonencounter* between the two paragraphs, both of which, however, point toward the *encounter* that will give birth to the son. "After many adventures, he had taken as his wife a maiden . . ."; "By dint of praying to God, a son came unto her." Like the contrast that will later be brought out by both the oracles and the parental readings of the oracles, these initial descriptions already prefigure the dichotomy between the paternal order—secular, assertive, realistic, and the maternal order—mystical, religious and ascetic.

Still, the semantic overload, the ironic tinge of the sentence which concludes the description of the mother—"By dint of praying to God, a son came unto her"—does more than just oppose the mother's religious and the father's secular disposition. By making quite plainly an allusion to the Immaculate Conception, it connotes a *nonrelation of the mother to the actual father* of her son. The mother's mystical perception thus involves not simply faith but a subtle syntax of denial, of negation: a denial—conscious or unconscious—of the sexual act that necessarily preceded the child's birth, a denial, therefore, of the mother's own sexuality as what motivated— and made possible—her maternity. Julian, then, will also have to consummate a double bind—to live out an aporia—between two paradigms of which one, the paternal, is a model of self-assertion and sensual affirmation, whereas the other, the maternal, is a model of self-denial and sexual negation.

This contradiction is, however, neither simply the result of the mother's faith nor a simple accident of psychology: it corresponds to the stereotypical sex roles of the man (Patriarch-Adventurer) and the woman (always, in some sense, Virgin-Mother) in Western culture. The mother's *mysticism* is, indeed, the *feminine mystique* par excellence. Thus the contradictions of which Julian is the incarnation are also, among other things, the symptom of a culture. However, Julian is a symptom only insofar as he is the very offspring of the gap, the very child of the discrepancy between his father and his mother: insofar as, paradoxically enough, he is *begotten by the nonrelation between the sexes*. What, indeed, could be more strikingly ironic than this vision of an *aporetic sexual act?*

The implicit motif of the nonrelation between the mother and the father is taken up again in a more explicit form in the scene of the oracular apparitions—solitary visions which the two spouses keep above all from communicating to each other. Thus the very image of the child stays with each parent as a private, unshared fantasy: the discontinuity between the father and the mother, the nonrelation between the two sexes, are thematized and sealed by the non-dialogue—the silence—between the two partners of the couple whose child becomes, ironically, the figure, not of what they share, but of what they *do not share*. The child of contradiction and division, Julian is the offspring, above all, of silence.

Dream or reality, it must have been a message from heaven; but she took care to say nothing about it, for fear of being accused of pride. . . .

He attributed this vision to his mental fatigue from having slept too little. "If I speak of it, I will be ridiculed," he told himself.

The spouses hid their secret from each other. But both cherished the child with equal love. [Pp. 178–79]

This silence which unites and separates the parents—and which makes the child into a *guilty secret*—is prolonged, extended, deepened, later on, by the child's own guilty silence sealing his first murder: the murder of the mouse in the church:

A drop of blood stained the flagstone. He wiped it up quickly with his sleeve, threw the mouse outside, and *said nothing about it to anyone*. [P. 179]

The silence of the child about the mouse—the real murder he has committed—is in turn prolonged by the silence of Julian's wife concerning the obsession that haunts her husband: the fantasy of the murder of his parents. But it is precisely *by keeping silent* to Julian's parents about their son's imaginary secret that Julian's wife brings about the fantasy's realization:

They asked a thousand questions about Julian. She replied to each one, but *took care to keep silent about the ominous idea concerning them*. . . .

Julian had crossed the park. . . . Everywhere there hung a great
silence. . . .

. . . .

His father and his mother were before him, lying on their backs with
holes in their chests; and their faces, with a gentle majesty, seemed to be
keeping an eternal secret. [PP. 183–85]

From the "secret" of the oracle that the spouses hid from each other,
to the "eternal secret" that the parents' corpses seem to keep, *The
Legend of Saint Julian the Hospitable* can be read as *the story of a
silence*. "Man," writes Freud in a formula itself oracular and lapidary, "man speaks in order not to kill." It is out of the reversal of this
formula that Flaubert's narrative is written: Julian *kills because he
does not speak*; in his legend, it is silence that engenders, motivates,
unleashes murder.

Paradoxically, however, it is also *what withholds speech* in the
legend that constitutes the very energy of its narration: it is *out of
Julian's silence* that Flaubert *writes*, that the text *speaks*, that the tale
is indeed *telling*.

The Ink Stain

The symbolism of color contrast draws out at yet another level the
opposition between the mother and the father. Thus the mother,
who "was very *white*" (p. 178), is repeatedly associated with the
signifier of the color white. When the mother is by mistake all but
murdered by her son, it is "two white wings" that Julian sees and at
which he throws his javelin, thinking he has seen a stork.

A piercing cry was heard.

It was his mother, whose bonnet . . . remained pinned to the wall.
[P. 182]

In the same way, the "little *white* mouse" (p. 179) killed in
church—the mother's space—is doubtless also a substitutive figure
for the mother.

The father, on the other hand, is symbolically associated with the
signifier black. So the prodigious stag which, "solemn like a pa-

triarch and like a judge," curses Julian for killing him and predicts he will one day "assassinate his father and his mother," "was *black* and monstrous in stature" (p. 181).

It is doubtless not by accident that the contradiction of black and white turns out to be the very one that produces writing. As Mallarmé suggestively puts it:

> You have remarked, one does not write, luminously, on an obscure background, the alphabet of the stars alone is thus indicated, sketched, or interrupted; *man pursues black on white.*[4]

What, then, is the *writing* which the contradiction between black and white—between the mother and the father in Flaubert's text—in effect produces, if not Julian himself as the very *text of contradiction*, as a marked, imprinted page?

> The spouses hid their secret from each other. But both cherished the child with equal love; and regarding him as *marked by God*, they bestowed infinite respect and care on his beloved person. [P. 179]

Produced by contradiction, difference, and alterity, the *mark*—at once the counterpart and the obverse of silence—is nothing other than a written letter. But what is, here, the page on which the mark is to be printed, the page on which the stained destiny of contradiction is to be inscribed and literally written down "black on white," if not, precisely, Julian's very body? Thus, in the metaphorical deer family, while the stag-"patriarch" is "black" and the doe-mother is "fair," the little fawn—obviously Julian's own reflection—is significantly "spotted" (p. 181).

But Julian's own skin is itself literally spotted, marked. It is indeed these very marks or spots that serve as signs of recognition by which Julian's aged parents, who are unknown to his wife, are able to identify their son for her:

> Nothing could convince the young woman that her husband was their son.
> They provided proof by describing certain *particular signs* he had on his skin. [P. 183]

Julian is thus "marked by God" very much like Cain, bearing in his turn the concrete inscription of a *writing*—of distinctive marks or signs—printed or imprinted on his very skin.

It is therefore not surprising that this legend of marked skin—of the epidermal stain and of writing in the flesh—should reach its pinnacle, or its epiphany, in the dramatic figure of the leper.

Julian saw that a hideous leprosy covered his body. . . . His shoulders, his chest, his skinny arms disappeared into *slabs* of scaly pustules. Enormous *wrinkles* dug into his forehead.

"I'm hungry!" he said. Julian gave him what he had, an old chunk of lard and a few crusts of dark bread.

When he had devoured them, the table, the bowl, and the handle of the knife bore *the very same spots that were visible on his body.* [Pp. 186–87]

Just like the spotted fawn and the signs marking Julian's skin, the leper's spotted skin is, once again, nothing other than a metaphorical image of Julian himself. But whereas Julian kills the fawn and plans to kill himself, he accepts—and saves—the leper: the ending of the tale marks the climactic moment at which Julian (at the actual point of dying—that is, of becoming in effect a saint) for the first time *forgives himself*—and accepts himself: forgives himself his spotted, tainted skin; forgives himself, in other words, for being *marked* by his own *otherness to himself*; accepts himself, therefore, as a stained, marred text, at once black and white, innocent and guilty: a text of contradiction he will no longer struggle to suppress (as he had attempted through the various killings), but to which he will henceforth submit, endeavoring to *pass through*, to traverse, to *pass beyond*. The crossing of the river, among other things, is also the symbolic crossing of his own division and his own contradiction.

II

The Voice Came from the Other Side

Since the passage became known, travelers presented themselves. They would hail him from the other bank. . . .

. . . The . . . voice . . . came from the other side. . . . The shadows were deep, and here and there *torn by the whiteness* of cresting waves. . . .

With each thrust of the oar, the backwash raised [the boat] in front. The water, *blacker than ink,* flowed furiously on each side of the vessel. [Pp. 186–87]

Why is the river's water said to be "blacker than ink"? In what way are we meant to read the crossing of the river as a metaphor of writing? And what, if so, is writing all about?

Navigating in the midst of *"shadows . . . torn* by the *whiteness* of cresting waves," passing through the *ink-black* river, Julian, struggling to survive division, crosses the contradiction between black and white (father and mother, innocence and guilt, sameness and otherness, consciousness and the unconscious). From one side of the ink-black river to the other, writing is this passage for survival, this repeated crossing of the contradiction of black and white, this constant shuttle movement between life and death. It is thus that Julian struggles to *traverse the ink stain,* to survive, pass through, and pass across the writing on his very flesh.

This struggle, this necessity of crossing, this agonizing passage through the ink stain is, indeed, Julian's predicament. But it is also the predicament of Flaubert who, elsewhere, writes in turn, for his part, to Louise Colet:

I fret, I itch. . . . I've got stylistic abscesses, and the sentence itches and cannot be quelled. What a heavy oar the pen is, and what a hard current is the idea, when one digs into it![5]

But what, then, is Flaubert's place in the legend of the Other, in the story of Saint Julian—which he writes?

The place from which the legend is enunciated is itself *marked* in the last paragraph of the tale:

And that's the story of Saint Julian the Hospitable, as one can find it—more or less—on a stained-glass window of a church, in my country. [P. 187]

It is out of this concluding, final sentence that the second question of the tale emerges: What, in the last analysis, is a legend?

A double blank, a silent gap marking a break in tone and a change of perspective, separates this final sentence from the narrative that precedes it. However, in order to attempt to grasp the import of the final sentence and the way it can shed light on what a legend is, we must try to look beyond—in fact across—this gap, for the *relation*— the articulation—on the contrary, between the apparently removed last sentence and the main (narrative) bulk of the text.

What is remarkable about this sentence—which is indeed unique in Flaubert's work—is the peculiar fact that it refers the text to a *first person* ("*my* country"), which could well be not just (fictitiously) the narrator's, but perhaps also (referentially) the author's. Even aside from the specific reference to the church window whose historical existence in Rouen did in reality motivate and trigger the writing of the tale,[6] the closing sentence—at least fictitiously—designates the narrator as the actual author. Placed just above the proper name "Flaubert," the "I" that so unexpectedly emerges in the closing sentence *in excess of the story*, so as to punctuate the text and bring it to a close, appears indeed to be, in relation to the (written) story, not just its narrator but its *signatory*. It therefore, in some sense, inscribes within the text the very signature of Flaubert.

The signature, however, says: *It isn't me*, it's not my person, that is the tale's originator: it's not from me that the narration springs, but from my homeland, from "my country." The question then becomes: what, exactly, is a country?

The Story of a Country

I have in me that melancholy of the barbarian races, with its migratory instincts and innate disgust with life that made them leave their country as if they were leaving themselves. FLAUBERT, *Lettters*

Julian crossed in this way an interminable plain, and at last he found himself on a plateau dominating a great expanse of country. Flat rocks were scattered among vaults in ruins. One would stumble over dead men's bones; here and there, worm-eaten crosses slanted lamentingly. But there were shapes moving about in the uncertain shadows of the tombs. FLAUBERT, *The Legend of Saint Julian*

What is a country? The answer to this question is, indeed, suggested in the tale: suggested by the way in which the signatory, final sentence implicitly rejoins the narrative's first sentence, which it remotely echoes; the ending is thus structured as a subtle counterpart to the tale's opening:

The father and the mother of Julian lived in a castle, in the middle of the woods, on the slope of a hill. [P. 178]

Much could be said about this sentence which, like the closing sentence, is rich in implications—beyond its innocuous appearance. One could stress the opposition it draws out between the *castle* and the *wood* (the animals' space, which will grow to be important in the story): an opposition between inside and outside, between the space of nature and the protected space of culture; "the slope of a hill" foreshadows, on the other hand, the possibility of a fall; and since this spatial description does not directly situate Julian himself, the implicit question which is left hanging is that of knowing, what space will belong to Julian? Indeed, as we will later learn, Julian will turn out to be the natural inhabitant of the woods and of the slope—far more than of the castle. What I wish to stress, however, is the fact, crucial in its simplicity, that the legend's opening—the very first sentence of the tale—gives information as to *where the hero's parents live*. The first sentence speaks, in other words, of Julian's country— of Julian's homeland, whereas the last sentence speaks of Flaubert's country—of the signatory's homeland.

What, then, is a country, if not, as the text suggests, the country where one's parents live? So, too, in the closing sentence, "my country" means *my parents' country*; that is to say, the country, at the same time, of the *cultural heritage* my parents have passed on to me.

But in this text "the country of my parents" necessarily implies the country of the *contradiction* which inhabits the relationship of those who have a child: the country of the gap, of the discontinuity which, paradoxically, is enacted by the very act of procreation. "My country," therefore, is the country of the contradictions embodied by the burden of the cultural heritage within which I am born, and with which my birth afflicts me.

The question of the meaning of a country thus begins to answer the initial question, concerning the nature of a legend. A legend is, precisely, the unconscious of the contradictions that beget us: the unconscious of the cultural heritage, articulating its *discontinuity with itself* in the form of this contradiction we, in turn, have to live, and to live out.

As if we didn't have enough of our own past, we chew over that of humanity in its entirety.[7]

In fact, beneath the allegoric figure of the very story of *birth into consciousness*, it is humanity's entire cultural and mythic past that Flaubert condenses into the *legend*. Almost all the myths of the Western heritage are present in it: the Greek and Latin myths of Oedipus, Narcissus, Ajax, Charon, the biblical myths of Adam, Noah, and Cain, the evangelical myths of the life of Christ and the trials of the saints.[8] "The story found in my country" being that of Occidental culture as a whole, "my country" is not simply France or Rouen, but rather Babel: the very Babel of the West.

But the Flaubertian inscription of this mythic Babel ruptures and subverts, for each myth, its autonomy of sense and its semantic unity and integrity. Out of the Western Babel of the myths, Flaubert's ironic writing registers precisely the contradictions which, opposing the myths to one another, oppose them—and make them discontinuous—to themselves.

Thus Julian, Christ and Oedipus,[9] is *crucified*, irreverently, not over his own death, but over someone else's death: over the corpses of two goats—prefiguring those of his parents—that the text specifically describes as his *cross*.[10]

Incarnating, in this way, the very irony—the very aberration—of the contradictory coincidence of Oedipus and Christ, Julian is also, at the same time, the embodiment of the conflicting myths of Adam and of Noah:

Sometimes, in a dream, he saw himself as *our father Adam* in the midst of paradise, among all the animals; stretching out his arms, he would make them die; or they would file two by two . . . as on the day they entered *Noah's ark*. [P. 183]

Adam, in the myth, did not *kill* animals: he *named* them. The

Flaubertian distortion of the myths suggests, in a revealing way, a textual correlation between *naming* and *killing*. In the case of Julian, the act of killing is suggestively substituted for the act of naming or of speaking, implying, once again, a relationship between silence and murder. Julian *kills* because he does not name; Flaubert, for his part, *names*—in order not to kill? Or perhaps rather to kill *by naming* him "our father Adam," to implicate himself in turn in the very parricide of myths? "The distortion of a text," writes Freud, "is not unlike a murder, in its implications. The difficulty resides not so much in perpetrating the crime, but in covering up its traces."[11]

What is there to cover up, however, if not the fact that the murdered father had already—from the outset—been dead, that there had always been *too many fathers*, too many myths?[12] What *The Legend of Saint Julian the Hospitable* reveals is, paradoxically enough, that *parricide is fundamentally impossible*.

Too many fathers, too many myths: behind "our father Adam" is already profiled, in the same breath (in the same paragraph), this other father of the human race, whose mythic function was, precisely, to start it over: "The animals would file two by two, . . . as on the day they entered Noah's ark." Noah, Adam: in coupling those two fathers of humanity, what is at stake in Flaubert's text is, once again, the inscription of a (yet another) contradiction between our parents. Whereas Adam, perpetrator of original sin, is the embodiment of guilt and of its irreducible human inheritance, Noah is, in contrast, the very figure of innocence par excellence: far from killing animals, he is rather their savior, the one who gives them life. The superimposition of these two myths in the same paragraph suggests that Julian—the very text of contradiction—is *at once* innocent and guilty: he who is most guilty, he from whom descends mankind's heritage of sin, and he who, of all mankind, is the sole innocent. Innocence is here no longer, in effect, *opposed* to guilt.

In this way Flaubert, inscribing "black on white" the myths of stain upon the myths of purity, writes innocence into the myths of guilt and guilt into the myths of innocence.

And that's the story of Saint Julian the Hospitable, as one can find it—more or less—on a stained-glass window of a church, in my country. [P. 187]

The story of a country: a story of the relation between Flaubert's land—that of the closing sentence—and Julian's (parents') land—that of the opening sentence. A tale of the relationship between where Flaubert comes from and where Julian comes from, between the country that locates the hero at the contradictory crossroads of conflicting dreams and parents, and the country that locates the signatory or the signature—the very energy of the writing—at the contradictory crossroads of conflicting myths.

Insiders and Outsiders: Hospitality

Since the native country of the signatory is thus related to the legendary country where "the father and the mother" live,[13] it should be stressed that Julian, nonetheless, is by definition one who cannot say "my country": his story is that of an *exile*, endlessly renewed. Structurally, the repeated scansion of Julian's displacement—his departure into exile—in effect constitutes the very punctuation of the three parts of the tale: each chapter ends with the hero leaving. Thus, at the end of the first chapter, Julian flees the parental castle and leaves his native country; at the end of the second chapter, he flees his own castle and leaves the country of his wife, which, through the marriage, had become his own; at the end of the third chapter, he leaves this world to ascend to heaven—the wayfarer's ultimate departure.

Since Julian is, by definition, he who has no land, but who nonetheless *inhabits my land*—lives in "my country" as the host of a church window, what else is a country if not, precisely, that which is *constituted by legends of exile?* If Julian, all the same, is defined as the story of "my country," then the story of "my country" is the story of an exile situated, not outside, but, paradoxically, *inside* my land.

This commingling of the inside and the outside of the tale itself, this relation adumbrated by the closing sentence between the (intrinsic) legendary hero and the (extrinsic) narrative first person of the signatory—between the legend and Flaubert's self-referential signing of the legend—suggests that writing is itself in fact an *inside job*: a relation—far more complex than we might think—between being an insider and being an outsider, between the stance of being in and the stance of being out of what one writes about.

Writing—but also murder. Julian consummates, indeed, his destiny as murderer both by virtue of his being an insider and by virtue of his being an outsider. On the one hand, it is because Julian has left his country that he—like Oedipus—ends up unwittingly killing his parents: the tragic mistake would not have happened had Julian not exiled himself out of his home and family, had he not cast himself on the outside.

But on the other hand, ironically enough, Julian kills in order to eliminate outsiders, to *protect the inside* of his home and of his family: finding his parents in his own bed, offered them—without his knowledge—by his wife, and tragically confusing his mother and his wife—whom he believes to have caught with a lover, Julian commits the double murder of his parents in a fit of jealousy that is clearly, in a metaphoric manner, Oedipal. But if Julian kills because he takes his own father for a stranger—an outsider—he kills because he in effect radically *confuses inside and outside* and thus mistakenly strives to protect what is *within* against what he believes to be an *intrusion from without*.

The attitude of the murderer, who endeavors to protect the inside from the outside and hence casts on the outside what is really only an unrecognized part of his inside, is diametrically opposed to the attitude of the Hospitable, who opens himself up to the outside and actually welcomes the outsider into his own home. It is not by chance, indeed, that "the Hospitable" figures in the legend's title. Hospitality, though hardly obvious or explicit—except precisely in the title—in effect plays in the tale an absolutely crucial role: crucial for an understanding of the way Flaubert *rewrites* the legend and of the irony with which he writes *into* the legend his sophisticated signature.

While it is true that Flaubert's title is no more than a recapitulation of the traditional title of the saint, as well as of the saint's title to sainthood—*Saint Julian the Hospitable*—Flaubert's writing does not fail to introduce *into the very title* (of the saint, as of the tale) an ironic split: the ambiguous tension, once again, of contradiction and division.

Hospitality itself, it turns out, is ironically divided in Flaubert's text: the title in effect refers not to just one but to *two* occurrences, to two displays of hospitality in the tale. The most obvious is that of Julian welcoming the leper and offering him everything he has, right down to his very body. That is, by all accounts, the ultimate in hospitality: the kind of hospitality that leads to sainthood. But the other textual occurrence of hospitality is when Julian's wife generously welcomes into her own bed the two strange visitors—the two impoverished and aged nomads—that the very parents of her husband have over the years become.

The symbolic link between these two narrative occurrences of hospitality is effected through the signifier of the bed: in both cases, the hospitable welcome is enacted by the gesture of *giving one's own bed*:

Julian's wife persuaded them not to wait up for him. *She herself put them in her bed*, then closed the window; they fell asleep. [P. 184]

The leper shook from limb to limb . . . and, in an almost silenced voice, he murmured: "Your bed!" Julian gently helped him drag himself to it. [P. 187]

Thus it is the bed which twice becomes the quintessential site of hospitality. But to what is the bed hospitable—what does a bed host? Sleep, of course, and dreams, and desire, and the erotic mingling of bodies ("Undress, so I can have the warmth of your body!" says the leper). But in the *legend*, the bed also becomes a tomb, since it is in bed that Julian kills his parents. The bed is thus equally hospitable to the murder of one's parents.

The ultimate gesture of welcome—*offering one's bed*—leads, then, on the one hand, to the sainthood of Saint Julian the Hospitable, yet on the other hand it leads to murder.

But it is precisely to the coincidence of these two scenes—to the ironic contradiction between these two displays of hospitality *taken together* and together issuing either in murder or in sainthood—that Flaubert's writing, in its turn, means to be hospitable. Hospitable to contradiction: hospitable to the voice of the Other, to a constant *countercurrent of meaning*; hospitable to silence, sleep, to its own silence, its own sleep, to its own difference from itself—hospitable, then, to a maximal number of mutually exclusive points of view within the same narrative statement, to a maximal number of opposed, conflicting readings (maternal / paternal, religious / sexual, supernatural-fantastic and / or natural-phantasmic, and so forth) within a single enunciation.

In the story as in its narration, on the inside as on the outside, what is at stake in hospitality is, therefore, not the simple gesture of inviting the outsider in—the welcoming of the outside inside—but, much more radically, the subversion of the very limit that distinguishes them from each other: the discovery that the outside is already within, but that what is within is, in effect, without—outside—itself.

Much Blood, Much Glory; or, The Stains of the Stained-Glass Window

A double, triple irony: not only is hospitality what leads at once to sainthood and to murder, but the Hospitable is, paradoxically enough, a man who has, himself, no country—no home of his own,[14] a man, moreover, who is himself received or welcomed by no one, and whose narrative—or message—will elicit nothing other than an absolute refusal of hospitality:

Out of the spirit of humility, he would tell his story; then everyone would flee him, making the sign of the cross. In the villages he had been through before, as soon as he was recognized, *the doors were shut*, threats were yelled out at him, and stones were thrown at him. The most charitable people set a bowl on their windowsill, then closed the shutters to avoid seeing him. [P. 185]

How is it that Flaubert can tell Julian's story while Julian himself *cannot tell*—or get anyone to listen to—his story? It must be because Julian's story is by definition the story of the Other—the story of no one: a tale in some way without language, which can be articulated in effect only by the *silence* of the stained-glass window. If Flaubert speaks, tells the deaf, mute story of the stained-glass visual image, he can only read, *translate* it. For his own protection, he is screened, precisely, by the stained-glass window, whose function is indeed to separate him from his own tale.

It is thus the stained-glass window of the church which can, alone, be host—hospitable—to Julian's story; but Flaubert's tale can in turn be hospitable to—host—the stained-glass window:

And that's the story . . . as one can find it on a stained-glass window of a church, in my country. [P. 187]

Is the window *hosted* by the tale inside or outside? What is the significance of the inscription of the window in the closing sentence? In what way does Flaubert's stained-glass in effect partake of the very nature of a signature?

The tale, quite literally, is *the legend of the stained-glass window*, since the word *legend* can also mean "any text that accompanies an image and gives it its meaning."[15] If the tale—like the account or interpretation of a dream—thus consists in the verbal translation of pictorial images into narrative, the stained-glass window constitutes a *legend* in the etymological sense as well: *legenda*—"what must be read." How, then, does the text define—or concretize—this figure of "what must be read?"

A stained-glass window is a painting; but it is also, at the same time, just a window; as such, it is, once more, a boundary, a limit that not only separates what is within from that which is without but also sets up the dependence of the inside on the outside: indeed, we could not see the painting on the inside were it not for the light that filters in from the outside. The stained-glass window thus enacts an ambiguous relationship of nontransparency, and yet of interfusion, between what is in and what is out. The outside—behind the painted window—is what the eye looking at the painting *does not see*, but it is also, at the same time, *what enables it to see*.

All these connotations of the stained-glass window are put into play by the tale itself. For the closing sentence, with its signatory gesture toward the referential church window that the narrator has just translated, is not the only mention of a stained-glass window in the legend. From within this signatory, painted window which in some sense frames the tale—apparently from outside the tale—another stained-glass window is outlined—and framed—inside the tale, in the very heart of the narrative itself. The story speaks, indeed, no less than three times of another stained-glass window: not that of Flaubert's home church, but that of Julian's castle. It must be significant that the three occurrences of this other stained-glass window all appear in proximity to the parental murder, which they literally frame.

The first appearance of the window introduces into the tale's silence a signatory note of tragic irony that mutely *signs* the parents' last sleep—the sleep from which they will never again awaken:

Julian's wife persuaded them not to wait up for him. She put them herself in her bed, then closed the window; they fell asleep. *Day was about to break, and behind the stained-glass window,* little birds began to sing. [P. 184]

In the bedroom, *in front of the window,* the invisible narrator seems to contemplate the parents' sleep—their unawareness. But what is there *behind the stained-glass window?* Apparently, behind the window day is breaking. But in reality, day will, for the parents, dawn no more: behind the stained-glass window it is nothing other than eternal night—and death—which in effect await them. The window, then, embodies here the very ambiguity of day and night: the ambiguous borderline that at the same time separates and links sleeping and waking, death and life, without our being able to know for sure which is inside, which is outside—what, exactly, lies behind the window.

The second textual inscription of the stained-glass window can be found just before the murder, when Julian, harrassed and frustrated by the final hunt, returns home:

Having taken off his sandals, he gently turned the key, and went in. *The stained-glass windows adorned with lead obscured the light of dawn.* Julian . . . made his way towards the bed, lost in the shadows spreading deep into the room. When he was at the bedside, in order to embrace his wife, he bent over the pillow, where two heads were resting side by side. Then, he felt against his mouth the sensation of a beard. . . . Definitely it was a beard . . . and a man! A man in bed with his wife!

Bursting with inordinate anger, he leapt at them, stabbing them repeatedly with his dagger. [P. 185]

The signifying chain of the stained-glass windows which constructs a link between the narrative and its frame, which subtly binds the windows framed by the legendary story and the framing window of the narrator-signatory, here takes on a curiously ironic tinge. For while the stained-glass window contemplated by the narrator is *what makes us see* the legend, giving the story visibility, the window at the same time turns out to be *that which obscures*, creates a blindness: it is because of the window that Julian, seeing nothing, kills his parents. The window thus maintains an ambiguous relation with light: its function is not just—by letting in the rays of light—to *produce representation*, but also—by screening them off—to *distort perception*. The stained-glass window, or "what must be read," at once gives sight and blinds.

And if, unlike those who "closed their doors" so as *not to see* Julian, so as not to look at—listen to—his story (p. 185), we agree to look at the stained-glass window, to listen to the legend, is it not precisely because of the blinding power of what a stained-glass window—or a legend—lets us see? Doesn't Flaubert suggest that the property of a legend (of a window) is to make us look, to make us see, while at the same time blinding us to the way the window in effect reflects on—has to do with—us?

The third occurrence of the stained-glass window takes place right after the murder. As day breaks, the rebus of the window lights up:

His father and mother were before him, stretched out on their backs with holes in their chests. . . . Splashes and *pools of blood* spread over the middle of their *white skin*, onto the bedsheets, onto the ground. . . . *The scarlet reflection of the stained glass window, now struck by the sun, lit up these red stains, and cast many more of them around the whole room.* [P. 185]

At its last appearance within the legend, the stained-glass window— hit by light—becomes itself a rhetorical figure of writing: a figure of the optical prism of language as what determines, motivates, compels, the performance of "the pen-man."[16] "Style being, in itself, an absolute way of *seeing* things,"[17] it is indeed the window that is writing: it is the window which, *multiplying stains of red* throughout the room, brings back the motif of color contrast—the textual inscription of the stain, the mark. "The scarlet reflection of the stained-glass window, now struck by the sun, lit up these red stains, and cast many more of them around the whole room."

In this way, the stained-glass window turns out to be *hospitable* to *blood:* hospitable, ambiguously, both to what in blood is most uncanny, most unsettling—the blood of mortal injury, of murder—but also, at the same time, to what in blood is most familiar, reassuring: the bloodline of the family, the very familiarity of heritage. Uncannily familiar and familiarly uncanny, the stained-glass window is inscribed throughout the text as a writing which consists, precisely, of staining white surfaces: a writing—a play of colors and a play of light, a chiaroscuro—which consists of tinting the white pages of the text with ink that, in effect, is blood, with blood that, in effect, is ink.

It is thus that, when the signatory brings the legend to a close by bringing out his own relation to the stained-glass window in his homeland, the referential, outside window is already *signed* from inside the text: signed, precisely, by the blood stain changed into an ink stain.

"Of all writing," asserts Nietzsche through the mouth of Zarathustra, "I love but that which one has written with one's blood. Write with blood, and you will learn that blood is spirit."[18] Has Flaubert told the story of, precisely, writing with one's blood?

It was a Bohemian with a braided beard. . . . With an inspired air, he stammered these disconnected words:
Ah! Ah! . . . Much blood! . . . Much glory! [P. 178]

In the end, what is the connection that uncannily emerges from behind these words' apparent disconnection? In telling us, along with Julian's story, the very story of the stained (glass) signature, the tale can give a different, unexpected insight both into the Bohemian's "inspiration" and into the nature of the "glory" he predicts. If the art of disconnection here turns out, indeed, to be inspired, if blood issues in glory and if the very glory of the "inspiration" is necessarily tied up with blood, the glory—like the blood as well—is Flaubert's.

"Almost everyone dies," writes Flaubert, "without knowing his proper name, unless he is a fool." A signature, indeed, is not the simple writing down of a proper name. A signature is nothing other than the story of one's writing with one's blood: the story of how *one does not know one's own name* and how, not knowing one's own name, one signs, instead, with one's own blood.

I, the Undersigned

It would be quite pleasant to spell out my thought in order to relieve Sir Gustave Flaubert by means of sentences; but what importance does this honorable Sir have? FLAUBERT, *Letters*

As for disclosing my own personal opinion of the people I put on stage, no, no, a thousand times no! I don't grant myself the right to do so. FLAUBERT, *Letters*

And that's the story of Saint Julian the Hospitable, as one can find it— more or less—on a stained-glass window of a church, in my country. [P. 187]

This highly complex signature in effect says in one breath: I am external to my text (an outsider); I am internal to my text (an insider). There is a gap separating me from my tale: the wall of the church window, for which I am not responsible. But on the other hand, it is only "more or less" that my text duplicates the stained-glass window: so I am also, at the same time, responsible for the discrepancy—the gap—that separates the stained-glass window from my tale. Just as the stained-glass window stands between my text and me, (the) "I" in turn stand(s) between the window and my text. Where, then, does the legend come from? With respect to it, I am at once responsible and not responsible, guilty and innocent.

To Georges Charpentier. Croisset, Sunday (16 February 1879). . . . I wanted to put the stained-glass window of the Rouen cathedral after *Saint Julian*. It was a matter of adding colors to the plate that's found in Langlois's book, nothing more. And this illustration pleased me precisely because it was not an illustration, but a historical *document*. In comparing the image to the text, one would have said to oneself: "I don't understand any of it. How did he get this out of that?"

All illustrations exasperate me, . . . and while I am alive none will be made. . . . The same is true of my portrait. [19]

Just as Julian's "I" enacts the gap—the *relationless relation* that at the same time separates and links his parents—the signatory's "I" enacts the relationless relation that at the same time separates and links the window and the tale. "And that's the story . . . more or less": the expression of approximation—more or less (*à peu près*)—marks the "I" as the play, precisely, of the undecidability between distance and proximity.

However, the very play of undecidability is itself decided and overdetermined: it is a play the "I" does not—cannot—decide.

One morning as he was returning through the colonnade, he saw on the crest of the rampart a large pigeon. . . . Julian stopped to look at it; since there was a breach in the wall at that point, *a splinter of stone met his fingers.* He cocked his arm, and *the stone knocked down the bird*, which fell straight into the ditch. [P. 179]

Just as the stone *meets* Julian's fingers—of its own accord, it seems—the stained glass window—"as one can find it" in the church—*meets* Flaubert's eye. The signatory's "I" itself is therefore nothing other than the acting out of the encounter between necessity and chance: the very writing of the unavoidable necessity of a chance encounter. Flaubert is the *instrument of the window*, just as Julian is the instrument of the stone.

Art has but the form we can give it: we are not free. Each follows his path, despite his own will. [20]

I've always guarded against putting anything of myself into my works, and yet I've put in a great deal. [21]

It is noteworthy that Flaubert, whose writing effort always tended toward the suppression of the "I," the effacement of the author's voice, nonetheless signs one of his last works by referring it back to the realm—discreet as it may be—of the first person, a first person, it is true, whose silent, subtle presence is denied and masked by an indefinite third person:

And that's the story of Saint Julian the Hospitable, as *one* can find it [telle qu'*on* la trouve] . . . in *my* country [dans *mon* pays]. [P. 187]

To understand the implications of this *mon* ("my")—beyond its contradition, its denial by the *on* ("one")—it is revealing to relate the signatory silence of this first person ("my") to all the other instances of the discourse of an *"I"* in the legend of Saint Julian. When we extract from the legend's narrative, told in the third person, the few fragments of *direct speech*—the several quotations reported in the first person—what we come up with is a stupefying textual precipitate which reads as follows:

CHAPTER 1

(Julian's discourse)   I cannot kill them!
                                 What if I wanted to, though? [P. 181]

CHAPTER 2

(Julian's discourse)   It's to obey you! At sunrise I'll be back.
                                 [P. 183]
(Julian's wife's discourse)   It's my father. [P. 183]

CHAPTER 3

(The leper's discourse)   I'm hungry.
                                 I'm thirsty.
                                 I'm cold.
                                 Undress, so I can have the warmth of
                                 your body.
                                 I'm going to die. [P. 187]

This is, then, what the "I" says, what the "I" *can* say, *all* the "I" can say—a quintessence of the discourse of the "I," an abstract of that, precisely, which Flaubert will never say in his own name, in his own right, with his own voice. Literature is, for Flaubert, *about the silence* of this discourse: the art of writing, in Flaubert's conception, is, precisely, the production of such silence.

What Flaubert will never say; what literature is all about:

I cannot kill them. What if I wanted to, though?
It's to obey you . . . I'll be back.
It's my father.

I'm hungry, thirsty, cold.
Undress, so I can have the warmth of your body.
I'm going to die.

This muted discourse of the "I," this summarily exhaustive spectrum of complaint, appeal, anxiety, protest, interrogation, and demand of the first person, is however, what the undersigned—the signatory "I" of the legend of Saint Julian—in the very gesture of denying it his own voice, at the very moment of his own lapse into silence, nonetheless refers back to his space—"finds in *his* country."

"And that's the story of Saint Julian the Hospitable, as one can find it—more or less—on a stained-glass window of a church, in my country."

Flaubert's signature: I, the undersigned, have found in my country that which I can tell, but which I cannot say—that which I deny myself the right to say.

"I, the undersigned, am going to die."

I am getting lost in my childhood memories like an old man. I expect of life nothing more than a succession of sheets of paper to stain with black ink. I seem to be traversing a loneliness with no end, to go I don't know where. And I myself am all at once the traveler, the desert and the camel. [22]

I feel mortally wounded. . . . I'll soon be fifty-four years old. At that age one does not redo one's life, one does not change habits. I'm devoured by the past, and the future has nothing good to offer me. I think of nothing other than of the days past and of the people that cannot come back. Sign of old age and of decadence. As for literature, I no longer believe in myself, and I feel empty. . . . In the meantime, I'm going to begin writing the legend of *Saint Julian the Hospitable,* just to occupy myself with something and *to see whether I am still able to craft a sentence,* which I sincerely doubt. [23]

Flaubert's signature: this is what *I* will not say.

I'm cold, I'm thirsty.
I, the undersigned, am going to die.

What Flaubert will never say, he nonetheless—in his own sophisticated, silent way—will *sign:* a crafted sentence. A sheet of paper stained with black ink.

"And that's the story." The legend of Saint Julian. The story of the ink / blood stain. As one can find it in my country.

Were it necessary to be moved in order to move others, I could write books that would make hands tremble and hearts pound, and, since I'm sure I'll never lose this capacity for emotion which the pen gives me of its own accord without my having anything to do with it, and which happens to me in spite of myself in a way that's often disturbing, I don't preoccupy myself with it, and what I look for, on the contrary, is not *vibration* but *design*.

Signed: GUSTAVE FLAUBERT[24]

[Translated by Brian Massumi, Rachel Bowlby, Richard Russell, and Nancy Jones, with the collaboration of the author]

Notes

1. Flaubert, *La Légende de saint Julien l'hospitalier*, p. 178, in vol. 2 of the *Oeuvres complètes*, 2 vols. (Paris: Seuil, 1964). All passages quoted from the French, here as elsewhere in this essay, are from this edition and have been rendered into English by the essay's general translators. In the texts quoted, emphasis is mine, unless otherwise indicated.

2. Only the oracle communicated to Julian appears in the form of a curse: "Accursed! Accursed! Accursed! One day, cruel heart, you will assassinate your father and your mother!" (p. 181). Thus the filial curse (Julian's oracle) is the obverse of the parental blessing (the parents' oracle).

3. For a different analysis of the significance of the opposition between Julian's parents—an analysis to which the present one is indebted—see Frank Yeomans, "*La Légende de saint Julien l'hospitalier:* This Side of Parricide," in "Flaubert's Trinity: A Psychoanalytic / Semiotic Reading of the *Trois Contes*," (Ph.D. diss., Yale University, 1979), pp. 56–132.

4. Stéphane Mallarmé, "L'Action restreinte," in *Oeuvres complètes* (Paris: Pléiade, 1945), p. 370.

5. Flaubert to Louise Colet, end of October 1851, *Extraits de la correspondance; ou, Préface à la vie d'écrivain*, ed. Geneviève Bollème (Paris: Seuil, 1963), p. 59. Unless otherwise indicated, references to the letters refer to this edition.

6. We know, by Flaubert's own account in his letter to his niece Caroline, dated 25 September 1875 (mailed from Concarneau), that it was

while looking at the reproduction of the Rouen cathedral window in E. H. Langlois's *Essai historique et descriptif sur la peinture en verre* (Rouen, 1832) that Flaubert began to write the tale (cf. *Préface*, pp. 266–67).

7. Flaubert, *Correspondance*, 9 vols. (Paris: Louis Conard, 1926–33) 2:6–7.

8. For Narcissus, compare the scene where Julian contemplates, with suicidal desire, his own reflection in the fountain (p. 186).

Like Ajax, Julian massacres animals which, here as well, are in reality substitutes for humans. In his letters, Flaubert mentions Sophocles' *Ajax*, which he read repeatedly.

Compare the crossing of the river, which recalls Charon welcoming passengers and taking them across the river (Acheron or Styx) to the shore of Hell.

For Adam and Noah, see my analysis below. Cain, like Julian, bears a mark on his skin—a sign imprinted by God to mark him as a murderer. Julian's parents, on the other hand, after the predictions about their son's future, think he has "been marked by God" (p. 179).

9. "He resembled a little Jesus. His teeth came in without his crying a single time" (p. 179).

10. "At the edge, two wild goats were looking into the abyss. . . . He finally got to the first goat and plunged a dagger through his ribs. The second, terror-struck, jumped into the void. Julian leapt to strike it, and, his right foot slipping, he *fell onto the other's corpse*, his face above the abyss and *his arms stretched out*" (pp. 180–81). Compare, during the parents' burial: "During the mass he stayed *prone* in the middle of the doorway, *his arms outstretched in the form of a cross*" (p. 185).

11. *Moses and Monotheism*, in *The Standard Edition of the Complete Psychological Works of Sigmund Freud*, ed. and trans. James Strachey, vol. 23 (London: Hogarth Press, 1964), p. 43 (translation modified).

12. Cf. Gérard de Nerval's retort when reproached for having no religion: "I, no religion? I have seventeen of them . . . at least!"

13. In an earlier version of this sentence, Flaubert actually wrote "my native town" instead of "my country."

14. "A small table, a stool, a bed of dead leaves and three clay cups, that was all his furniture. Two holes in the walls served as windows" (p. 186).

15. *Le Petit-Robert*'s definition of *légende*.

16. "I am a pen-man. I feel through it, because of it, in relation to it and much more with it" (Flaubert to Louise Colet, Le Croisset, 1 February 1852, *Préface*, p. 64).

17. To Louise Colet, 16 January 1852, ibid., p. 63.

18. Friederich Nietzsche, *Thus Spoke Zarathustra*, trans. Walter Kaufmann, in *The Portable Nietzsche* (New York: The Viking Press, 1968), p. 152 (translation modified).

19. Flaubert, *Préface*, p. 285.

20. Flaubert to George Sand, 3 April 1876, ibid., p. 272.

21. Flaubert to Louise Colet, 14–15 August 1846, ibid., p. 39.

22. Flaubert to George Sand, 27 March 1875, ibid., p. 264.

23. Flaubert to Madame Roger des Genettes, 3 October 1875, ibid., p. 267.

24. Flaubert to Louis Colet, Rouen, 11–12 December 1847, ibid., p. 48.

Flaubert's Libidinal Historicism: *Trois Contes*

Fredric Jameson

We need to think the writer's relationship to history, to dead history, to the past, in some new way, which is no longer dominated by static ideas of representation or of some "vision of history" in which a given artist is supposed to "believe." Preferable, it would seem, is the notion of a libidinal investment in the past—indeed, of a libidinal historicism, of which Nietzsche's famous cry, in the delirious letters of the final days, may stand as an emblem: "I am all the names of History!"

Flaubert's is also surely a libidinal historicism; but we will not be able to describe its peculiar rhythms and attractions and repulsions without insisting (but the same is true for Nietzsche himself) that, no, finally, he was only some of the names of History after all. Let us look at once at one of those names, one of the most important, which rises to the surface in a dense and fascinating letter to Louise Colet (7 August 1846):

I have just about as much sympathy for caged birds as I do for enslaved peoples. The only thing about politics I understand at all is *riot*. I am as fatalistic as a Turk, and I think there is little to choose between giving our all for human progress and doing nothing whatsoever. And as far as progress itself is concerned, I am particularly dense when it comes to vague ideas. This kind of language bores me to tears. Actually, I have little but contempt for modern tyranny, which strikes me as stupid, weak and timid, but I have a deep veneration for ancient tyranny, which I consider one of the most beautiful manifestations of the human spirit.[1]

In this "cult of ancient tyranny"—what Karl Wittvogel's political fantasies will revive for our time under the name of "oriental despotism"—a whole complex of practical political and ideological attitudes and libidinal investments in images of the past are figured and arrested in the moment which precedes their official aesthetic figuration, their crystallization into so many formal representations.

I want to argue in what follows that such libidinal investments are essentially matters of shifting relationships, whose content is not fixed: the representational frame, however—whether of *Salammbô* or even of *La Tentation de saint Antoine*—seeks to freeze this mobility and to endow it with some more permanent, quasi-material symbolic value. Fortunately, we possess, in *Trois Contes*, a peculiar form, which I have elsewhere called the triptych, in which the temptation to interpret is at every moment subverted by the impossible triangular relationship between the three panels, such that one corner is always eccentric to the stable meaning the interpreter seeks desperately to establish between the other two. The triptych is thus an object of endless meditation, like the mandala, across which the eye and the mind trace seemingly interminable paths. Let me take one at once: the debris, the broken objects and commemorative traces that surround the elderly Félicité as so many signs of a subordinate life, lived by proxy through her masters:

. . . rosaries, medals, several pictures of the Virgin, and a holy-water stoup made out of coconut. On the chest of drawers, which was draped with a cloth just like an altar, was the shell box Victor had given her, and also a watering can and a ball, some copy-books, the illustrated geography book, and a pair of ankle-boots. And on the nail supporting the looking glass, fastened by its ribbons, hung the little plush hat.[2]

Caricature of Walter Benjamin's strong form of the Collector, Félicité here assembles so many metonymic objects around her one metaphorical icon, the stuffed parrot Loulou.

We must not expect this object cluster, this complex of multiplicity, to return untransformed in the narrative of Saint Julian. Rather, we must search for whatever interrupts the movements of agents and of *actants* with a descriptive cumulation that seems irreducible to narrative meaning, that offers the contingencies of Barthes's pell-mell and enumerative "effet de réel," yet in another register, in a register, precisely, where such resistance to narrative meaning, far from taking on the appearance of the contingent, and the inertly material, may well interrupt the narrative fabric with an excess of meaning, an indecipherable surplus of enigmatic signifiers that, as Rimbaud says, "look back at you." This is evidently the phalanx of oneiric beasts, the ladder of the animal kingdom, that nags Julian's steps like a remorse, even as he slaughters them in a frenzy of blood lust:

Sometimes, in a dream, he would see himself like our father Adam in the middle of Paradise, with all the birds and beasts around him; and stretching out his arms he would put them to death. Or else they would file past him, two by two, according to size, from the elephants and lions down to the stoats and ducks, as they did on the day they entered Noah's ark. [P. 49]

The Adamic reference, meanwhile, underscores the secret relationship, in this second panel of the triptych, between objects and their names, between language and desire, which the language of representation magically gratifies, without any delay, in the oneiric weightlessness of the text, at the same time that the words for things fatally kill the things themselves, a process theorized by Mallarmé.

But now a final transmutation of these collections, under the stark light of classical history and the Holy Land, and some final inassimilable narrative meaninglessness, which is neither that of metonymic seriality nor that of the inaccessible signifier, but rather that of sheer quantitative potentiality:

Vitellius came and looked at them, and insisted on having the underground rooms in the fortress opened up for inspection.

These rooms were hewn out of the rock in the shape of high vaults, with pillars at regular intervals. The first contained old pieces of armour, but the second was crammed with pikes, whose points stuck out of bunches of feathers. The third looked as if it were lined with reed mats, the slender arrows in it were stacked so straight and close together. Scimitar blades covered the walls of the fourth. In the middle of the fifth were rows of helmets, which, with their crests, looked like a battalion of red serpents. In the sixth there was nothing but quivers to be seen, in the seventh greaves, and in the eighth brassards; while in the other rooms there were forks, grappling irons, ladders, ropes and even poles for the catapults and bells for the dromedaries' breast-plates. And as the mountain widened out towards its base, hollowed out inside like a beehive, there were still more and even deeper rooms under these. A winding passage led downwards; they followed it, and eventually reached the threshold of a cavern which was larger than the other underground rooms. At the far end an archway opened on to the chasm which defended the citadel on that side. A honeysuckle clung to the roof, its flowers dangling in the sunlight. A thin trickle of water was purling across the floor.

There were perhaps a hundred white horses there, eating barley from a shelf on a level with their mouths. Their manes were all dyed blue, their hooves were enveloped in esparto mittens, and the hair between their ears was puffed out over their foreheads like a wig. They were lazily whisking their exceptionally long tails against their hocks. The Proconsul was struck dumb with admiration. [Pp. 102–4]

To hold the identity and the difference of these passages is to fix an object which is neither form nor content, but rather, following Louis Hjemslev, something like the form of a content or the content of a form. The thematic thread of animal life—parrot, Adamic beasts, invincible cavalry—is deceptive in this sense, not really a theme so much as a relationship and a category generated by the opposing one of the dead or inert, in a complex which includes objects, multiplicity, and the like. It will be somewhat more satisfactory, although no less ultimately problematical, if we coordinate these three passages under the currently fashionable notion of "signifying practices," practices which can then be approached across a series of distinct perspectives: affective content, models of force, spatial representation, transcendence, and temporality, of which the last is perhaps the easiest to convey, since it can be distributed across the three panels in terms of the persistence of the past, the mirage of a full oneiric present, and the accumulated potentiality of a power still to be exercised.

But if we want this text to remain open, and to continue to

generate its aleatory relationships in the sense in which Umberto Eco has described this process, we must be careful not to stabilize the movement of interpretation too hastily, nor prematurely to reify the play of association, something it would be only too easy to do. The category of sainthood, for instance, offers an all too convenient "theme" in terms of which to immobilize the narrative materials of a lost object, a visionary or beatific union, and the annunciation of a Messiah yet to come and beyond the text itself.

I want to argue that the invention of a theme of this kind is not at all the same as the description of a meaning, indeed, that there is a way in which the recourse to such thematic unification in reality betrays the *absence* of a narrative meaning, the hole at the center around which the quest for meaning turns, and which must ultimately be our object of inquiry. As for sainthood, it is not really a theme at all, but rather an ideological motif, part of a whole ideological complex, or *ideologeme*, which may be termed "aesthetic religion"—a projection of the religion of other people which informs the nineteenth century's sense, from Chateaubriand to Conrad to Max Weber, of the mirage of value of precapitalist societies and the desacralization of the emergent market system. An ideologeme of this kind—a most ambiguous ideologeme, whose other face Edward Said has described under the name "orientalism"—far from emitting a coherent narrative message, is rather to be grasped as the imaginary resolution of a very real and insoluble contradiction. To see the text in this way is to make a place for the properly interminable generation of interpretive meanings—interminable owing to the antinomy, or double bind, which cannot cease its restless search for an impossible closure—at the same time that we grasp the contradiction in terms of which that movement, but none of its provisory positions, is comprehensible. The sham endings of the tales—the Holy Spirit or Christ soaring, the severed head—by their own immobilization in the Imaginary, their sudden stasis as the reified images into which these narratives have been transformed offer testimony enough to the impossibility of closure here by their shift to a different discursive register, that of sheer decoration and of the impressionistic.

To attempt artificially to reconstruct the contradiction of which this text stands as an imaginary resolution means leaving the safe terrain of textual commentary and venturing some hypotheses whose usefulness can be tested only after the fact. Perhaps a question can be framed to guide this process: why, we might ask ourselves, should this unquestionable nineteenth-century *present*, the object of a henceforth classical Flaubertian realism, project, not one, but two distinct *pasts*, two distinct and seemingly irreconcilable historical trajectories? The desacralized world seems indeed to fantasize its own genealogy in two separate semic systems: the medieval world, the world of miracles, faith and legend; and the classical world, which we have heard Flaubert admire for its despotism, the world of aesthetic sadism and "bloodlust," of Delacroix's *La Mort de Sardanapale*, the world of *Salammbô* and of what will shortly be termed, by the fin de siècle, *décadence*. This second system is evidently also characterized by the presence in it of religious belief, but to put it that way is to realize that *Hérodias* makes of the otherness of religion a very different use than *Saint Julian*.

While ox-kidneys were being served, together with dormice, nightingales, and minced meat wrapped in vine leaves, the priests discussed the problem, of resurrection. Ammonius, a pupil of Philo the Platonist, thought they were stupid, and said so to some Greeks who were joking about oracles. Marcellus and Jacob had struck up acquaintance. The former was telling the latter of the happiness he had experienced on being baptized into Mithras, and Jacob was urging him to follow Jesus. Palm and tamarisk wines, the wines of Safed and Byblos, flowed from jars into bowls, from bowls into cups, from cups into gullets, and soon everyone was talking and exchanging confidences. Jacim, although a Jew, was no longer making any secret of the fact that he worshipped the planets. A merchant from Aphek was dazzling the nomads with a description of the marvels of the temple of Hierapolis, and they were asking how much a pilgrimage there would cost. A German who was nearly blind sang a hymn in praise of the Scandinavian promontory where the gods appeared with their faces bathed in light, while some people from Sichem refused to eat any turtle-doves, out of respect for the dove Azima. [P. 117]

Here the evocation of belief projects the vision of a dizzying multiplicity, of Babel and the infinite generation of superstitions, heresies, and sects. This sudden transformation of faith into superstition then allows us to complete the ideologeme of this particular tale and to identify its characteristic combination of despotism and superstition as the classical Enlightenment stereotype of the Ancien Régime. There is, therefore, in these two tales a process which Freud called splitting, in which the phenomenon of religion is broken into positive and negative semes: the corrosive, Voltairean, scientific, Enlightenment Flaubert will produce an orientalist image of tyranny and bloodlust, while the Flaubert who loathes the modern world and its bourgeoisie will project a wish fulfillment of precapitalist organic society in the henceforth familiar nostalgic and conservative terms of the loss of an age of faith.

But even these semic poles are far from being unambiguous. This same Flaubert will evoke the desacralized world of modern Paris over and over again, in *L'Éducation sentimentale*, in terms of the babel of codes and the proliferation of private languages, while socialism and the Commune will be ferociously denounced by a once more Enlightenment Flaubert as so many medieval survivals. As for science itself, if it knows a negative opposite in the form of error and superstition, it also generates a positive counterpole in the mindless innocence of Félicité herself and the well-nigh Wordsworthian celebration of imbecility and nonconsciousness.

The turning mechanism of these antinomies may indeed be clarified by another look at the eccentric position of Félicité in these representations: unlike the figures of the other two panels, and owing to metonymy itself, a serial displacement of the center away from its signs, Félicité as a woman and a servant—a quite different class determinant from those determinants of working woman or peasant—cannot register the truth of the modern world except by proxy and as absence and marginalization. A fourth term is conspicuously absent here, which would represent the modern world as Julian does the medieval or Herod the classical: and that is the Bourgeois himself, caricatured as M. Bourais in a corner of the text. It is on this structural absence that the complicated semic machinery of the *Trois Contes* turns perpetually, as in the void. It can be schematically described according to those equations or relations of equivalence and analogy with which Lévi-Strauss accounted for the operations of mythic narrative: bourgeois enlightenment (or science) is then to despotism and superstition as sainthood (or the no-power position and innocence of the servant) is to the secular diversity and babel of codes of the secular bourgeois world. The two terms of precapitalism and capitalism thus return on either side of the equation in positive and negative, dominant and subordinate forms: and these desperate relationships, which the mind is unable to think, then realize themselves in so many distinct and discontinuous images. In this way, a meditation on history, ideologically blocked, secures a resolution for itself in the languages of the Imaginary.

Yet this peculiar message is not articulated on the level of the individual *récit:* it appears only when the discontinuous relationships between these three separate narratives are grasped by way of the mediation of their formal systems: the juxtaposition of the three panels thus generates a second-degree space in which the essential interpretive theme becomes the ideology of form itself, the juxtaposition of three distinct modes of representation: realism, theatrical representation, and that more enigmatic third thing which we may, following Walter Benjamin's classic essay on Nikolai Leskov, *The Storyteller,* call the classical tale or *récit* in its strict sense. But this second-degree and reflexive narrative message, whose content is a differentiation of formal languages and their projection worlds—that mechanism which Barthes used to call connotation—is not to be taken as an ultimate either: *Trois Contes* emits a message about art language, only in order thereby to free some deeper fantasy about history itself. In Flaubert's political unconscious then, the mode of representation has become the vehicle for an unresolvable libidinal meditation on the nature of modes of production.

Notes

1. Gustave Flaubert, *Correspondance,* 2 vols., ed. Jean Bruneau (Paris: Pléiade, 1973), 1:278. Translation is mine.

2. Gustave Flaubert, *A Simple Heart,* in *Three Tales,* trans. Robert Baldick (Harmondsworth: Penguin Books, 1975), p. 49. All page references to the *Three Tales* of Flaubert in the text refer to this edition.

A Little Story about the *bras de fer;* or, How History Is Made

Françoise Gaillard

Open the *Dictionnaire des idées reçues* (*The Dictionary of Platitudes*). [1] Under the letter *B*, entry "Bras" ("arm"), we read: "In order to govern France a 'bras de fer' is necessary" (p. 305). The choice of the entry alone provokes laughter. A serious attitude would have placed such a statement under the patriotic heading "France," or the political one "Government," followed in parentheses by "the ways of." In the first case such an attitude could have been labeled as paternalistic, since it clearly shows solicitude toward the immature country, in whose place its own true needs must be precisely articulated. In the other case it could be denounced as political realism: there must be no hesitation in telling a country—in order to prevail—wherein lies its welfare.

In all cases a presupposition induced by the nature of the entry (empirical knowledge of France, or scientific knowledge of the art of government) would have sufficed to characterize the assertion and eventually ensure (be assured of) its comprehension. Since the sentence is hitched to an anatomical term, the word "bras," the most obvious consequence is that the entry falls between "braconnier" ("poacher")—

Freed convicts, every one of them. They must excite a frenetic anger: No pity, sir! No pity! Yet one goes to them when looking for a hunting dog [P. 305]

and "Bretons"—

Great folks, but stubborn [Ibid.]

and the sentence thus loses some of its specific resonance because of the echo caused by an implicit isotopy. A sort of meteorite of opinion fallen into a space composed of alien elements, the statement seems to be on unfriendly semantic terms with its lexical neighbors, unless we understand the exclamation "No pity!" and the call to the "bras de fer" as the expression of the same desire for authority and firmness, the manifestation of the same rigid conception of the exercise of power, or unless we find some kind of formal resemblance among all these definitions, which are, indeed, so many judgments, given their strongly assertive, in fact, peremptory, character! Does this suffice to justify their copresence in an enumeration that is more closely akin to a list than a dictionary, despite the alphabetical ordering?

"In order to govern France a 'bras de fer' is necessary"[2]—syntactically correct and semantically significant, such a statement is, from a logical and pragmatic point of view, totally devoid of meaning since it at once falls outside the jurisdiction of truth and is beyond verification by the discursive situation. Even this initial formulation is too lax, for it is difficult to dissociate from its semantics the logical relation of a sentence to the state of things it sets forth, but no more so than to dissociate this logical relation from the pragmatic relation of the sentence to its users. Might it be precisely this dissociation which Flaubert stigmatizes by calling it "la bêtise,"[3] which must henceforth be understood outside any reference to intelligence? In other words, might this scotomization of referential reality (to what do such remarks refer? what knowledge of France, of politics, and so forth is voiced here? who is uttering such things?) possibly be one of the sure signs of *la bêtise*, one of the objective means of spotting it?

To answer positively, as we are tempted to do at first, is to lay the basis for the establishment of a possible formal criterion of *bêtise*. It would be to declare *bête* (for the moment we will keep this Flaubertian denomination) all statements which, like the one we are analyzing, lend themselves, by their fixed enunciative forms, their *inertia*, to this operation of decontextualization that the dictionary makes them undergo. Everything, therefore, presenting itself in the barely disguised form of a proverb, a maxim, a postulate, or a law, can emigrate into other discourses, sprinkling them with truths as intangible as they are incontestable (since they are beyond the concrete sphere where contestation can take place).

We know that this is the position of Roland Barthes, for whom *la bêtise* is above all a matter of form, a manner of speaking, of offering one's opinion in the traditional enunciative forms of opining discourse. A Flaubertian theme if ever there was one! I give as proof only this fragment from a letter to George Sand: "What form must one adopt occasionally to express an opinion on aspects of this world without running the risk of later appearing to be a fool?"[4]

In order to avoid the risk of being accused of foolishness—that most fearful of things for Flaubert, who, let us note in jest, tries less not to be stupid than not to seem so—it is necessary, above all, to avoid amplifying the voice of *la bêtise* by speaking *like* it. Little does it matter that one says the same things that *la bêtise* does: the essential thing is not to say them *as* it does! In this perspective our sample statement is undoubtedly *stupid*, since it offers all the stylistic traits of total disjunction from reality, beginning with *grandiloquence*. This *bras* ("arm"), metonymical figure of a power reduced to its executive function, and this *fer* ("iron"), conventional symbol of firmness, end up digesting reality which generally withstands poorly the salivating and dissolving action of tropes. Although it may be a mouthful, it will nevertheless have lost the specific flavor of the syntagm that was meant to be diagnosis and prescription, the analysis of a specific situation and the instructions for its remedy. The rhetorical call to the *bras de fer* raises the statement to the level of a constant in the art of governing. Because this is valid at all times, in all places, it is possible to generalize the notion, and this by erasing the concrete traces of its emission. Such a dictum, thus made impersonal, might well have acquired the thrust of a maxim. However, this anonymity, which ends up hardening the statement by dipping it in a bath of universality, also has the paradoxical consequence of making it fragile. It changes it into an utterance that, while having cultural references (a whole imaginary realm of power traversed by phantasms of the bogeyman), has no referent. A word, therefore, that belongs to the language of wind, a *flatus vocis* . . . symptom which, upon further inquiry, indicates the illness of the time, this aerophasia that inflates words to the size of bourgeois bellies! Another indication is the fixity of the syntagma. What is *bête*, Jean-Paul Sartre tells us, "is the sentence whose mechanical rigidity excludes any live relation with the situation, the truth." And in his lexicon, Roland Barthes takes it up once more: what is *bête* is that which is stable, indivisible, indecomposable. Basically, the *idée reçue* ("platitude") would be the idea which has received its definitive form and which, once struck like a medal, would be exchanged without being changed.

"Mechanized life":[5] this expression ought to provoke laughter, but this is far from the reaction of Flaubert. In his correspondence he lets out the roar of an old lion feeling dispossessed of his kingdom, or worse, condemned to do his turn at the wheel like all the others, chained down by the inexplicable power of these hollow words. What, then, rankles him most about them? An enunciative arrogance? A will to intimidate? It is true that this will leave one speechless. Indeed, it is characteristic of this type of sentence construction not to provoke a reply, but to be its own final word! However, everything that we have just recalled, all too briefly, about the formal structure of *la bêtise*—which has commanded so much critical attention lately—shows that the will to power of stupidity's statements, which know, among other things, how to disguise the constative as the obligative, is paradoxically destroyed by their linguistic irresponsibility with respect to reality. The *Dictionary*'s "bras de fer" is a hollow expression! The laxity of the commonplace—an utterance absolutely worn out from overuse—contradicts the violence of its semantic power. The political program, uprooted from any referential stump, is consumed and absorbed into the triumphal quality of language. If, therefore, as we have been led to believe, *stupidity* were language which has attained the ultimate degree of extenuation of its contents, by erosion due to repetition; if it were simply empty thought, great soft words—not the *bras de fer* but its opposite, the *bras de velours* ("velvet"), verbally and verbosely gloved in iron—it would be easy to avoid it and escape from its grasp. It would suffice to abstain and to preach abstinence to others by taking up again the words of warning proposed by Nathalie Sarraute: "Take care, don't come near it, this object contains a time bomb. . . . It's too late to defuse it, it must be surrounded with interdictions, with signs on which is written the word 'danger.' . . . All who refuse to heed this warning should know what awaits them: they will be fools."[6]

This could be the function of the *Dictionnaire des idées reçues*: to be the manual of improper language usage, the sum of linguistic traps into which one must not fall. But in the tone and vocabulary of Nathalie Sarraute's warning, another relation with stupidity is indicated: that of *fear*. It seems to possess an explosive force, and one must above all fear its shock waves. Who is "one"? Intelligent people? Would these be the people most endangered by the exploding fragments becoming lodged in them, forming hard deposits? But they have remedies, and Flaubert knows it well; he has the choice: muteness or quotation marks. Sarraute tells us again:

It's the only effective, inexpensive, simple, quick way. . . . We recently had a fine demonstration of this. It should be a lesson to you. It was really—and no mistake—a stroke of genius. One of our teachers, one of the greatest, spotted a sort of limp, slippery idea, he isolated it, he compressed it as he knows how to do, reduced it to a few words, put it between quotes, and without further ado, without an additional touch, without running the risk of getting soiled, without deigning to lose his precious time, he added the simple warning: "fools say."[7]

The weapon is absolute except when turned against its wielder, as in the children's game "He's It if he says 'it.'" So who is seriously threatened by *la bêtise*? Answer: everyone, and Flaubert in particular. Not Flaubert as an intelligent being who, through contact with *la bêtise* risks his very intelligence, no! Rather, Flaubert as a social being who risks being dragged into the disastrous turbulence of its action.

Interest in stupidity has been largely limited to its passive aspect: Barthes's "noyau dur" ("hard kernel") or Sartre's "pratico inerte." In fact, it is just the contrary. *La bêtise* is active, activating; indeed, this is one of its fundamental characteristics, and the impact produced by stupidity on Flaubert is not comprehensible unless measured by the effect of stupidity on the course of events. The writer's epistolary outburst must not be compared with the dead utterances (rather laughable!) of the *Dictionary*, but instead with the vivid sentences (rather disturbing!) of the novels. Such outbursts do not strike at a language paralyzed by its own inflation, floating a few steps above the real situation, but rather at a language whose lexical poverty and syntactical rigidity are the secret of its efficacy. A question of form, if you will, but above all a question of force! Indeed, *la bêtise* is so intolerable to Flaubert only because it always triumphs in the power dealings of languages. For *la bêtise* isn't an open set of discrete utterances which are intrinsically stupid (*bête*), but a system with its own lexicon, syntax, tropes, and "tropisms," too . . . in short, what we call a language. And, contrary to what Barthes thought, who believed it sterile, confined by its own repetition, it is fertile, and this is in direct proportion to the number of people who speak it: "Because of the mere fact that the crowd exists, the seeds of stupidity that it contains develop, and from this result *incalculable* effects";[8] and Bouvard and Pécuchet remain dreaming, overcome by dizziness when faced with this fathomless proliferation!

Coming back to our statement, which Charles S. Peirce would call a model sentence, what permits us to consider it *bête*, except its apparent (formal) conformity with other lexical and syntagmatic formations belonging to this subcode of the general French code that we agree upon in order to name or designate *la bêtise?* For, by considering only its representative content, the matter is undecidable. At the most, the content could be said to be true or false (nevertheless, it is necessary to be able to referentialize it!), but in itself, it is neither stupid nor intelligent. Indeed, stupidity never derives from any sort of relation with truth, since this relation can change depending on the context and the enunciative situation. So what renders an utterance stupid? Essentially, the speakers. What is stupid is that which fools say—or could say. Now a new question arises: who, then are the fools? Is the tautology monster stalking us at this point in the investigation? For, if a sentence is defined by its speaker, inversely, the sentence is the predicate of the individual who says it; it defines him synthetically. A fool is therefore a person who says stupid things—"stupidities," as the young Gustave would say. The utterance makes the man; that at least is what Flaubert thinks, who, in one of his preparatory scenarios, underscores, in the following terms, the importance of the dinner offered by Bouvard and Pécuchet to the prominent people of Chavignolle: "This dinner should set in motion the action of the secondary characters. It is there that they discuss (in order to establish the identities of the secondary characters, source of the action) gardening, curios, religion, medicine, politics, literature, and, finally, socialism as it applies to the vagrant."[9] Note that in this narrative outline the transcription of the conversation is worthy of a descriptive presentation in Balzac's style—for saying is being—and that the characterization initiates the action—for being is doing—from there to conclude that saying is doing. . . . This tempting short circuit would betray Flaubert, who, between saying and doing, does not establish a relation of equivalence, but rather of correspondence.

In his eyes, there is a continuity between saying and doing, which is assured by the double coincidence of a person with his *speech* and with his *action*. If we follow Flaubert closely, it appears that the conversation taking place during this dinner derives all of its importance for the novel from its function as regulator of the identities of the characters. It serves in a way as a prelude to the action which it also conditions. This is to say that to the definitional value of the spoken word (the establishment of personalities) is added, in the novelistic situation, an actuational value, if only in a conjectural manner: the probable behavior, deducible from the undercurrent of the spoken sentences. The story of Bouvard and Pécuchet, which implicitly contains that of the coup d'état, reveals the diegetic and historic importance of the stupid word. This would be the novel about the actualization of opinion, of its taking hold, and of its ascendancy, of the emergence of its formidable power which has a name: *democracy*.

In order to find out how to get out of the revolving door that seems to send us from the statement to the speaker, from stupidity to fools, without permitting us to steady ourselves on the stable ground of indisputable judgment, one must listen once again to Flaubert. In the game of definitions, he accords primacy to the spoken word. We do not speak as we are; we are as we speak—which does not mean that we are what we say.

This ought to induce us to look for the unifying factor between word and action elsewhere than in the character who is only a middle term, an executive relay. Accordingly, we will now turn to an analysis of the key episode at Chavignolle.

By taking the floor at that famous dinner, during which, according to Flaubert, "all great subjects" must be touched upon, each diner *enters into language* and *situates himself in public opinion*—takes up (his) place in the ready-made language of public opinion—which defines his own social position. *Manner of speaking, manner of thinking*, and consequently *manner of acting* all have a common referent which immediately becomes conspicuous: the sociological position of the speaker. Indeed, it is there that the agreement between words and actions finds it justification; and opinion, which sideswipes them, in order, so it seems, to elevate them toward the heights of the universal, is revealed to be only the expression of a relative, conformist position. Confirmation of this is provided by Flaubert himself in these very same scenarios: "To show how and why each of the secondary characters loathes Science, Truth, Beauty, Justice—first, by instinct, second, by interest."[10] We might want to add, by personal interest. This exposition takes the place of all ulterior motivation. Indeed, the plot, slight as it is in *Bouvard et Pécuchet*, always advances through conflicts of opinion. There is no antagonism that at the first reading could seem to be merely personal, that might not originate in a difference in point of view. If Bouvard and Pécuchet are gradually quarantined, it is because in the chorus where every Chavignollais voice sings its part, they are off key. They sing out of tune (wrongly) to the ears of their citizens, who are sensitive to the harmony and tuning between the song and the role. In fact, being always a note too high or too low . . . they are the only ones lacking the voice of their condition. Does this suffice to scratch them from the great book of *la bêtise*, despite their progenitor? Perhaps: for their case interrogates *la bêtise* instead of illustrating it. It is because of their false notes that people resent them, and the "Your opinions are known" thrown out at them during a day of near-rioting in Chavignolle, by a Foureau driven to distraction by their paradoxicalness, is a threat which will be carried out at the moment of final ostracism.

A preliminary and provisional conclusion that contradicts all the defenders of the anonymity of *la bêtise*, those who think that it could be only systematically recorded (the *Dictionary*), or picked out from the continuum of texts (the cultural code of Barthes), would be: *Stupidity is a situated utterance.* The call to the *bras de fer*, alone capable of firmly holding the reins of the country, is no more the statement of a real political need in France (criterion of truth), than it is, in itself, the sure sign of stupidity. It is, first of all, the transcription of an opinion, which furthermore takes on the appearance of a wish.

Thus we read in *L'Éducation sentimentale*: "Monsieur Roque wished to have a 'bras de fer' in order to govern France" (p. 254). Summoned by Monsieur Roque, this *bras de fer* is an utterance whose stupidity, always evident to the narrator, proves to be indissociable from the enunciative situation, that is, from the person of the speaker (in this case, his position on the social scene) and from the circumstances of its utterance (a conversation at the home of the Dambreuses after those June days of 1848 when everyone was scared stiff!).

The decontextualized sentence of the *Dictionary*, which could make us believe in the existence of an *en soi* of *la bêtise*, was only understood after we had arrived at a common factor which is the implication, not "Fools say" (vague formulation with a high tautological risk), but "All the Messieurs Roque in France say." All that is necessary is that a statement be signed for, so to speak, by an owner, who, without having invented it, makes it his own merely by assuming ownership, so that the statement which seemed to owe its stupidity precisely to its complete ignorance of referential reality (grandiloquence, stereotyping, and so forth) proves to be completely appropriate. Appropriate to what? Neither to the state nor to the needs of France in general, no, but to Monsieur Roque's interests, which have instinctively known how to mold themselves into the right sentence which we must henceforth consider less agreed upon than agreeable, appropriate . . . to the point of view of its proprietor, which is a proprietor's point of view!

This stupidity is perhaps not so stupid; as the voice of the instinct of self-preservation, it is simply formidable! And it is what makes the hermit of Croisset howl with impotent rage. The inertia of *la bêtise* lies entirely within the word *conservation* itself. For when it comes to putting this plan for stability into action, *la bêtise* is very restless and active: it gears down, spending itself in words and actions, in words that metamorphose into action upon reality. For as long as the phrase of Monsieur Roque is confined to the conversational space, it remains a social act (underscored by an act of sociability); but written out on the voting ballot, it is a political act that has repercussions on the development of the country. Miracle of universal suffrage (above all when its universality is reduced merely to the Messieurs Roque), it is a machine to *execute la bêtise*, to make it the *executive power of France*. For who governs France? Not the *bras de fer*, but the *bêtise* that enthroned it. The weapon of *la bêtise* is its indifference to truth. *La bêtise* has no need of verification; that is, the state of things that it sets forth need not be true, in this case that France really has need of a *bras de fer*. It suffices that stupidity be obeyed, that what it says be brought about, which in this case is that France elect a *bras de fer* in the person of the president prince. Its reality test is *efficacy*, a posteriori confirmation. Barthes expressed his satisfaction at the fact that discourse had no responsibility towards reality, adding: "Suffice to imagine the disorder the most orderly narrative would create were its descriptions taken at face value, converted into operative programs and simply executed."[11]

Now this disorder feared by Barthes is precisely the *order of la bêtise*, which breaks the traditional equilibrium established between words and things, by seeking to impose upon things the order of the words of *la bêtise*. The stupid word does not care about coinciding with reality; rather, it summons reality to submit to *la bêtise*, and, what is worse, reality does so, as if sucked in by the attractive force of stupidity's void. Reality is swallowed up by the gaping chops of all the mongrels ("roquets") who eat their fill of it . . . satisfied, strengthened. The submissiveness of things plays into the hands of *la bêtise*. They docilely follow along as if subjugated by the catchy triumphalism in the iron words of *la bêtise*. Could it be the brassy sounding syntagm *bras de fer* that, acting as a magnet, has attracted all the votes? In short, could it be the expression that has been put to a plebiscite for having, by its vivid form, bodied forth a veritable imagery? The effective adherence of the populace to the formula must not be attributed to shady manipulations or electoral frauds. At least that is what Bouvard thinks: "I believe rather in the foolishness of the people. Think of all those who buy Revalescière, Dupuytren cream, 'chatelaine' water, and so forth! These simpletons make up the electoral mass, and we suffer their will. . . ." "Your skepticism appalls me," says Pécuchet (p. 254).

Virtue of congealed syntagm: language of wind becomes language of wood! Must we envisage the *coup d'état* as a *coup de force* of language? No doubt so, but the expression owes its power less to the imprint it leaves on minds—hypnotized to such an extent that they will never give up trying to actualize its content—than to the vagueness of its most dogmatic formulations. For the characteristic (and the force) of this type of declaration is to mark off (*baliser*) a field of understanding by unmarking (*banaliser*) a portion of language: the common place is first of all a meeting place of the community, where it restores and reknits itself. The stupid statement does not trouble itself over nuances. It works in the mass of language and acts upon the masses in proportion to its consistency, density, and strength. Contrary to the critical statement, which is necessarily divisive, it is *unifying*. From this comes the danger: it takes! Henceforth, the stupidity of a proposition is measured less according to its decisive, conclusive—in a word—totalizing, character than by its ability to make each individual a part of an *all*, to transform a social unit composed of discrete elements into a consenting and active totality.

At the very moment that Monsieur Roque is expressing his opinion (faithfully rendered by the narrator in free indirect discourse) to a soused and rowdy postdinner crowd, the mayor of Chavignolle, Monsieur Foureau, is expounding his views on the political situation to the guests of the count of Faverge: "I'm not making a speech, not I! I'm not a journalist! And I maintain that France wishes to be governed by a 'bras de fer!'" (p. 256). It is clear that the little dig at journalists, those opinion-makers, is intended to affirm, by contrast, the independence of Foureau's ideas. Like Monsieur Roque, he says (and very loudly) what he, Foureau, thinks. When it is his turn to take the floor, he believes that he is installing himself in speech as a free subject, as a particular subject, highly individuated, as shown by his hammering-out of first-person pronouns (*I, me*). But the subjective space which he imagines having carved out for himself by the sheer illocutionary force of his speech reveals itself to be a collective space: a *common place!* There is no private opinion, and true stupidity is to believe in the singularity of one's point of view. That does not mean that Foureau is a madman, that the voice is *similar* to the other's, to the others', for it comes from further away than he does: *from the id of his interests.* The question of the origin of the stupid statement, which is correctly considered impertinent, if we understand by this word *originality*, is no longer so once the question takes into account the problem of the sociologically concrete place of its emission. It has often been said that stupidity is speech without an origin. Yes, but only in the sense that it lacks the name of an author, for, as to its actual utterance, speech, as testified to by the Flaubertian dialogues, is solidly *originated*. We have to understand that Foureau is not to be suspected of plagiarism. He does not repeat Monsieur Roque any more than the latter repeats some illustrious predecessor. The matter is simpler still: *Foureau and Monsieur Roque meet*, and if spontaneously the same word comes to their lips, it is because this word which speaks their interest also speaks to them.

A problem, then, of *convergence*, and not of repetition, as it has been too often . . . repeated; of stereophony rather than of stereotype. An echo chamber, would this be *la bêtise profonde?* Perhaps, but the musical metaphor that fits best is that of unison.

In the Babel of conversations, where babblings battle for hegemony, the intervention of Foureau restores a sort of endangered linguistic unity, not so much lost as recently *forgotten* in the convulsive period between revolutions. And the guests, relieved, take up in chorus, in a single voice: "Everyone was pleading for a savior" (p. 256). Perfect moment, moment of stasis, which has a suspensive effect: "They were drinking liqueurs, and the cigar ashes were falling between the furniture cushions" (p. 256). There remains the mystery of this utterance, spoken by a few people, which immediately speaks to all, so that everybody in turn begins to speak it, as much on the private stage of conversation as, in no time, on the public stage which rests upon the ballot boxes of democracy. To speak it, did we say? Rather, to speak oneself in it, thanks to it, that is, to reveal themselves to themselves and to communicate among themselves. What we continue to call *la bêtise*, and which must now be given a new name (ideology?), is shown to be the social instrument of communion just as much as of communication. The epithet "language of cement" would be more appropriate to it than "language of wood," for it points, repoints the joints of the conversational or social edifice which is in the process of coming apart.

One question remains, however. The lapidary content of the statement to which everyone seems to rally, at the home of the count of Faverge just as at that of Monsieur Dambreuse, is, in fact, nothing but the generalization of a narrow point of view which, while shared by their peers, is nonetheless particular to the Roques and the Foureaux. . . . Where does it get such a unifying power? From its objective truth, confirmed by events? For this to be so, it would be necessary to believe in stupidity's perspicacity and to suppose either that this is the fitting and proper way of seeing or that stupidity is in the right place, the place from which to see the vanishing point of history, where the eye can take in totality. But if, as the Flaubertian text tells us, *la bêtise* is the voice of instinct and of interest, its (conjectural) clairvoyance is only due to the accidents of a historical situation, where the interest of the speakers is synchronized with what might well be called the general interest, which is never but a deformed representation: the projection on the screen of the social imaginary of diverse private desires. By its enunciative transparency, the sentence of the Roques and Foureaux has the effect, the function, of a lark-mirror. Everyone in turn is taken in by it, thinking that he recovers himself and regains self-control by looking in it. He recognizes himself in it and identifies with it, as with the symbolic mirror where every community puts itself to the test through its perception of itself. The efficacy of this speech that wishes to be made of iron is due to its nature and its role as a mirror: it reflects as a national identity, as a common will, the multiple figures of particular interests. Also, the coincidence between the (expressed) desire of (and by) some people and the latent desire of others, all others, that seems to us to be only a tag-along phenomenon, is less the result of a deep or final congruence of opinions than the product of a double exposure, the imprinting one upon another, of the various imaginary representations by which everyone gives form to his will, imagines it (for himself). The *bras de fer* is a synthesizer with a more metaphoric than iconic character: it serves as hieroglyph for the saving power in all political jargons that, without it, would draw in their own way, in their own words, the conclusions of the lesson of history.

From *L'Éducation sentimentale* to *Bouvard et Pécuchet*, the call to the *bras de fer* passes from the expression of an individual will: "Monsieur Roque wished, in order to govern France . . . ;" to that of a general wish: "France wishes to be governed." This expansion of the subject of the statement, which supposes in the speaker an identification of his point of view with the point of view of the universal—a procedure whose legitimacy is doubtful, even if the historical and novelistic reality confirm, in this case, its lucidity—is the characteristic of *la bêtise*. Any and every utterance which universalizes itself, which absolutizes itself is stupid. Contrary to what the sequence of events might lead us to believe, Foureau was not in a position correctly to hear France's heartbeat, was not prepared to be an accurate interpreter of its desire, which would imply that the understanding of history was on his side. In fact, it is not France which speaks through his mouth, despite what he thinks and what the narrator lets us think, it is his mouth which restores to France *a* language, *its* language! In this sense, and only in this sense, can one truly say that he expresses the *desire* of France: its desire for a common language, for a koïné, its dream of political stereophony rather than cacophony. It is not the real content of its opinion which has come to be promoted as truth, but rather it is the will to give its idea a universalizable form which translates a collective aspiration. This brings up, in other words, the question of the representativity of *la bêtise*.

La bêtise representative? Yes, its influence on the course of history in Flaubert's time suffices to prove this. But representative of what? Of desires? Or of French interests which no one knows how to describe very well any more? Neither one nor the other. Stupidity is representative of France's single will to homogenize. Whence the headiness of representation that seizes all who, speaking this unified language, believe themselves invested with representativity. Not a single prominent person from Chavignolle or from Paris who does not let himself be seduced by the mirage of a seat in parliament!

No doubt about it, *la bêtise* succeeds, imposes itself. But these undeniable successes are due less to the persuasive power of stupidity's speech than to its linguistic imperialism: because of its inability to promote successfully a universalizable interest that, at the level of content, would bring about a consensus, *la bêtise* replaces it by a universalist language ethic. After the revolutionary shake-up which has left each person separated and enclosed in his fear, French society can recompose itself only on the level of language, reunify itself only with the aid of a common language, and *la bêtise* is this koïné, this common front, not of interests, or of opinions, but of tongues that speak them, and of which the *Dictionnaire des idées reçues* is the glossary. In any koïné there is, as dominant, the language of some, but this domination can escape notice through formulations which are so vague and so abstract that they seem to be the resultant of all idiolects, of all the regional particularities. This is the very definition of general interest!

In order to be the unifying agency which it is, and which it must be, stupid language has to erase all traces of its origin. This expunction of sources (*déssourcement*) is the very condition of a possible revitalization (*ressourcement*) of national unity. It is necessary that each person be able to enter this new language, take possession of it, and feel at home in occupying the place that it has provided for him. Each person must be able to speak it in his own name and say, like Monsieur Roque, that he wishes for France . . . , or, like Foureau, "that France wishes . . . ," no matter the particular content that one or the other puts into this proposition, no matter the idiolect that hides within it! And it is thus that the *bras de fer*, called forth out of hatred of the people, or of the bourgeoisie, or of the republic, or of everyone, indeed, of itself, called to be the executant of all ideological passion and of all personal rancor, becomes, one day, the *executive of history*. Put into power by *la bêtise*, it is only its agent, or rather, its straw man. In fact, it is *la bêtise* that is at the command post, and the impotent Flaubert belches, cursing the language of opinion, and striving to nullify it by turning it against itself, without truly understanding how this demonetized language imposes its rate of interest on the currency of things.

[Translated by Elizabeth Aubé]

Notes

1. Gustave Flaubert, *Dictionnaire des idées reçues*, in *Oeuvres complètes*, ed. Bernard Masson, 2 vols. (Paris: Seuil, 1964). All page references to works of Flaubert in the text will be to volume 2 of this edition. [Translations are by the translator.—EDS.]

2. *Bras de fer* translates literally as "iron arm." However, since the equivalent English expression is "iron hand" we have chosen to retain the French term. This also facilitates comprehension of the article's opening paragraph, which makes much of the *Dictionary*'s alphabetical listing.—TRANS.

3. *La bêtise* carries a connotation of animallike simplicity which is lacking in the English terms "foolishness" and "stupidity." Also, the notion and the term *la bêtise* have been associated with Flaubert and his thought. For these reasons, we have often used the French term or its adjectival form *bête*.—TRANS.

4. Flaubert to George Sand, 18–19 December 1867, quoted by Claude Mouchard in his article "Déchirer l'opinion," *L'Arc*, no. 79 (1980), pp. 69–76.

5. This is an allusion to the famous definition of laughter offered by Henri Bergson in *Le Rire*: "du mécanique plaqué sur du vivant."—EDS.

6. Nathalie Sarraute, *Fools Say* (*Disent les imbéciles*), trans. Maria Jolas (New York: George Braziller, 1977), p. 50.

7. Ibid., p. 44.

8. *Bouvard et Pécuchet*, p. 254. The italics are mine.

9. From the preparatory scenarios for *Bouvard et Pécuchet* published with the novel in the edition of Claudine Gothot-Mersch (Paris: Gallimard-Folio, 1979), p. 450.

10. Ibid., p. 451.

11. Roland Barthes, *S/Z*, trans. Richard Miller (New York: Hill and Wang, 1974), p. 80.

Flaubert and the Status of the Subject

Victor Brombert

Contemporary criticism is fond of quoting Flaubert's proclaimed desire to write a book with hardly a subject, a book about nothing at all ("un livre sur rien") that would be held together through sheer power of structure and style. A number of other sallies or paradoxes have been found useful in this effort to enlist Flaubert in the cause of modernity. "One can write anything at all as easily as whatever one likes," Flaubert affirmed to Louise Colet, whom he liked to impress with his literary extremism. Or: "I would like to create books which require only the *writing* of sentences." It is almost as though Flaubert coined the by now commonplace chiasmatic opposition between the story of an adventure and the adventure of a story. Did he not, in speaking about his own uneventful life, describe the act of writing as the real drama "in which the adventures are the sentences"?[1] All this feeds the prevailing notions that Flaubert is interested above all in form; that he engages, as an *experimenter*, in a game of literary structures; that his fiction, projecting the bad conscience of the traditional novel, is committed to the ultimate disappearance of the personage; that he is the first of the nonfigurative novelists; that his books reflect essentially the problematics of textuality.

According to modernistic doxa, Flaubert, though choosing the medium of the novel, attempts to escape from the tyranny of story-telling; he not only subverts narrative movement but eludes meaning and aims at undecidability; he reaches toward the essence of litera-ture which perversely is its own disappearance. His is the tragedy of a vocation which ultimately tends toward a spoken silence.[2] Recent critics have chosen to find and to stress in Flaubert: Maurice Blanchot, the intransitive nature of the literary work; Pierre Bergounioux, the elusiveness of the center of meaning; Claude Bur-gelin, the self-referential nature of the text; Jonathan Culler, the fundamental questioning of the communicative act. And even Sartre, though he continued until the last to believe in intentionality and meaning, has seen Flaubert as one of the original Knights of Nothingness.[3]

All this is not sheer critical fantasy and willful (wishful) reading. Flaubert's literary habits and pronouncements, even if one discounts the consciously playful or aggressive nature of some of the paradoxes, do provide more than a hint of the essentially ironic, perverse, and aporetic nature of his literary idiom. The dogmas of impersonality ("One must not *write oneself*"), of the autonomous value of art, of the priority of language (words precede experience), all seem to undermine the conventional notion that literature is *about some-thing* and that the subject is centrally important. Throughout his correspondence, Flaubert repeatedly questions the prestige of the subject and appears to deny the mimetic function of literature.[4]

The insignificance of the subject is by him affirmed, not merely as a challenge to the vulgarian and utilitarian thinking of the *caboches épicières*, but as axiomatic: "In literature there are no beautiful artis-tic subjects." Style, form, and point of view (they are often inter-changeable) are all that count; and their efficacy and prestige grow in inverse proportion to the deflation of subject matter: "style by itself being an absolute way of seeing things." Increasingly so, it would seem, Flaubert moves toward the aesthetics of formalism. In a letter to George Sand, in 1876, he wonders why a book, independently of what it purports to say, could not produce the same architectural effect as a Greek temple, through the precision work of its articulations, the texture of its surfaces, the harmony of its structures—thus reaching out toward a form of abstract perfection. But even much earlier, at the time he was still at work on *Madame Bovary*, he could assert that from the point of view of "pure Art" one might say that the subject did not exist.[5]

Such statements amount to a declaration of independence of art. If Flaubert irascibly maintains that the word *subject* is without meaning ("ne veut rien dire"), it is because, long before Edouard in Gide's *Les Faux-Monnayeurs*, he is convinced that the truly great works are those that are least dependent on an external reality: "The most beautiful works are those containing least subject matter." The creative pride behind such affirmations casts light on the provocative final sentence of *La Légende de saint Julien l'hospitalier*:

And that is the story of Saint Julian the Hospitaller, more or less as it can be seen on a stained glass window in a church in my part of the country.

Not only is the referred-to reality here an art work in its own right (the stained glass window of the Rouen Cathedral), but between text and what it refers to no true mimetic relation exists. Flaubert in fact comments revealingly on this fake relation and on the importance of the discrepancy. In a letter to Gustave Charpentier, he imagines with delight the puzzlement of the reader had an illustration of the cathedral window been added to the text: "Comparing the image to the text, one would have said: 'I don't understand a thing. How did he get this from that?' "[6]

Of course, Flaubert abhorred the very idea of having his books illustrated. And the gap between text and referential reality, as he sees it, not only serves the prerogatives of art but intensifies the power to perplex and bewilder. The combination of ironic and poetic mystification is a potent temptation for Flaubert. He repeatedly stated that the loftiest works of art, the ones that unleash the power to dream, are also *incomprehensible*. Hence the lasting ambition to conceive works that would puzzle and even madden the reader. Two years before his death, he put it explicitly: "This is my (secret) purpose: to astound the reader so much that it drives him crazy." The aim was already formulated years before he published his first novel.

In a letter to Louis Bouilhet, he dreams of a text so written that the reader would be totally disconcerted ("that the reader not know whether he is being made fun of or not").[7]

The antirepresentational, antimimetic bias of Flaubert is further sustained by an early conviction that art and life are distinct, even antagonistic realities, that the former is clearly superior to the latter. From his earliest texts on, he repeatedly suggested that life cannot measure up to books. He openly declared his preference for a factitious existence ("vie factice"). Hence the advice given to Louise Colet to indulge, not in real debauches, but in those of the imagination. "One must create harems in one's head, palaces with one's style." Writing is perceived, all at once, as derivative, legitimate self-defense, and hostile substitute to life. Nonliving becomes, as it were, the precondition of the artist's vocation. Conversely, nonwriting appears as a form of death: "My nonwriting weighs heavily on me," he confides to Jules Duplan in a depressed mood. More dramatically still, in a letter to Mademoiselle Leroyer de Chantepie: *In order not to live*, I immerse myself in Art, in my despair."[8]

Statements such as these help us understand why Flaubert's aesthetic bias so often takes the form of the very opposite of what his contemporaries, perhaps because it suited them, chose to praise as his "realism."[9] For Flaubert's particular love-hate relation to reality nurtures his antimimetic stance, making him at times stress the unbreachable hiatus between art and life ("Art is not reality . . . one has to choose"), at others point to the need for transcendence: "Reality, in my view, should only be a springboard." Not only is "exact narration" considered impossible and undesirable, but literature's superiority over the plastic arts is largely attributed to its nonreferential status. One might ponder the following declaration in a letter to Duplan: "A drawing of a woman looks like a woman, that's all . . . whereas a woman described in words makes one dream of a thousand women."[10]

One could go on and on marshaling evidence. From where we stand, a century after his death, Flaubert can only too easily be made to loom as a prophet of modernism. There is, however, something partial and self-serving in this critical perspective. To be sure, Flaubert the "homme-plume" ("human pen"), as he called himself, lived out the writer's craft as a total vocation; he approached each work as a new problem, as a new challenge; he sought, in the literary experience, the essence of literarity. And between this literarity and the subject matter there existed for him a fundamental gap. Art he always saw as a matter of *excess:* that which could not be made to correspond. He was, at the same time, haunted by the specter of repetition, the paralyzing and silencing effect of any linguistic act, the fear and consolation of being no more than a redundant scribe. Much like the budding poet in *Novembre,* who discovers that he is only a *copyist,* much like Frédéric, who is discouraged by the numerous literary echoes he detects in his own writings, Flaubert himself is plagued by the pervasiveness of the *déjà-dit.* Only with him, this self-consciousness turns into an ironic and parodistic strategy that blurs genres and becomes, one might say, creatively deconstructive. And the case for Flaubert's modernity is further strengthened by his deliberate view of himself as a transitional figure preparing and anticipating the literature of the future. With arrogant humility, he liked to see himself as achieving "that which is most difficult and least glorious: the transition."[11]

Yet there is something simplistic and downright falsifying in a critical position that sets up Flaubert as the progenitor and exemplar of modernity. His fascination with the past, his allegiance to classical culture, his reverence for those he calls the "pères de l'Art" are demonstrably keener than any of his attitudes towards the to-be-created future. Homer and Shakespeare are literally referred to as coworkers with God: they are the conscience of the world. Throughout his life, and increasingly so as his own art matured, he felt that only the classics deserved to be read and studied. "Devote yourself to the classics . . . do not read anything mediocre," he advised Amélie Bosquet. "Read the classics . . . you have read too many modern books," he admonishes another correspondent. As a first rule of literary hygiene, he urges the daily reading of the great texts of the past: "Every day . . . read a *classic* for at least one full hour." More significantly, as Sartre so aptly put it, Flaubert saw himself, while alive, as already posthumous, as integrated into the freemasonry of all the great dead writers of the past, as writing uneasily, not for the future (and even less so for the present), but for all those readers who have already, or will have, their place in the vast cemetery of culture.[12] One might add that, temporally speaking, the future anterior is the symbolic tense of Flaubert's literary calling.

It could be argued, perhaps too cleverly, that a particular type of uneasy relation to past culture is precisely a characteristic of modernity. But such an argument would hardly dispose of deeper contradictions. Flaubert, it should be noted, was quite aware of some of them. "In me there are . . . two people [deux bonshommes]," he declared: one is in love with lyric outbursts or gueulades, the other is determined to observe reality, to seek out and analyze the truth. He himself diagnosed the compartmentalization of his mind, allowing the most scabrous contradictions to coexist: "I live by pigeon holes; I have drawers, I am full of compartments." Flaubert's correspondence, so justly praised for its theoretical interest, is in fact a fascinating web of contradictions, of confusing overlaps and blurrings. The key notions of representation and reproduction—at times opposed to each other, and others almost interchangeable—are shifting in meaning and context. The notion of illusion is ill defined, and the concept of truth whether in the guise of vrai or vérité, remains thoroughly inconsistent. "From the moment something is true, it becomes good," he writes late in life to George Sand, echoing an early conviction that all great works do reveal a truth ("the truth they manifest and expose"). But his reaction to Zola's L'Assommoir, which he qualifies as "ignoble" to the Princess Mathilde, rings another bell. "To achieve reality [faire vrai] does not strike me as the prime condition of art." And pondering over the poor reception of L'Éducation sentimentale, he comes up with an altogether ambiguous statement: "It is too real and . . . is lacking the distortion [la fausseté] of perspective."[13]

Granted that some of these inconsistencies have to do with changing contexts and changing interlocutors, it remains that Flaubert's theoretical pronouncements, unless one systematically represses the ones that do not fit into a system, seriously complicate the task of defining his critical position. This is especially so if one examines Flaubert's unsteady and constantly shifting attitudes towards the priorities of art and experience. On the one hand, the inferiority of experience is posited as a precondition of art: it is the poet's voice, not lived life, that is to provide the raw material for reverie. But on the other hand, experience is considered ineffable, too overwhelming to be spoken. In Beyrouth, looking at the sea and the snow-capped mountains, he scorns the nerve ("toupet") of those who dare write descriptions. The one literary lesson of his oriental trip, he claims, will have been to discourage him from ever writing a single line on the Orient. The impossible mimesis: again looking at the sea, he muses on how radically false any attempted artistic "reproduction" would be. The vanity of art in the face of reality impressed him during his earliest literary efforts. "What vanity is art," he writes in *Mémoires d'un fou*, "to want to portray man in a block of stone, the soul in words, feelings through sounds, and nature on a painted canvas." The unsayable haunts the young writer, struck by the inadequacy of language. "Pitiful human weakness! With your words, your languages, your sounds, you speak and you stammer"—while the essence of the experience cannot be expressed.[14]

This inexpressible experience, often defined as the *Idea*, is thus surprisingly perceived as beyond words, indeed, as independent from words. Flaubert goes so far as to suggest—and this may seem incongruous in our era of linguistically oriented criticism—the existence of a style without words. The narrator of *Mémoires d'un fou* has learned Byron by heart—in French. The fact that it was a translation does not seem to matter. "The flatness of the French translation disappeared in the face of the ideas themselves, as though these had a style of their own, independent of the words." The corollary of this wordless style is obvious: an experience that lies beyond words, beyond art. "I vaguely yearned for some splendid thing which I would not have known how to formulate in any words, or define in my mind in any form."[15]

The problematic relation, in this sentence, between the terms "chose," "mot," and "forme" does point to a wavering between two fundamental frustrations: the unattainability of unmediated experience and the futility of the mediation of writing. Flaubert's drama as writer will somehow remain situated between two opposing negations: the denial of the subject and the discredit of linguistic expression. The ambiguity outlasts his adolescence. While writing *Madame Bovary*, he observes, in a manner that seems to displace *bovarysme* from the character to the act of writing: "We have too many things and not enough forms." Just as Emma's dreams are too big for her house, so Flaubert suffers from a sense of oppressive limitation. The overabundance of available subject matter ("Oh, *subjects; how many there are*") becomes as crushing and as paralyzing to the anguished writer as the endless cortege of heresies in *La Tentation* is to the anguished saint. Already in the first *Éducation sentimentale*, the one he completed when he was twenty-four years old, Flaubert had commented on the relation between wealth of subjects and artistic paralysis. The nineteenth century with its revolutionary background, its Napoleonic saga, its collapsing and reborn regimes, its ideological fermentation, provided a dizzying marketplace of topics. But this wealth itself strikes the young Flaubert as a threatening plethora: "The overabundance of subject matter causes the difficulty of art."[16]

We are compelled to return to the central issue of the subject and its status. For while it is indeed tempting to draw up a catalogue of Flaubert's pronouncements deflating the import of the subject, thus lending weight to the declared ambition to write a book "about nothing," it is possible also to come up with a no less telling list of conflicting statements, all of which proclaim the subject's centrality. "Everything has to come out of the subject," he peremptorily informs Louise Colet. It is hard to imagine a more categorical statement. What Flaubert means is that the literary devices, in a viable work, derive from the conceptual thrust of the subject. The subject-as-matrix: we are far removed from the notion of the generative power of language and rhetoric. Flaubert says as much in a colorful letter to Louis Bouilhet. Literary know-how (the *ruses*, the *ficelles*) and sophisticated self-consciousness are simply not enough. Masterpieces are conceived only when there is an organizing central principle which Flaubert defines as "the heart of the matter," and more specifically as the "very idea of the subject." And he pursues this with a series of bawdy metaphors to stress his misgivings about a literary virtuosity that ultimately remains impotent: "Nous gamahuchons bien, nous langottons beaucoup, nous pelotons lentement, mais baiser! mais décharger pour faire l'enfant!"[17] ("We're good at sucking, we tongue a lot, we pet for hours: but—the real thing! Can we ejaculate [*décharger*], can we engender a child!")

The conviction that there exists an original bond between subject matter and creativity lies behind countless comments on the importance of the subject. When Flaubert writes that the secret of masterpieces is the concordance between the subject and the temperament of the author, when he repeatedly hopes to find a subject suitable for his own particular temperament ("a subject in *my register*"), when he flatly states that for a book to be oozing with truth the author must be stuffed with his topic, what is involved is the belief in the generative power of the subject. He could not be more explicit about this than in a letter of 1861 to Madame Roger des Genettes: "A good subject for a novel is one that comes all in a piece, a single shot. It is a matrix that gives birth to all the other ideas." The belief in the subject's matricial virtue would explain why, in flagrant contradiction to the claim that there are no "beautiful" subjects, that all subjects can be indifferently good or bad, Flaubert nonetheless remains stubbornly faithful to the notion that the African desert is more inspiring a subject than a vegetable garden or the even more pedestrian *trottoir*. And this would explain why he can get angry with his friend Ernest Feydeau for supporting precisely the paradoxical notion he himself advocated: "Why do you insist on getting on my nerves by maintaining that a cabbage patch is *more* beautiful than the desert?" This disputation with himself has its fictional projections. Thus Pellerin, in *L'Éducation sentimentale*, whose ideas echo Flaubert's own pronouncements, yet seem to mock them, at the same time rejects the doctrine of realism ("Leave me alone with your hideous reality!") and reaffirms the priority of the subject's intrinsic value: "Better . . . the desert than a sidewalk."[18]

The reaffirmation of the subject's preeminence would also explain why, despite disclaimers, Flaubert never gave up an interest in satire, why topicality remained a steady temptation, and why, far from signing the death warrant of the personage, he continued to believe in the independent, nontextual reality of his own characters. In a letter to Taine, he makes a revealing comment about the unwritten presence of his personages: "There are many details that I don't write. For instance, Homais is slightly pock-marked." The unwritten physical detail matters, however, less than the pretextual, or extratextual, psychological individuation. Flaubert, in his early thirties, speaks of himself proudly as "an old psychologist like me." He will continue to view the creative effort of the novelist as an inductive process leading to the reconstruction or reproduction of a psychological reality which has a preexistent, independent status. He in fact congratulates himself precisely on this psychological intuition and reconstruction. "Bovary will be . . . the summa of my psychological knowledge"—and, as he explains to Louise Colet, "will only be original because of that." Even more telling, for it clearly denies the priority of formalistic concerns, is the following appraisal of his achievement in _Madame Bovary:_ "The reader will not be aware, I hope, of all the psychological labor hidden under the literary form, but he will feel its effect." This notion of form as hiding a deeper truth certainly does not give much support to linking Flaubert's name to the generation of the nouveau roman, a generation that so scornfully denounced what Alain Robbe-Grillet called "the old myths of depth."[19]

Thus Flaubert himself places curious difficulties in the way of any attempt to canonize him as an apostle of a formalistic, self-referential, intransitive literature devoted to the problematics of its own textuality, a literature whose subject, as Jean Ricardou wants us to believe, is "the functioning of the book" and nothing else.[20] And the greatest difficulties Flaubert places in the way of a postmortem conversion to this brand of fashionable modernity have to do with his insisting that the prime function of literature is to _reproduce_ and _represent._

Reproduction and representation are, of course, far from the same thing, though they tend to overlap in Flaubert's usage. The greatest poets, Flaubert asserts, reproduce the world. But with equal axiomatic assurance, he declares that the greatest geniuses have never done anything but _represent._ Though the two notions blur, their distinct meanings for Flaubert can be traced. When he refers to reproduction, it seems quite obvious that he means something both more precise and more limited than a totalizing of experience, a _speculum mundi._ The reproduction is, first, that of material reality. His literary self, as he puts it, wants "the things he reproduces to be felt almost materially." The outer physical reality must come into focus; it is the objective: "The external reality must become part of us . . . in order to reproduce it properly." And Flaubert not only advocates but claims to practice the close observation of the physical model. While at work on *Un Coeur simple*, he kept a stuffed parrot on his desk, "so as to paint from life."[21]

Three images—the eye, the mirror, and the mime—preside over the Flaubertian doctrine of reproduction. Seeing sharply comes first. For anything at all to become interesting, it is enough, he is convinced, to look at it for a long time. Beyond the "voluptuous sensation" that comes with the contemplation of the object, the steady gaze has to do with the conception and delineation of the object as subject. If Flaubert is so pleased to have what he calls a "myopic" vision ("I know how to see, and see the way the nearsighted see, the very pores of things"), it is because he is convinced that all great works depend on the abundance of functional details ("détails intrinsèques au sujet"). This reaffirmation of the subject's centrality and of the detail's specific role in the larger economy of the work suffices to cast strong doubt on Roland Barthes's somewhat hasty affirmation that the concrete detail in Flaubert, serving only the illusion of reality ("l'effet de réel"), remains resistant to any structure or meaning.[22]

Flaubert's symbolic myopia is in fact the prerequisite for a larger vision. Flaubert speaks of the need to become the eye of the world ("être oeil, tout bonnement"), to lose oneself in the subject, much as Saint Anthony dreams of becoming matter. "As a result of staring at times at a pebble, an animal, a painting, I felt myself becoming part of it." A great literary artist, in turn, provides his reader with a supreme ocular and specular experience. On reading Shakespeare, "one is no longer a man, but an eye." The mirror image serves indeed as a mediation between the visionary eye and the spectacle of the external reality. "Let us be magnifying mirrors of external reality." Appropriately, the transition between the reflecting eye and the spectacle is provided by the metaphor of the imitative actor, and more specifically the *mime*. But the imitative process depends first of all on the ability to observe. "To be a good mime, one must . . . first of all *see* people, be imbued with them."[23]

But this mimetic function of art, precisely because of the mediating specular and theatrical metaphors, does not really imply a *reproduction* of a fixed reality. It is here that the other key term, *representation,* serves, not as a contradiction, but as a corrective. Art, says Flaubert, is representation: "We must think of nothing but representing." Yet even to "represent" such immaterial realities as "the passions" or as "humanity of all times," Flaubert feels driven to the most painstaking documentation: on agricultural fairs for *Madame Bovary,* death by thirst for *Salammbô,* the symptoms of croup for *L'Éducation sentimentale,* provincial sites for the setting of *Bouvard et Pécuchet.* Flaubert's principle remains invariable: "to know things before describing them." That of course includes books. The powerful attraction to erudition is, however, not a mere yearning for a sheltered life spent counting "fly spots"; it corresponds to the conviction that only encyclopedic knowledge can give literary mastery. "In order to write, one should know everything." And Flaubert stresses the encyclopedic nature of this literary documentation: "Books which have given rise to entire literatures, such as Homer and Rabelais, are encyclopedias of their time." What lurks behind this respect for knowledge and its fecundating power is not only the potential of caricature (and self-caricature) which Flaubert was to exploit fully in *Bouvard et Pécuchet* but the conviction that, no matter how omnipresent the specter of eternal redundance, there is a worthwhile something-to-be-written, that the subject exists, and that it can be communicated—though perhaps only in an enigmatic, or as Flaubert puts it, "incomprehensible" manner. This indeed, for Flaubert, is the paradox of the subject: "I have a need to say incomprehensible things."[24]

Flaubert himself provides the qualifier to his perplexing relation with the "subject." In the same sentence that prominently features the word *sujet,* the word *illusion* appears as the ironic companion. Literary form, he explains, is achieved only when "we are obsessed by the illusion of the subject." Illusion may even be seen to achieve priority in Flaubert's theory of mimesis. The first quality of Art and its purpose is *illusion.*" Though he boasted that *Madame Bovary* would make his fellow Normans roar with indignation because of the absolutely lifelike *Norman color,* Flaubert was obviously not a dupe of the mimetic fallacy. Writing to Léon Hennique, shortly before his death: "Do you take me for enough of a fool to be convinced that in *Salammbô* I created a genuine reproduction of Carthage, and in

Saint Anthony an accurate depiction of the world of Alexandria?" Raymonde Debray-Genette has very shrewdly made the point that when Flaubert speaks of reproduction, the verb *to reproduce* comes heavily loaded with connotations of craft and artifice. What is to be imitated is, not nature itself, but its devices. It is because of this *artistic* imitation of nature that art appears as a second nature, an analogue. Or rather, it is nature itself that here functions as the metaphor for artistic creation: "Let's get used to seeing the world as a work of art whose devices we must reproduce in our works." The verb *reproduire* is thus emphatically linked to literary technique (*procédés*) rather than a fixed reality.[25]

Mutability is indeed of the essence. Transmutation, recasting, transformation, metamorphosis are the key images associated with the creative act. "I wish . . . to transform through Art everything I have felt." Or again: "I am presently devoured by a need for metamorphoses. I would like to write everything I see, not as it is, but transfigured." One might justifiably claim that the profound and unifying *subject* of Flaubert is, not this or that character in a given setting, but the struggle against the very conditions of existence by means of what he himself defines as the "plastic and total recasting through Art."[26]

Raymonde Debray-Genette scores another important point: the *structures imaginaires* are indeed far more significant in a given textual space than the imperatives of the so-called subject.[27] But such structures are also the precondition for thematic unity, and the elaboration of the themes represents the real subject of the work. To be sure, this thematic subject, ultimately the organizing principle of the writer's total vision, is harder to define; it always partially eludes both reader and writer, camouflaging its powerful singularity behind a surface variety, reaching out to the unsayable, the *indisable*.

And this precisely is the merit of thematic reading and thematic criticism when, at their best, they focus on textual strategies: they decipher, through a careful reconnaissance of linguistic and figural patterns: the hidden subject of the work. This "other" subject which, in the case of Flaubert centers on the superiority of artifice and imagination over life, cannot be reduced to what has come to be known as textual self-referentiality. Just as the book "about nothing" is not the same as the book about pure textuality, so the writing of fiction is a self-projecting as well as self-transposing activity: "A book for me is a special way of living"; and more clearly still: "I have always placed myself in everything I have written. Instead of Saint Anthony, it is I who am there."[28]

It is most revealing that Flaubert, in his fiction, avoided the portrayal of the artist as hero. This figure makes the briefest appearance—and at that in a work Flaubert refused to publish. Jules, in the first *Éducation sentimentale*, achieves a kind of salvation through suffering, solitude, and the struggle with the demon of art. But even in this novel, the artist-hero appears only in order to disappear. The priority of art implies, it would seem, the death of the artist. "The more I detach myself from artists, the more enthusiastic I become for art." If Flaubert confesses to having dispersed himself in his works ("Mon moi s'éparpille . . . dans les livres"—"J'ai toujours péché par là"), this only strengthens the latent hostility to the artist-hero.[29]

Yet it could be argued that, in the deepest sense, all of Flaubert's writings extol the artist. Even the caricatures of Pellerin or of Bouvard and Pécuchet, deal—perversely, to be sure—with ideals and ideas dear to the author. And *bovarysme*, this yearning for the unattainable, this confrontation of dream and reality, is certainly not Emma's monopoly. Baudelaire was uncannily perceptive when he identified Emma, in pursuit of the ideal, as the "poète hystérique." Of course, Emma's flaw is that she uses art to feed her dreams, instead of placing her dreams in the service of art. In a subtle way, Frédéric and Madame Arnoux move closer, if only by preterition, towards an esthetic possession of their own existence. During their last encounter, they become the narrators of their own past ("Ils se racontèrent leurs anciens jours"). Abstracted from their passion, they place themselves at the supreme vantage point of a transcending future anterior: "No matter, we will have loved each other deeply." Albert Thibaudet, as perceptive a reader as Flaubert could have hoped for, went so far as to hint at Frédéric and Madame Arnoux's status as proto-novelists: at the end they possess their dream instead of being possessed by it. The *livre sur rien* may well turn out to deal latently but powerfully with a subject and with meanings that go

beyond intransitivity and the sophisticated playfulness of a nonsig-
nifying signifier![30]

Notes

1. Gustave Flaubert, *Correspondance*, 9 vols. (Paris: Louis Conard,
1926–33), 6:2. Subsequently referred to as *CC*. The translations are mine.
2. See Gérard Genette's article "Le Premier Écrivain moderne," *Le
Monde*, 25 April 1980.
3. Maurice Blanchot, *L'Entretien infini*, (Paris: Gallimard, 1969), p.
492; Pierre Bergounioux, "Flaubert et l'autre," *Communications* 19 (1972);
Claude Burgelin, "La Flaubertolâtrie," *Littérature*, no. 15 (October 1974),
pp. 5–16; Jonathan Culler, *Flaubert: The Uses of Uncertainty* (Ithaca, N.Y.:
Cornell University Press, 1974), p. 13; Jean-Paul Sartre, *L'Idiot de la famille*, 2 vols. (Paris: Gallimard, 1971). For perspectives on Flaubert's modernity, see also Jean Rousset, "*Madame Bovary*; ou, Le Livre sur rien," in
Forme et signification (Paris: Corti, 1962); Nathalie Sarraute, "Flaubert le
précurseur," *Preuves*, February 1965; Jeanne Bem, "Sur le sens d'un discours circulaire," *Littérature*, no. 15 (October 1974), pp. 95–109.
4. *CC*, 4:164.
5. *CC*, 7:322, 3:249, 2:345, 7:294, 2:345.
6. *CC*, 4:225, 2:345, 8:207.
7. *CC*, 3:322, 8:175; *Correspondance*, ed. Jean Bruneau, 2 vols. (Paris:
Pléiade, 1973), 1:679 (subsequently referred to as *CB*).
8. *CC*, 3:45, 351; 5:91; 4:356.
9. Jean-Paul Sartre, in *L'Idiot de la famille*, has given complex analyses
of this fundamental (and willful) misunderstanding.
10. *CC*, supplement, 4:52, 5:26. The hierarchy of the arts was obviously
a conviction of Flaubert. See his letter to Turgenev: "Je vous soupçonne de
vouloir . . . entendre de la musique ou voir de la peinture, *arts inférieurs*"
(ibid., 4:59).
11. *CC*, 2:364; *Novembre*, in *Oeuvres de jeunesse inédites*, 2 vols. (Paris:
Conard, 1902), 2:184; *L'Éducation sentimentale* (Paris: Garnier-Flam-
marion, 1969), p. 59; *CC*, 2:279.
12. *L'Éducation sentimentale: Version de 1845*, in *Oeuvres complètes*, 2
vols. (Paris: Seuil, 1963), 1:244. *CC*, 1:302, 8:300, 2:353. For a concise
discussion by Sartre of the "posthumous" stance of both Flaubert and

Baudelaire, see his introduction to Baudelaire's *Écrits intimes* (Paris: Editions du Point du Jour, 1946).

13. *CC*, 2:343; 4:5; 7:285; *L'Éducation sentimentale: 1845*, p. 237; *CC*, 7:351; 8:309.

14. *CB*, 1:652, 637; *Mémoires d'un fou*, in *Oeuvres de jeunesse inédites*, 1:526, 540.

15. *Mémoires d'un fou*, 1:496; *Novembre*, 2:164.

16. *CC*, 3:157, 66; *L'Éducation sentimentale: 1845*, p. 246.

17. *CC*, 2:439; *CB*, 1:627–28.

18. *CC*, 4:464; 3:268; 4:212, 463; *L'Éducation sentimentale*, p. 81.

19. *CB*, 1:37; *L'Éducation sentimentale: 1845*, pp. 246–51; *CB*, 1:679, 680; *CC*, supplement, 2:92; 3:100; 2:457; 4:3; Alain Robbe-Grillet, "Une Voie pour le roman futur," *Nouvelle Nouvelle Revue Française*, July 1956, pp. 77–84.

20. Jean Ricardou, "L'Aqueduc et le piédestal," *Tel Quel* 18 (Summer 1964): 87–88.

21. *CC*, 1:385; 5:3; 2:343; 3:269; 7:331.

22. *CC*, 1:178, 192; 2:343; Roland Barthes, "L'Effet de réel," *Communications* 11 (1968): 84–89.

23. *CC*, 2:169; 3:210; 1:339; 3:384; 9:3; supplement, 2:95.

24. *CC*, 3:21; 5:338; supplement, 2:118; 7:230; 4:249, 52; *CB*, 1:495.

25. *CC*, 3:388, 344, 161; 8:374. Raymonde Debray-Genette, "Flaubert: Science et écriture," *Littérature* 15 (1974): 41–51. *CC*, 3:138.

26. *CC*, 3:317, 320; 4:18.

27. Raymonde Debray-Genette, "Du mode narratif dans les *Trois Contes*," *Littérature* 2 (1971): 39–70.

28. *CC*, 4:357; 2:461.

29. *CC*, 2:38; 4:441; 2:461.

30 Charles Baudelaire, *Oeuvres complètes* (Paris: Pléiade, 1963), p. 654; Albert Thibaudet, *Gustave Flaubert* (Paris: Gallimard, 1935), p. 150.

Madame Bovary and the Question of Pleasure

Dennis Porter

One of the more interesting developments in narrative theory over the past decade or so has been a renewed interest in pleasure. Subsequent to the structuralist enterprise there have grown up a reader-centered, a psychoanalytic, a new textual, and a feminist criticism which in their different ways have been attentive among other things to the experience of the reader reading a literary text and to the subject positions the reader is required to assume. For those interested in that experience and those positions, the guiding critical questions have been, neither "What does the work tell us, and how well is it made?" (New Criticism) nor "What is the model narrative structure of which this particular work is an example?" (structuralism), but "What does this work do to us as we read it, and how does it do what it does?" (reader response) and, to paraphrase Roland Barthes, "How is this text to be unmade, exploded, disseminated?" (poststructuralism).[1] As the result of such inquiry, we have come to appreciate more fully that reading literary works is not like breathing. It is, on the contrary, a complex learned activity with a corporeal and psychic as well as a social dimension, and one that we choose to

engage in under certain conditions for a variety of reasons, para-
mount among which is the pursuit of pleasure. Through an interest
in the way a reader is both constituted by and processes a text, we
have been led back to ask the question why it is we enjoy reading
literary works at all.

Probably the most suggestive account of the varieties of pleasure to
be derived from reading, if not the most comprehensive and systematic, remains Barthes's *The Pleasure of the Text*.[2] And I would like in
what follows to consider how Barthes's work can help in rethinking
the question of pleasure as it relates to a more traditional form of
narrative than he once championed. *The Pleasure of the Text* is, of
course, in itself a characteristically allusive piece of writing that
raises almost as many questions as it suggests answers. But it is a work
that conveniently gathers together much that has been thought about
literature in France over the past decade or so and reformulates it
with a provocative incisiveness. It has, in fact, something of the
character of a manifesto of the postmodernist sensibility that draws
on Lacanian psychoanalysis, deconstructionism, and French feminist theory. Consequently, I have chosen to put Barthes's thought to
the challenge of *Madame Bovary*, a novel that for many readers still
has a canonical stature as the most fully developed example of classic
French realism. The exchange is suggestive not only for the challenge Barthes's book throws down to reread a monument but also for
the questions that Flaubert's novel in its turn raises about postmodernist narrative theory.

As far as *The Pleasure of the Text* is concerned, it will be remembered that Barthes distinguishes there between two major categories
of texts, the *texte de plaisir* and the *texte de jouissance*, and makes a
passing reference to a third category, the *texte de désir*, that he
mentions only to dismiss. Further, a hierarchy of literary value based
on these three categories is established whose two extremes are more
easily defined than the middle term. The despised *texte de désir* takes
the form of a popular work of erotica or a detective story that represents not so much a scene of sex or violence as its imminence—"its
expectation, its preparation, its rise" (p. 92). At the other extreme a
texte de jouissance is one which "leaves you in a state of loss, which
disturbs . . . which causes the reader's historical, cultural and psy-

chological foundations to wobble . . . provokes a crisis in his relation to language" (p. 25). As for the middle category, the *texte de plaisir*, the range of sensations encompassed by the word *plaisir* itself suggests the ambiguity of the concept. *Plaisir* is the general term which includes the particular experience of *jouissance* but which also needs to be distinguished from it. In Barthes's scheme, the former generalized concept of *plaisir* refers to an "excess of the text" and includes such notions as "euphoria, satisfaction, comfort, the sensation of fullness into which culture freely enters." It does not include "shock, agitation, loss" (p. 34), which are exclusive to *jouissance*. On the one hand, there is, in Stephen Heath's phrase, "a pleasure (*plaisir*) linked to cultural enjoyment and identity, to the cultural enjoyment of identity, to a homogenizing movement of the ego; on the other, a radically violent pleasure (*jouissance*) which shatters—dissipates, loses—that cultural identity, that ego."[3]

Isolated from Barthes's work, such categories appear to have a peculiarly abstract quality of a kind that one associates with pre-Freudian psychologizing in spite of the obvious Lacanian derivation. They also suffer from the imprecision inherent in definitions founded on the effects of a text on a reader—what is experienced as "euphoria" by one reader may be felt as "shock" by another. Yet in practice Barthes's categories are useful because they go further than any other contemporary critical text in introducing the idea of a range of qualitatively different pleasurable emotions that may be excited in a reader by a work of literature.

From Barthes's point of view, the highest level that a traditional work of prose fiction such as *Madame Bovary* might attain is that of a *texte de plaisir*. However, the effort to rethink the responses that Flaubert's novel excites in the light of Barthes's theory shows how at least two of the categories are present at the same time and that there are occasional intimations of the third.[4]

In the first place, then, *Madame Bovary* is a *texte de désir*. That is to say, like popular romantic fiction, it has an erotic theme and engages the reader in the progress of not one but three love affairs—named respectively Charles, Léon and Rodolphe—the second of which is suspended in medias res in order to be resumed in a spirit of intenser expectation after the third has run its predictable course. As in that popular romance which takes the crooked path to coupling or in the detective story that goes the long way round to an unveiling and the reconstruction of an original scene of suffering, Flaubert's novel alternately promises and postpones gratification. *Madame Bovary* offers an example of the familiar tension-building device of trebling, but it is complicated here by an overlapping—the affair with Léon begins and ends after the affair with Rodolphe—and in each case the author lingers over scenes of anticipation, preparation, and arousal. The titillation of deferment is particularly marked in the affair with Léon, but in each case there is an important element of the suspense that is inherent in narrative structures at all levels and that may be exploited more or less thoroughly. Before they are anything else, the novels of James and Proust are also novels of desire whose complex sentences are paradigms of halting progression toward an anticipated end. And in *Madame Bovary* many of the celebrated early episodes that involve Emma are designed to arouse desire in a reader through the lingering evocation of female sensuality. But after Emma's wedding there is no representation of the night of love. Moreover, the climactic moments in the subsequent affairs with Rodolphe and Léon are also deliberately elided—the first, in the woods, evokes the sharpness of sensations after the act; and the second, in the closed cab, is represented from outside as grotesque pantomime.

The only scenes which follow Emma through preparation to a kind of consummation are those evoking her suicide and death. In this case, suspense as an unresolved narrative sequence that alternates in the reader fear of the worst and hope for the best sustains reader concentration down to Emma's final paroxysm. Thus Emma is represented in the labor neither of love nor of childbirth but in that of death. Flaubert exploits for his own purposes a strange morality that imposed a taboo on the representation of sex, yet finds no indecency in dying. But more of that later.

At the same time that it is a *texte de désir*, *Madame Bovary* is also a *texte de plaisir*. That this is the case it confirmed early on through scenes that are not simply designed to stimulate desire; they are more than brief stopping places on the journey to fulfillment. The story of Emma is, in fact, chiefly told through the device of matching scenes of expectation with others that represent apparent plentitude and final disillusionment. Those equivalences which in the poetic function of language Jakobson found projected from the axis of selection onto the axis of combination are constituted here by *scenes à faire* in paired relationships. As a result, the linearity of basic narrative is overlaid in Flaubert's novel by a complex patterning that on the level of the action is cyclical in nature. As she moves from anticipation to fulfillment to disillusionment, Emma is made to repeat herself before the alerted eyes of the reader. Moreover, Flaubert's novel is rich in such equivalences at all levels from that of episode, scene, paragraph, and sentence down to word and phoneme. Consequently, the work's texture is thickened to a point where its linear sequences come close to being overwhelmed by complex cross-references. It frequently happens that the reader ceases to be impelled by the dynamism of the end-oriented forces of desire and is invited to enjoy the play of the text; in Jakobson's terminology, the reader is distracted from the referential function by the pull of the poetic function of language.

It will be remembered that in Barthes's view one sign that we are in the presence of a *texte de plaisir* is the apparent excess of signifier over signified. And the realist subject matter of Flaubert's novel is not enough to prevent a characteristic indulgence in such excess on a number of fronts. The classic example, in fact, sits astride the entrance to the text and presents its challenge to each fresh critical probe of the work's significance. I refer, of course, to the description of Charles's hat that can, if one is so inclined, be reduced to narrative sense, recuperated by reference to plot and character, but whose verbal extravagance on the printed page always remains uncomfortably in excess both of any signified in the text and of any referent in the world.[5]

The description of Charles's hat is a verbal *pièce montée*, which is introduced as "one of those hats of a composite kind."[6] In other words, the hat that is produced at this early point in the novel faces the reader with the category of the monstrous. A *monster* according to the *Concise Oxford* is: "1. [A] Misshapen animal or plant. 2. [An] Imaginary animal compounded of incongruous elements." And Charles's hat is just such an imaginary beast. In brief, Flaubert's apparently realist novel begins, not with an "effet de réel," not with the ordinary, but with the extraordinary. Flaubert imagines a hat that is five different hats in one. In its composition, he knowingly confuses a variety of shapes and orders; it is familiar and exotic, organic and inorganic, formless and geometric. The description combines references to three animals—a rabbit, an otter, and a whale—to food, fur, gold, and an acorn. In other words, largely as the result of the juxtaposition of disparate elements, a verbal context is established such that beyond the derived meanings of *baleine* ("whalebone stiffners"), *boudin* ("roll") and *gland* ("tassel") their concrete sense reasserts itself. The effect is particularly marked in the sentence beginning "Ovoïde et renflée de baleines, elle commençait par trois boudins circulaires" ("Oval and reinforced with whalebone, it began with three circular rolls")—a line of print that manages to combine references to eggs, whales, and blood-sausages. At the same time, because of its exposed position at the opening of the sentence, the peculiar sonority of *ovoïde* ("oval") forces itself briefly on the reader's attention. Two full-sounded back vowels echo each other across the labio-dental fricative, and the second [o] is followed by a glide into the high thin front vowel, which is terminated by the voiced dental stop consonant, [d]. Further, that prominent *ovo* anticipates the *ova* of the mumbled "Charbovari" a few lines later. And it is the spelling of the name which provides a further clue to the ways in which *Madame Bovary* occasionally promises to transcend *plaisir* in the direction of *jouissance*.

Charbovari is a Joycean neologism that contains an ox and a cart and a discordant noise—"un charivari." After a composite hat, a composite word; the monster here is metalingual. The linguistic sign is suddenly made to lose its self-evident discreteness, and the code itself is put into question. Moreover, one might urge against Culler that at the center of the hat paragraph itself Flaubert seems to invite the kind of symbolic interpretation that the object's eclecticism apparently mocks. The passage is a signifier that claims as its signified "la laideur muette" ("the mute ugliness"). By virtue of the following simile, however—"comme le visage d'un imbécile" ("of an idiot's face")—Flaubert makes such interpretation specular. The hat is like the human type of which it is the image. Like a pun or a misspelling, words whose referents seem limited to other words are, I assume, capable of provoking the sudden sense of loss which can follow the collapse of an order. Depending on one's point of view, therefore, speech may appear as beyond culture and thrillingly carnivalesque or shockingly irresponsible. At such moments, one is reminded that *Madame Bovary* is the product of the same mind that conceived the outrageous figure of the Garçon, bred different monsters in the *Tentation de saint Antoine*, and typically reinvented an adjective in his youthful correspondence to express the world's outrageousness, "Hénaurme" ("He-normous"). That splendid orthography is in itself an example of the way in which the extravagance of a signifier may lead to one of those vertiginous moments when the word subverts the word. If Flaubert brings classical realist representation to a new level of fullness in *Madame Bovary* in the celebrated pictorial tableaux, he also subverts such representation by rematerializing his medium.

Similar if less spectacular effects are to be found throughout the novel, including the apparently straightforward episode which describes the operation Charles performs on Hippolyte's clubfoot (part 2, chapter 11). On the level of the signified, the extravagance here is in *bêtise* made visible in its actions upon others; it is in particular an example of the macabre which begins with the verbal construction of another monstrous object, namely the strangely material box destined to contain the deformed foot: "a kind of box that weighed about eight pounds and in which there was no shortage of iron, wood, metal, leather, screws, and nuts" (p. 633). At the same time, the episode turns out to be a characteristically disturbing and comic example of linguistic self-reflexiveness in which categories are collapsed and cultural identities are blurred. In short, the register of the reader's pleasure alternates between *plaisir* and *jouissance*.

As so often in *Madame Bovary*, long sections of this chapter are constituted of pastiche in one form or another. The narrator's voice is not absent, as was once thought, but it tends to disappear because it is only one voice among many others, a tissue of voices. That hierarchy of discourses which characterizes classic realist narration and which is dominated by the privileged discourse of the narrator is temporarily subverted. The technique used is that of quotation, both direct and indirect, handled in a less obvious way than in the *comices agricoles* section.

In the form of a foregrounded intertextual exchange that is related to the novel's central theme of the duplicity of language ("La parole est un laminoir"), the chapter begins with Homais *reading* about the operation and, assisted by Emma, *talking* Charles into performing it, with Charles *reading* up on the relevant medical *literature* and with Homais *talking* Hippolyte into undergoing the operation: "While he Charles was studying equinus, varus and valgus, that is to say, strephocatopody, strephendodopy and strephexopody (or, more precisely, the different malformations of the foot, downwards, in-wards or outwards) with strephypopody and strephanopody (or, in other words, torsion below and straightening above), Mr. Homais used all kinds of arguments in exhorting the boy to undergo the operation" (p. 633). The passage is characteristic above all because it reveals a word-merchant's delight in words as material objects inde-pendent of any referent. Thus the page is briefly overwhelmed by the alien wordhoard of the medical lexicon. The echoing Greek syllables in particular amount, in the context of French, to a formidable obstacle for the tongue and are also experienced as a comic cacoph-ony by the ear. Moreover, there is interlinguistic irony in the fact that Flaubert takes the opportunity to turn the tables and make Greek for once seem "barbarous." Such prose in any case may be said to provoke a crisis in the reader's relation to language insofar as it objectifies speech in its material strangeness. It effects a shift out of the geometrical space of theatrical representation or narrative tab-leaux into nonrepresentative music, Barthean stereophony.

Further, in the rest of the chapter the circulation of words con-tinues, either in the form of dialogues in direct and indirect speech or in the form of musings in *discours indirect libre* or in the form of reproductions of the written word. Flaubert quotes a nineteenth-century druggist, an incompetent medical man, an unhappy house-wife, a parish priest, a chorus of village characters, a medical text-book, and a newspaper article. Yet the voice of his hidden narrator is finally made to emerge from the network of borrowed words in order to confront the reader with the reality of a gangrenous leg: "A livid tumefaction spread over the leg with here and there phlyctena whence oozed a black liquid" (p. 635). The task of the words here is different. It derives from the familiar Flaubertian intention of mak-ing his reader feel the material impact of what is evoked or, in other words, to disguise the fact that this reality, too, is only verbal. Moreover, in order to achieve such an effect, Flaubert steps outside the circle of quotations and reverts to realist reportage, employing a privileged narrative discourse that presents itself as the discourse of knowledge. Such sentences are an expression of his continuing trust in the power of words to communicate with the force of experience. Thus, in spite of the fact that so much in this chapter is put into inverted commas, by no means everything is self-reproducing speech. *Madame Bovary* is not simply an echo chamber in which all combinations of words have the appearance of having come from somewhere else. The conception of the novel itself as a *Dictionary of Received Ideas* will have to wait for *Bouvard et Pécuchet*, but Flaubert's first major work sometimes points in that direction.

On such occasions as those just referred to, then, and there are many others, *Madame Bovary* hints at the form a sustained *texte de jouissance* might take. From time to time it invites what Barthes has called reading "à la dérive" ("adrift"): "Drifting occurs whenever I *do not respect the whole*, whenever apparently borne away here and there at the whim of the illusions, seductions, and intimidations of language, like a cork on a wave, I remain still, pivoting upon that intractable *jouissance* which binds me to the text (to the world)" (*The Pleasure of the Text*, pp. 32–33).

As far as Flaubert is concerned, the paradox, of course, is in the fact that the great craftsman of fiction, the inventor of the novel as grand poetic design, should have created a work that seems to encourage irresponsible readings, readings which do not "respect the whole," but which dismantle what was so carefully laid together. Yet such insidious encouragements are only intermittent and are perhaps perceptible chiefly to those who share something of our postmodernist sensibility. For the most part Flaubert submits the fragmenting potential of his text to the traditional discipline of end-oriented narrative. Consequently, excess as a characteristic of a *texte de plaisir* mostly takes quieter forms in *Madame Bovary* than those mentioned above and is carefully delimited as an episodic unit within an advancing action. A famous passage suggests how:

Elle le reconduisait toujours jusqu'à la première marche du perron. Lorsqu'on n'avait pas encore amené son cheval, elle restait là. On s'était dit adieu, on ne parlait plus; le grand air l'entourait, levant pêle-mêle les petits cheveux follets de sa nuque, ou secouant sur sa hanche les cordons de son tablier, qui se tortillaient comme des banderoles. Une fois, par un temps de dégel, l'écorce des arbres suintait dans la cour, la neige sur les couvertures des bâtiments se fondait. Elle était sur le seuil; elle alla chercher son ombrelle; elle l'ouvrit. L'ombrelle, de soie gorge-de-pigeon, que traversait le soleil, éclairait de reflets mobiles la peau blanche de sa figure. Elle souriait là-dessous à la chaleur tiède; et on entendait les gouttes d'eau, une à une, tomber sur la moire tendue. [P. 580]

[She always accompanied him outside as far as the first step of the stairs. When his horse had not been brought up, she waited there. They had said goodbye; no further words were spoken. The open air surrounded her, carelessly lifting the soft little curls at the nape of her neck or raising on her hips her apron strings which twisted in the wind like streamers. Once during a thaw, when the bark of the trees in the courtyard was oozing and the snow of the roofs of the buildings was melting, she stood on the threshold. She went to fetch her sunshade. She opened it. The silk sunshade was pigeon-breast in color, and the sunlight passed through it to illuminate the white skin of her face with shifting hues. She smiled as she stood there at the gentle warmth, and drops of water could be heard, falling one by one on the taut silk.]

At first glance the passage appears to be a tableau of the kind associated with classical realism, namely, a word painting that in its transparency offers itself as an equivalent for a slice of already given reality. It turns out, however, that the passage is an example of the way in which representation may achieve the status of a "text," of a "writable" potential within a "readable" work. Such potential is experienced first of all by a reader as a consciousness of thickened verbal texture, of the materiality of the medium.

On a first reading the passage gives the impression of a *plein-air* Impressionist canvas. That is to say, it imitates a scene from life that appears to be flooded with light and air. Yet, as we all know, if one comes too close to an Impressionist canvas, the represented scene suddenly disintegrates into a chaos of brush strokes. One step too many leads the observer out of the illusion of a dappled world and into the presence of paint. And a comparable attention to the verbal medium of Flaubert's scene may give rise to a similar effect. The passage is perceived to exist simultaneously on a referential and a material level. A form of play occurs that is dependent on the double nature of the linguistic sign. And it becomes clear at such moments that if Flaubert was, in fact, the first novelist to write as a poet, the first to pay systematic attention the acoustic substance of words, it is because he was the novelist of the "gueuloir." He put his prose to the test of declamation. In formalist terms, he worked the verbal texture of his fiction so hard his linguistic signs became palpable; by trying out his words in the mouth he foregrounded in his text those sound values that are the units of word-units, thus disclosing phonemic equivalences which communication usually dissimulates.[7] On the one hand, therefore, the passage evokes erotic expectation on the representational level. On the other hand, it is a tissue of patterned sounds that generates a concurrent pleasure in the reader, not because of some supposed imitative harmony, of a posited natural connection between sound and sense, but because as we read—and to read Flaubert properly is to read him as he wrote, aloud—we are obliged to play the instrument constituted by our organs of speech. Flaubert's text is a score to be played in the mouth.

Like any *texte de plaisir*, like the *Sarrasine* that Barthes analyzes in S / Z, the passage speaks to the reader on a number of levels in the same way as the novel which contains it. From the beginning it displays the referential and sequential qualities of realist narrative, but by the third sentence the complex interrelatedness of the concepts and sounds is clear. Word music begins to subvert word painting.[8] Repetition in the form of assonance, alliteration, rhyme, words, and syntactic structures insists on a recognition that impedes the forward momentum of the narrative. The two consciously unremarkable opening sentences suggest a potential for union in the play of the gender-specific personal pronouns and the personal adjective—"Elle le reconduisait" ("She always accompanied him"), "son cheval, elle restait là" ("his horse, she waited there")—a union that takes a grammatical form with the opening "On" ("They") of the third sentence. But it is the second half of that third sentence which reveals how in a *texte de plaisir* pleasure is located as much, if not more, in the play of the signifiers as in the signifieds, in the decomposition and recomposition of acoustical images in unaccustomed proximity as in the concepts they speak.

". . . le grand air l'entourait, levant pêle-mêle les petits cheveux follets de sa nuque, ou secouant sur sa hanche les cordons de son tablier, qui se tortillaient comme des banderoles" ("The open air surrounded her, carelessly lifting the soft little curls at the nape of her neck or raising on her hips her apron strings which twisted in the wind like streamers.") As is often the case in Flaubert, the semicolon preceding this passage signals the fixing of the attention; it is a sign of the intention to linger and savor sensation through and across words. On this occasion, the author makes use of the capacity of language to isolate a part in the absence of a whole—in painting before cubism a breast was never detached from its body. And Flaubert isolates a part in order to focus with fetishistic relish not so much on a woman as on the nape of a neck and a hip. In such a context the linguistic signs constituted by *nuque* ("nape") and *hanche* ("hip") are calculated to excite desire on the conceptual level. But before considering the peculiar power of this passage as erotic scene, I would like to look briefly at its phonetic complexity, paying attention not only to audition but also the production of speech.

The opening clause—"le grand air l'entourait" ("the open air surrounded her")—breaks down into two sequences of three syllables, both of which begin with an [l] and end with an open [ɛ], either followed or preceded by the liquid [r]. All the phonemes used occur at least once in each sequence with the exception of the [g]—the voiced dental consonant [d] recurs in the unvoiced form [t]. Liquid consonants, open [ɛ]s and the nasal [ã]s dominate. And the same sounds are repeated in the following phrase, "levant pêle-mêle les petits cheveux follets de sa nuque" ("carelessly lifting the soft little curls at the nape of her neck"), the [l] no less than five times, the open [ɛ] three, the [ã] once. Moreover, in this phrase the open [ɛ]s and the [l]s combine in "pêle-mêle" to form a back-to-back rhyme which is introduced by two bilabial consonants, so that a closing of the mouth is followed by an opening of the mouth and a final rise of the tongue behind the teeth. The phrase, "les petits cheveux follets de sa nuque," with the play of the [l]s, is most marked for its series of fricatives—[ʃ], [v], [f], [s]—and the surprise of the velar positive [k], a new sound. Fricatives dominate in the next phrase, no less than four in the following four words. Also, the word "hanche" which ends the series repeats the open nasal sound before sliding into the palatal [ʃ]. In the final dozen words of the sentence, the sound texture is chiefly dominated by the phoneme [k] that originally appeared in "nuque," by the voiced and unvoiced dentals, [d] and [t], and by open or nasalized [ɔ]s.

From the point of view of phonetic analysis, the most striking feature of the last three sentences is the frequent repetition of the two phonemes [ɛl], either alone or combined with the nasal [ɔ̃] in "ombrelle" ("sunshade")—"Elle était sur le seuil; elle alla chercher son ombrelle; elle l'ouvrit." ("She stood on the threshold. She went to fetch her sunshade. She opened it.") The combination of the two phonemes [ɛ] and [l] involves, of course, an opening of the mouth followed by a darting forward of the tongue against the teeth. In the word "ombrelle" the production of the two phonemes together is preceded by the full sound of the rounded nasal vowel, a shift forward in the mouth to the bilabial stop consonant [b] and a swift movement back again to the resonant velar [r]. In short, the production of the five phonemes of the word "ombrelle" involves considerable motor activity on the part of the organs of speech, so much so that as a result of repetition the sound values achieve a substantiality we can almost taste. It is at such moments that one is forced to recognize that speaking is, like eating, an oral activity capable of engendering a similar range of pleasures.

That Flaubert is the novelist of the "gueuloir" is confirmed finally by the second half of the final sentence—"et on entendait les gouttes d'eau, une à une, tomber sur la moire tendue" ("and drops of water could be heard, falling one by one upon the taut silk"). Within the space of little more than a dozen short words, Flaubert uses six of the eleven regular vowels of French and two of four nasals, most of them more than once, and one, [y], no less than four times. The effect is the same as that of playing musical notes in sequence at different points on the scale on an instrument whose range of sonorities is unusually wide. If one isolates the phrases beginning "gouttes d'eau, une à une," for example, and concentrates on the vowels, one notes a slide down the rounded back vowels from [u] to [o], followed by a shift forward of the point of articulation to the rounded middle vowel [y]. Further, in this play of similarity and difference, the postponed infinitive "tomber" finds an echo first in the opening nasal phoneme of "moire" and then in the resonant last word of the paragraph "tendue." Moreover, both "tomber" and "tendue" are two-syllable words, and both begin with the unvoiced dental [t] followed by two relatively similar nasal sounds, which in their turn are followed by two consonants pronounced well forward in the mouth, [b] and [d]. And they end with two fairly closely related front vowels, [e] and [y].

If I have concentrated so pedantically on the sounds of what is after all a familiar passage, it is because Flaubert's prose here illustrates so well how the different elements in a text that trigger pleasure begin with motor activity in the mouth. And in this respect the technical terminology of phonetics is suggestive to the extent that it locates speech precisely in the bodily organs—lips, teeth, tongue, and palate—which produce it, and supplies a word for the manner of its production—fricative, resonant, sibilant.

Not only qualities of sound but also most of the other forms of pleasure that I have so far discussed find an analogue in this passage. In the first place, it has the power of a *texte de désir* insofar as it is a tableau that generates sexual suspense by representing, not an erotic scene, but its preparation; it is on its most obvious representational level a scene of early courtship. At the same time it is a *texte de plaisir* to the extent that it is suggestively polysemic and, in effect, manages to represent figuratively what it merely looks forward to literally, namely, physical union. The fact that it is only the wind which touches a bare neck or a hip does not prevent the gesture from being read as delicate foreplay. And from that point on the passage moves successively through images of unfreezing and flowing to the offering of an "ombrelle"—a word that both through the shape of its referent and through the combination of two syllables evoking respectively the concept of shadow and of the female gender may be said to suggest the traditional essence of femininity. From "ombrelle" it moves on to refer to a face expressing pleasure— "sourire" ("smile")—humid warmth and the insistence of drops on a taut membrane—"moire tendue." The erotic charge concentrated in that final "tendue," in any case, is unmistakable. And it is an erotic charge that depends for its power on all the verbal factors isolated above, including, finally, the word's emphatic position at the end of a developing narrative sequence.

In brief, the passage is a paradigm of narrative at the level of a *texte de plaisir*. It moves in a linear fashion from an initial neutral situation to a point of climax via a series of sentences whose syntactic variety is calculated to produce an alternating rhythm of advance and delay. At the same time, like a dream, it embodies effects of displacement and condensation that are, nevertheless, controlled by considerations of secondary revision in the interest of narratability. As a result, it suggests a latent significance that it does not declare; like certain gauzy Victorian portraits of women, it manages both to profess innocence and to invite the spectator's erotic absorption. Insofar as it is a portrait of a woman, it also serves to remind us how in literature as in film women have been traditionally produced by and for the male gaze, within a regime of pleasure, in other words, whose characteristic perversions are voyeurism and fetishism. The effect of such production, as Laura Mulvey has noted in connection with film, is to freeze the flow of the action.[9] Where women are concerned, classic realist representation in both the literary and the film media has typically combined spectacle with narrative.

The passage achieves the polysemic suggestiveness of a *texte de plaisir*, then, but it stops short of *jouissance*. If *jouissance* is a symptom recognizable by the loss of self and the collapse of meaning and is produced by the play of detached signifiers, it is not a symptom excited by Flaubert's prose here. His linguistic signs retain for the most part their dual status. They achieve through juxtaposition a new substantiality that one is obliged to stop and taste in the mouth, but they are at the same time under traditional syntactic control, and their location in an unfolding realist narrative limits signification.

In a remarkable passage at the end of *The Pleasure of the Text*, Barthes refers to "a writing aloud" ("une écriture à haute voix") whose goal is not communication. Instead, it promotes "desiring incidents, it is language hung with skin, a text in which one can hear the grain of a throat, the patina of consonants, the sensuousness of vowels, a whole stereophony from deep in the flesh" (pp. 104–5). It is a passage whose choice of words makes particularly clear how a mouth supplied with appropriate combinations of words is a formidable organ of pleasure-taking. It is also clear that such a noncommunicational goal for the written language is only possible in the form of a nonreferential writing that subverts the traditional order of words by employing such devices as the dislocation of syntax, the absence of punctuation, multiple punning, or calculated misspellings. Under such conditions it is possible to offer the pleasures of sound pigment in place of sense; the written word is made simply material. But this is not the case with the Flaubert passage quoted above. More systematically than any other novelist before him, Flaubert obliges his reader to refer his printed words back to their production by the organs of speech. Yet context is not dissolved in pure auto-referential play. Instead, the reader's attention is solicited now by the scene represented, now by the acoustical material of the linguistic signs. The passage has the status of a Monet canvas, not of a Jackson Pollock; to read it carefully is to be absorbed in a game of now you see it, now you don't.

It could hardly be otherwise, since without such a play of the text between the referential and poetic functions of speech in the sole interest of the latter, the story of Emma would disappear. In short, the price of *jouissance* is the end of narrative. But it is a price that Barthes, along with other postmodernists, including particularly certain French feminists, has seemed willing to pay. In common with moralists from at least the seventeenth century, Barthes recognizes that novel reading is an erotic activity. However, what he advocates in the theory of *jouissance* is eroticism with a difference, eroticism that is not end-oriented. The fundamental distinction affirmed in "Diderot, Brecht, Eisenstein" between mathematics and acoustics, on the one hand, and geometry and theater, on the other, is finally one between the voice and the look, between stereophony and representation. And it is precisely this distinction which has been taken up by French feminists who, extrapolating from Freud and Lacan, affirm the qualities of (feminine) voice over the phallocentric representation of the (male) gaze.[10]

In any case, whereas narrative has traditionally been constructed according to principles similar to those which Freud viewed as characterizing normal adult sexuality, a *texte de jouissance* repudiates such principles. It stands in relation to a *texte de plaisir* as in Freud's theory the sexual perversions do to the genital aim of the mature sexual norm. In the second of the *Three Essays on the Theory of*

Sexuality Freud contrasts infantile sexual life in which "its individual component instincts are upon the whole disconnected and independent of one another in their search for pleasure" with that of the normal adult "in which the component instincts . . . form a firm organization directed towards a sexual aim attached to some extraneous sexual object."[11] And Freud goes on to speak of "organization" and "subordination to the reproductive function." As the key terms "organization" and "subordination" make clear, it is a view of sexuality that is both directional and hierarchical in its structure and is, therefore, subject to the same strictures that Barthes applies to the sentence and a fortiori to the form of narrative which is the sentence writ large, namely the novel.

In effect, the theory of textuality as elaborated by Barthes in collaboration with a certain French avant-garde amounts to what was once known as a polymorphous perversity of the written word and has more recently been seen as a feminine form of sexuality, an *écriture féminine*. In a *texte de jouissance* the reading aim is diverted from taking pleasure in the parts of a text in the anticipation of an end to a total absorption in those parts—"like a cork on a wave." The goal of writing has become "a definitive discontinuity" (*The Pleasure of the Text*, p. 79). The new criteria of literary value are founded on such concepts as semantic undecidability, sonic reversibility, and a text's energy in transgressing all taboos, including particularly those which hold that narrative should be both linear and representational. The reader is invited to join in the play of the self-dismantling text in the same way that in the activity of critical deconstruction the text itself is made to collaborate in dethroning its authorial subject and in exposing the failures of authorial intentionality. The ideal of the text is a writing in which nothing is privileged. And a similar purpose is served through the critical subversion of the hierarchies in a canonical text. There is *jouissance* in a world without categories and identities where everything reverberates with utopian possibility. The utopian character—in the sense of desired but unrealizable—of an unlimited textuality is conceded by Barthes himself: "How could art, in a society that has not yet found peace, cease to be metaphysical? that is, significant, readable, representational? fetishist? When are we to have music, the Text?"[12]

If among nineteenth-century novels *Madame Bovary* seems particularly receptive to analysis along Barthean lines, therefore, it is in part because Flaubert's novel embodies attitudes that are sympathetic to the postmodernist and post-Freudian sensibility. And this is the case not only in the ways suggested above but also in relation to the work's central themes. *Madame Bovary* knowingly thematizes the question of the relationship between erotic pleasure and the reading process, both in the novel's content, or in its account of Emma's experience in the world, and in the novel's structure, to the extent that it exploits the mechanisms of popular romance in order in the end to entrap its reader.

First, then, the theme of eroticism and reading is represented directly in a heroine whose experience of life is shown to be less satisfactory than her early novel reading had prepared her for. But this is not simply because men in reality prove to be inferior to the heroic lovers of literature. It is rather because in Emma's case the sharpness of sensations stimulated by the reading activity itself is never quite matched, let alone sustained, in the world. Neither the content of reading-inspired fantasies nor the intensity of feeling aroused by the activity of reading literary romances has, in fact, been suggested with greater precision than in the sixth chapter of *Madame Bovary*. The sight and touch of "keepsakes" and novels as objects stimulate an anticipatory physiological reaction in Flaubert's adolescent heroine: "Delicately handling their beautiful satin bindings, Emma fixed her dazzled eyes on the names of unknown authors whose signature lay there. . . . She trembled as she lifted with her breath the silk paper of the engravings which rose half-folded back and then fell again gently on to the page." Emma's most important discovery will perhaps be that, though they have much in common, making love turns out in the end to be less exciting than reading or writing it. [13] Although she is not let into the secret, it is clear that the only alternative to suicide—the author's alternative—was aestheticism.

Second, the theme of the relationship between erotic experience and reading is embodied in the structure of *Madame Bovary*. If as was noted earlier, Flaubert consciously employs the mechanisms of a *texte de désir*, however, he only does so in order to frustrate his reader at the denouement. The promise of fulfillment seems implied by a great many scenes in *Madame Bovary*; the early representations of Emma particularly excite expectations in the reader—"the rise"— that the text does not satisfy. In the end, however, apart from the clubfoot operation, the only scene which represents directly down to its denouement a physical action carried out by a body on a body is that of Emma's suicide. Instead of a consummating act of generation, Flaubert inflicts on his reader a scene of self-destruction. As the text makes clear, Emma's suicide is the gesture of a *révolté* in which the means of death is particularly significant. The cramming of arsenic directly from her hand into the mouth is not only a defiantly self-destructive act, it is also a regressive one. It has in itself the force of an anti-Freudian, radical feminist gesture. By that I mean that there is a return to an oral form of gratification which under the circumstances is the essence of perversity,[14] in Freud's sense, since it is a return that occurs after the disappointing experience of three male lovers, of sexuality under the regime of the phallus. In other words, the mode as well as the choice of Emma's death constitute a bitter comment on male sexuality. Autoerotic gestures are associated with Emma from the beginning—witness the early incident when she pricks her finger and sucks it and the subsequent reference to the movements of her tongue licking the bottom of a glass. Moreover, such moments knowingly appeal to that voyeuristic reader pleasure which consists in observing someone else taking their pleasure. Nevertheless, the climax of all the rich foreplay of Flaubert's novel is an autoerotic *Liebestod* that can please nobody. No wonder Lamartine was so upset. The reader gets something significantly stronger than he bargained for. If Flaubert seems for long stretches of his novel to be appealing to the reader of a *texte de désir*, the denouement reveals that such an appeal is only simulated. Flaubert punishes the reader of Madame Bovary as *texte de désir* at the same time that he rewards anyone who is responsive to his work as a *texte de plaisir*.

In short, if in the end Flaubert's first and apparently most traditional novel continues to interest us so much, I suggest it is because a consciousness of the Barthean registers as well as of male desire and female sexuality is embodied in his fiction on a number of levels. *Madame Bovary* is exemplary because it implicitly acknowledges the existence of the three kinds of reading pleasure that Barthes isolates. It consciously combines the characteristics of a *texte de désir* and a *texte de plaisir* and occasionally confronts its reader with the thrilling vertigo of a *texte de jouissance*. Unlike the latter, however, it always locates its auto-referential digressive elements within a strongly articulated progressive structure. It displays to an unusual degree the features of "organization" and "subordination" that characterize linear narrative, but it does so at least in part because of the powerful centrifugal pull of its parts down to the level of its phonemes. The lesson of *Madame Bovary*, in fact, is that unlike a run-of-the-mill traditional novel or a *nouveau nouveau roman*, it manages to maintain a balance of tension such that the reader's interest is invariably divided between local excitements and the expectation of yet greater rewards. The risk run by a *texte de jouissance*, on the other hand, is similar to that described by Freud in the section of his third essay on the theory of sexuality entitled "Dangers of Fore-pleasure." There is, in Freud's view, "danger" "if at any point in the preparatory sexual processes the fore-pleasure turns out to be too great and the element of tension too small. The motive for proceeding further with the sexual process then disappears, the whole path is cut short, and the preparatory act in question takes the place of the normal sexual aim" (p. 77).

If *Madame Bovary* continues to exercise a hold over its readers, I would suggest that it is because, in spite of the richness of its preliminaries, "the whole path is not cut short." It still leads its reader on through promise and postponement toward an end. The verbal distractions of Flaubert's text are multiple and operate on the registers of both *plaisir* and *jouissance*. Above all, perhaps, the story of Emma is accompanied throughout by a sonorous subliminal buzz, by a stereophony which is registered by the reader as a reading in the body. At such moments the reader enjoys the play of language released briefly from the tyranny of sense and representation. Yet it is this (male) reader's experience that he is not unhappy in being returned to them. Although *Madame Bovary* submits its reader throughout to the various regimes of pleasure, it comes down in the end on the side of the currently despised phallocentric closure.[15] In spite of Barthes, therefore, Flaubert's novel persuades me that the most pleasurable fictional mode my own male difference can learn to love is one which navigates between the shores of *désir, plaisir,* and *jouissance* without stopping off at any single one. In the back and forth movement between such loss and reappearance is the *Fort / Da* of narrative itself.

Notes

1. Roland Barthes, *Image-Music-Text: Essays Selected and Translated by Stephen Heath* (Fontana: London, 1977), p. 127.

2. Roland Barthes, *Le Plaisir du Texte* (Paris: Éditions du Seuil, 1973). With the exception of the Barthes quotations from *Image-Music-Text*, translations from the French throughout are my own.

3. Barthes, *Image-Music-Text*, p. 9.

4. Barthes himself is, of course, aware of the provocative originality of Flaubert's writing. He refers in passing to the fact that "a generalized asyndeton takes hold of the whole enunciation so that this very readable discourse is beneath it all one of the craziest one can imagine" ibid., (p. 18).

5. See Jonathan Culler's nice account of how Flaubert's description resists the traditional interpreting process, in *Flaubert: The Uses of Uncertainty* (Ithaca, N.Y.: Cornell University Press, 1974), pp. 91–94.

6. It hardly seems necessary to repeat once more in print what is by now one of the most celebrated artifacts in literature. Yet critical good manners perhaps require it. "C'était une de ces coiffures d'ordre composite, où l'on retrouve les éléments du bonnet à poil, du chapska, du chapeau rond, de la casquette de loutre et du bonnet de coton, une de ces pauvres choses, enfin, dont la laideur muette a des profondeurs d'expression comme le visage d'un imbécile. Ovoïde et renflée de baleines, elle commençait par trois boudins circulaires; puis s'alternaient, séparés par une bande rouge, des losanges de velours et de poil de lapin; venait ensuite une façon de sac qui se terminait par un polygone cartonné, couvert d'une broderie en soutache compliquée, et d'où pendait, au bout d'un long cordon trop mince, un petit croisillon de fils d'or en manière de gland. Elle était neuve; la visière brillait." In *Oeuvres complètes*, 2 vols. (Paris: Seuil, 1964), 1:575. ("It was one of those headgears of the composite kind in which one can find elements of a fur hat, a shako, a billycock hat, a sealskin cap and a cotton bonnet. It was, in short, one of those poor things whose mute ugliness has the expressive depths of an idiot's face. Oval and reinforced with whalebone, it began with three rolls. There

followed in order, separated by a red band, lozenges in velvet and rabbit skin; then came a sort of bag which culminated in a cardboard polygon covered with ornate braid and to which in turn was appended by means of a long, excessively thin cord a tassel of plaited gold. It was new; its peak gleamed.") Subsequent page references in the text are to volume 1 of this edition.

7. The spelling of French shares with English the advantage of often disguising congruences of sound behind graphic difference. From the point of view of the poetic function of speech, therefore, there is pleasure in the surprise of an identity heard but not seen. Spelling reform would be a disaster for poetry.

8. In a typically suggestive essay, Barthes notes aphoristically on Western theater: "Thus is founded—against music (against the text)—*representation*" ("Diderot, Brecht, Eisenstein," in *Image-Music-Text*, p. 69).

9. "The presence of woman is an indispensable element of spectacle in normal narrative film, yet her visual presence tends to work against the development of a story line, to freeze the flow of action in moments of erotic contemplation. The alien presence then has to be integrated into cohesion with the narrative." "Visual Pleasure and Narrative Cinema," *Screen* 16, no. 3 (Autumn 1975): 11.

10. "All the feminine texts that I have read are very close to the Voice, are very close to the flesh of the language, much more than in masculine texts" (Hélène Cixous). "Investment in the look is not privileged in women as in men. More than the other senses, the eye objectifies and masters. It sets at a distance, maintains the distance. In our culture, the predominance of the look over smell, taste, touch, hearing has brought impoverishment of bodily relations" (Luce Irigaray). Quoted by Stephen Heath, "Difference," *Screen* 19, no. 3 (Autumn 1978): 83–84.

11. Sigmund Freud, *Three Essays on the Theory of Sexuality*, trans. James Strachey (New York: Basic Books, 1962), pp. 63, 65.

12. Barthes, "Diderot, Brecht, Eisenstein," p. 77.

13. When toward the end of her affair with Léon, Emma feels obliged to conform to her received idea of the role of a mistress by writing letters to her lover, she manages once again to relocate the ideal lover of her fantasy. Once the letter is finished, however, "she collapsed, broken, since these outbursts of vague love tired her more than grand orgies" (p. 672).

14. One is also reminded of Freud's formulation that "poison is nourishment that makes us ill." *The New Introductory Lectures on Psychoanalysis*, trans. James Strachey (New York: Norton, 1965), p. 122.

15. Commenting on the relationships between male desire and feminine

sexuality, Jane Gallop has noted that they both function in the same dimension of metonymy: "The difference is that desire is metonymical impatience, anticipation pressing ever forward along the line of discourse so as to close signification, whereas feminine sexuality is a '*jouissance* enveloped in its own contiguity.' Such *jouissance* would be sparks of pleasure ignited by *contact* at any point, any moment along the line, not waiting for a closure, but enjoying the touching." *The Daughter's Seduction: Feminism and Psychoanalysis* (Ithaca, N.Y.: Cornell University Press, 1982), pp. 30–31.

Quidquid volueris: The Scriptural Education

Already and Always

The signs of a future perfection are often looked for in Flaubert's juvenilia. Using the works of his mature years as the model and telos, the imperfections in his early works have been disclosed and pardoned, and only that which sheds light on the great works to come has been valorized. According to this evolutionist reasoning, in *Rêve d'enfer* (1837) Flaubert reveals his promise and talent, in *Mémoires d'un fou* (1838) he is doing better, with *Novembre* (1842) he has progressed further, and so on. In literature, as in life, the adolescent must be surpassed by the mature man, the apprentice must give way to the master; it is all a question of education, whether sentimental or stylistic.

In this way the works of the adolescent Flaubert have been seen as rough outlines in which we can read the precursive signs of his geniality and of his neuroses. In his early works critics have noted Flaubert's first literary influences and the traces of his first traumas; in them they have observed imperfections of style and composition—exaggeration, repetition, a declamatory tone, a lack of taste and proportion—and have attributed these to the immaturity of his character. All of this is progressively rectified; and if the critics are not in agreement when it comes to the "first important work" by Flaubert, they all agree that in 1857 his education was complete.

Meanwhile, in spite of their assertion of Flaubert's evolution, numerous critics have arrived at the conclusion that he never changed. Flaubert always takes up the same subjects, often the same scenes, the same comparisons. The temptations are never overcome, the educations are never finished; the *garçon* survives, aged and incorrigible, in Bouvard and Pécuchet. Thus the work of Flaubert is the perfect place to study at once evolution and permanence. Already in 1909, René Descharmes sees in the juvenilia "the seeds of his future masterpieces." In following the evolution of the young Flaubert, he says, "I watched a transformation of his character and of his aesthetic . . . but at the same time I found throughout the survival of primitive tendencies."[1]

That Flaubert could have developed over the years and that nonetheless he could have remained always the same is not an inextricable paradox. It is what happens to most writers, to most people. What is particularly interesting in Flaubert's case is that he could have changed in such a radical, voluntary manner and at the same time could have stayed so thoroughly and obsessively the same to the end.

What I propose to do here is to look at one work from Flaubert's juvenilia from a nonevolutionist point of view; to highlight in it what is not only *already* but *always* there, to expose not only that which is to endure but also that which was silenced, that which was killed in Flaubert so that the great works could be written. This silence and this death, which are the basis for the evolution of Flaubert, command our attention, not because they came to fruition, but, on the contrary, because they were never perfected: the howling remains audible over the measured thoughts and phrases, the corpse has always been the active fertilizer of their flowering. I propose to examine this other Flaubert, the adolescent, not as the potential, yet imperfect one, but as a writer already mature after a fashion.

Quidquid volueris, the psychological tale written in 1837, has always been seen by the critics as an adolescent's extravagance.[2] Even after 1931, when D. L. Demorest showed the richness and the subtlety of the images in this tale, the last two decades of criticism have turned a deaf ear to the poetic *gueuloir* of the adolescent Flaubert. This text has been used as a document of biographic interest; it has been analyzed as a failure. It has been consigned to romantic sources, easily interpreted by psychoanalysis, accused of referential or stylistic unseemliness; in it the critics have seen, each in his turn, *lacks* or *excesses*.[3]

Djalioh, the sentimentally ineducable ape-man, first monster of the temptation of Saint Flaubert, shrieks like a hysterical woman. It has been said that he shrieks too much to be taken seriously, and rightly so. The defenders of style do not like hyperbole. *Quidquid volueris* is thus nothing but a curiosity, the flawed beginnings of the extremely educated prose to come or the first sign of a neurosis which was to evolve also.

If, on the contrary, one were to read this tale outside the evolutionist perspective, Djalioh might be understood differently. Let us for a moment take ourselves out of the context of Flaubert's great repertory, by asking a hypothetical question: if Flaubert had died young, like a Lautréamont, would a work like *Quidquid volueris* still be readable? And how?

The Ape-Man

Djalioh, the hero of this ultra-Romantic short story is not a René or an Adolphe, nor is he a Quasimodo, while he owes more than one trait to all of them. René and Adolphe are socially inept characters who ask themselves psychological questions and answer with metaphysical ones. Quasimodo's maladjustment is accentuated more strongly, but this "monster" is still an error of human genetics. Djalioh is a complete mistake, an aberration, the impossible: the ape-man, son of an orangutan and a black woman.

The ape-man comes from a much vaster mythology than the personal phantasms of our young romantic author. While the subject is fascinating and has been the object of numerous studies, I am going to concentrate here on only a few. According to André Leroi-Gourhan, this myth, common to several prescientific peoples, is the result of a spatial merger, the result of an ethnocentric point of view: "The prescientific thinker considers as an essential people those who constitute his ethnic nucleus, beyond which, in increasingly distant aureoles, less human beings appear with stranger and stranger hybrids."[4]

Among the hybrids imagined by man, the ape-man is one of the most constant and most perturbing, in so much as it represents the limit between the fantastic and the probable. In our culture this being appears among the monsters of medieval architecture and in the navigational maps of the fifteenth and sixteenth centuries.[5] These maps confirm the ethnocentrism noted by contemporary anthropology: the unknown seas were inhabited by hybrid peoples, less and less human the further one got from Europe. The more recent discovery of the great apes in Africa and Asia seemed to confirm at least one of the medieval fantasies; to the eyes of the travelers, these apes were hardly more shocking than the American Indians, and if they admitted the humanity of these beings, then they could easily speculate about the humanity of the animals as well.

By the eighteenth century, in the West, the myth of the ape-man was fixed as a possibility which should be examined by science. Rousseau discusses this question at length in the tenth note of his *Discours sur l'inégalité* and shows himself strongly inclined to admit the humanity of the great apes:

All of these observations about the variety that thousands of causes can produce, and have, in fact, produced in the human species, make me doubt whether various animals that resemble men—taken by travelers for beasts through a lack of investigation or because of some differences which they noticed in their exterior conformation, or only because the animals did not speak—are not in effect veritable savage peoples, a race dispersed long ago in the woods, that has not had the occasion to develop any of its faculties, has not attained any degree of perfection, and which finds itself still in the primitive state of nature.[6]

By the nineteenth century the discovery of prehistoric remains, such as those of the Grotto of Engis in 1833, had suggested other similarities between men and apes. These fossils were still anthropologically illegible, but they invited a more disturbing reading than the previous spatial one. It is not until 1859, some twenty years after Flaubert's tale, that Darwin cleared up this mystery with his theory of evolution, which met with no small resistance. Meanwhile, the phantasmatic force of myth continues to exert itself alongside science. The myth of the ape-man has persisted to this day, passing through Tarzan (whose animal side, as Leroi-Gourhan observes, is assumed by his companion Cheeta), it is reincarnated in King Kong and the inhabitants of the *Planet of the Apes.*

Flaubert's character appeared at this time of uncertainty, when the presence of the animal in man was beginning to be suspected, no longer as the symbolic existence of evil in a foreign body, but as an essential coexistence. At the time of *Quidquid volueris,* large monkeys were first exhibited at European fairs and circuses, provoking extravagant commentary in the press.[7] While the human appearance of the apes was shocking people, interest grew in cases of the reverse like Victor de l'Aveyron and Kasper Hauser.

Flaubert, like Rousseau, is firmly on the side of the apes. The narrator of *Quidquid volueris* puts all of his sympathies in the character of Djalioh, with whom he identifies. "That which is best in me is poetry, is the beast," Flaubert will say later. Opposed to the narrator are the "civilized men" of the tale, who, in an exemplary incarnation of the ethnocentric attitude, make fun of Djalioh. The monster comes from far away; he is born in Brazil. What is more, he is born of an inferior, ethnically and socially: his mother is black and a slave, "a silly little Negro woman" (p. 108), according to Paul de Monville, the tale's civilized character. This relation to the other, whom one would like to keep totally distinct but whom one finds to be a part of oneself, raises the whole question of racism. Thrice removed from men by his foreign, animal, and black origins, Djalioh is kept at a distance by this society. Paul de Monville and his friends test the ape-man by their criteria for humanity and conclude, relieved, that "it is an inert animal without intelligence" (ibid.). What are these criteria of humanity?

Whereas contemporary anthropologists define mankind by its vertical posture, the presence of a shortened face, freedom of the hands during locomotion, and the use of interchangeable tools, in M.

Paul's circle the conditions for humanity are as follows: the ability to smoke cigarettes, to hunt, work, read, write, and to love horses and women. Now since Djalioh does not satisfy these conditions, they can affirm that "decidedly he is an idiot" (p. 108). M. Paul and his friends' ethnocentrism is even more deeply rooted than that of the prescientific peoples: their criteria for humanity came from the habits of an extremely closed circle inside a given social group.[8]

Like Rousseau, who ends his note on the apes by remarking on the almost inhuman stupidity of the observers who described them, Flaubert emphasizes the brutishness of men in relation to Djalioh. As we all know, the sympathy of the Romantics for primitives and savages is proportional to their aversion to a society in which their aspirations were unrealizable. For Flaubert, and like Flaubert, Djalioh is the antibourgeois par excellence.

Gustave was the idiot of the family, Flaubert was the idiot of the salons, according to Théophile Gautier. As an adolescent he felt like an ape: wild, clumsy, he managed poorly with language; in short, he was monstrous. *Quidquid volueris* is thus the story of an ape told by another ape. Even the subject of the tale is that of a failed education. Raised by the Frenchman who is his adoptive father, Djalioh ends up by raping and killing this man's wife, after having murdered his child and before eliminating himself. Djalioh is not a "noble savage." His sentimental education will have been a resounding failure. The amorous initiation proves to be radically antisocial: instead of an apprenticeship, we witness a rite of passage so bloody that the hero dies from it. The subjective is revealed here as not assimilable to the social: Djalioh, the excessive individual, must die so that society can continue to live by its preconceived ideas. The adolescent's social and sexual conflict is resolved through the elimination of his alterity.

The evolutionary side of the question is what interests us here: the fact that this backward little boy *became* a great writer, the fact that this child was *transformed* into a master of style. It is about this that we marvel ceaselessly, just as we are unendingly moved by the fact that a species of monkey could become the human wonder that we are. As Jacques Lacan puts it, "It is not because of Darwin that people think themselves any less on the top of the heap of creatures, since that is precisely what he convinces us of."[9]

Two questions are then worth asking: At what price this evolution for Flaubert? And, what do we eliminate, we critics, in order to maintain this vision of an evolving Flaubert, who progressively corrected the excesses (faults) of his juvenilia to arrive at the perfection of *Madame Bovary*?

By approaching the savage discourse of *Quidquid volueris* like salon critics, we react to the young Flaubert like M. Paul's friends confronted with Djalioh: according to the criteria of our lettered tribe, we will be surprised by certain "invocatory exaggerations, certain religious obsecrations," by "the excessive romanticism of comparisons," we will ask that "the plot remain full and sustained,"[10] and we will perhaps conclude like Anatole France, who says of Flaubert: "That man who had the secret of infinite words was not intelligent." We will wait for him to evolve in order to recognize in him a master of literature, underestimating the adolescent-ape-writer on behalf of the mature civilized writer.

Deferred Alterity

Djalioh is aphasic, but he has verbal and even oratorical thoughts, organized according to grammatical rules and decorated by rhetorical ornaments. Of all the implausibilities in the tale, this is certainly among the least implausible, and like all the rest it requires no explication.

Nevertheless, Djalioh's aphasia is psychoanalytically plausible. I am not invoking a clinical psychoanalysis of Flaubert the man, but a general psychoanalytic knowledge which this text, like all great literary works, possesses and makes explicit. Djalioh does not speak, because he lacks an *imago*. His relation to his own image is blocked, he does not arrive at a spatial auto-identification which would facilitate his access to language. When he looks at people, he does not see himself in them: they seem too animallike, a fact which the narrator ceaselessly emphasizes throughout the ball sequence. On this occasion, Djalioh appears extremely civilized in his sullen reserve, in contrast to the beelike women who "buzz," the carp-men who "jump about," and the couples who "gallop" (pp. 108–9).

On the other hand, when he looks at Madame de Lansac's monkeys, he feels "drawn toward them by a strange sympathy" (p. 111). But here also, there is an irreducible difference: the monkeys look too much like people, they act like "kings," "lawyers," "women of pleasure" (ibid.). Faced with his half-brothers and sisters, Djalioh awaits an impossible "birth," immobilized in the fetal position, that of the newborn before speech: "seated on the ground, his knees drawn up to his head, his arms on his legs, and his half-dead eyes fixed on a single spot" (p. 111).

M. Paul tells us that when he had taken Djalioh to a brothel, he fled carrying a "rose and a mirror" (p. 108). Placed in a sexual situation, Djalioh reveals his double nature. As an animal, his sexual instinct is a need, which, like all needs, can be satisfied. As a man, Djalioh invests this instinct with desire which, as we know, is by definition without object and thus doomed to frustration. His escape from the brothel is due to his inability to decide between need and desire. At the first level of interpretation, rose and mirror correspond to nature and culture. But a subtle network of associations which runs throughout the tale invites us to read many other things: in the rose, woman, inaccessible but perishable; in the mirror, the lure of identity, vanity, which in this tale is mainly masculine. In the final scene of the tale flowers and mirrors are again present. The frustration of the animal, thwarted in his need, leads him to kill; that of the man frustrated in his desire leads him to kill himself. On the symbolic level the rose is crushed and the mirror is broken. Suicide is the definitive proof of Djalioh's humanity.

During the whole tale Djalioh never looks at himself in a mirror; his aspiration for an *imago* remains unsatisfied. The mirror is the attribute of humans: M. Paul "looks at himself in the mirror" (p. 105) and finds himself handsome; Adèle (his wife), in the last sequence of the story, "seeing herself nude in the mirror in the arms of Djalioh, let out a scream of horror and prayed to God" (p. 112). Djalioh, seen in the mirror, concretizes the specular fascination that the ape holds for mankind.[11]

Djalioh remains at an intermediary stage between the absence and presence of an *imago*, between need and desire. He remains on the verge of speech, and he very nearly speaks at his most human moments, which are his moments of desire. It is for this reason that the simple opposition between nature and culture, evoked by several critics, is not sufficient here. At the moment of Paul and Adèle's marriage, "his fat lips, cracked by fever, and covered with pimples, moved actively like someone speaking fast" (p. 107); and the moment he approaches the young woman: "Djalioh did not answer; he only stammered and hit his head in anger" (p. 112). According to Lacan, "The moment when desire is humanized is also the moment when the child is born to language."[12] Djalioh remains on the edge of desire, of language, of humanity. Deprived of speech and humanity, he is at the same time preserved from the social indignity of men, and he possesses that language of the heart which the Romantics dreamed of; he expresses himself by purer means than verbal language, as, for example, in the strange music that he draws from the violin.

For Djalioh every being is the irreducible other: half identified with people, half identified with apes, he cannot but desire, in distress and aphasia, this mixture of identity and alterity which he discerns in the other.

For M. Paul, the other is Djalioh. This "son" produced by "unusual means" is the perverse result of his white man's desire. Paul bought Djalioh's father, the orangutan Bell, from a black; with this ape as intermediary he impregnates a black woman.[13] Paul's virility and paternity pass through the relay of the animal and the black race. The birth of Djalioh, he says, filled him with joy, an ambiguous joy which resembles that of a father but which is given a scientific alibi (as a successful experiment): "I was certainly very happy, the question was resolved" (p. 108). Perhaps the real question resolved here is that of his virility.

Not only does Paul see his virility confirmed by the production of a child, but this exploit also gets him a supplementary penis: the Cross of Honor, awarded by the Institute of Sciences. Of this cross, he says to his friends: "It pleases women; they look at it smilingly when you talk to them" (ibid.).[14] The impregnation of a black woman by an ape bought from a black is for Paul the realization of a racist phantasm: "In the wildness of our *jouissance*," says Lacan on the subject of racism, "there is nothing but the Other that situates it, but only in so much as we are separated from it."[15]

Djalioh's very name marks this distance, this alterity: "That?

That's Djalioh." "What is Djalioh?" "Oh! It's a long story" (p. 107). J. Piaget Shanks observed that Esmeralda's goat in *Notre-Dame de Paris* is called Djali, as is Emma Bovary's greyhound. All one has to do is to add to the name Djali the exclamation "Oh!" as Flaubert emphasizes in this dialogue, to obtain the shocking name, the name of the monster. Djalioh is born "in Janeiro" (p. 108). This designation of the city of Rio de Janeiro by its last word, contrary to French and Portuguese usages, must be due to the homophony of Djalioh-Janeiro, which associates the two words in the same linguistic oddity. Even by its phonetics this name designates someone who is radically foreign.

The essence of the other is topographic: everyone is the other of his or her other, it is a question of one's point of view. In this way Djalioh is a monster for Paul and his friends, and the handsome Paul is a monster for the black woman who rejected him: "The stupid thing never wanted me; she probably found me uglier than a savage" (p. 107). Flaubert himself voluntarily hesitates: "Here is the monstrous aberration of nature who was in contact with M. Paul, that other monster, or, rather, that wonder of civilization who had all the right symbols: grandeur of spirit and hardness of heart" (p. 105).

Remember that Djalioh's father was named Bell and "that it was the most handsome [*bel*] orangutan ever" (p. 107). By naming and designating it in this way the narrator makes fun of Paul, the handsome (*bel*) man, "who was conceited enough to believe that all the women were in love with him" (p. 105). A subtle reversal of esthetic categories is under way here, unsettling the ethnic hierarchy at the same time.[16]

If Djalioh, animal and black, is M. Paul's other, for Djalioh and for M. Paul, as males, the other is Adèle. Woman simultaneously awakens in them sexual desire and the death instinct that accompanies the consciousness of the other. For the narrator, himself male, woman is that attractive and repellent other, fixed in the vegetative metaphor, throughout the whole story: woman as a wilted flower, always close to decomposition, a metaphor that achieves two objectives at once: it dehumanizes woman by giving her another nature and then kills her. Woman is at one time a flower, at another she is an animal (bee, mare), but most frequently she is a thing. M.

Paul includes her in his inventory among his furniture, paintings, and property, and she imagines herself as "a Lady, that is to say, something which bears a big shawl and walks alone in the streets" (p. 107).

The tale also poses the question of the otherness of childhood. As a backward adolescent, Djalioh is in the way of the adults. "Stop it, little monster!" the adult says to the child. Flaubert, himself having matured and progressed beyond literary aphasia, represses the little monster that he was; and we, the others, the readers, regard his juvenile compositions with an adult condescension.

For the narrator and the reader, Djalioh, as an ape, is the closest other to a person, equipped with all the attractions that derive from this resemblance-difference: "I never liked apes, says the young Flaubert, but perhaps that's wrong because they seem to me a perfect imitation of human nature. When I see one of these animals—I'm not speaking here of people—I think I am seeing myself in a magnifying mirror." It is not by chance that Lacan's text about the mirror stage is full of references to apes: "an operation which, though carried out within nose-shot, so to speak, would be almost the quality of this *aha!* which enlightens us about the chimpanzee's intelligence, amazed as we are to sense this miracle on the face of our equals, it does not fail to bring about a deplorable result."[17]

In the end, Djalioh's alterity is seen as demonic.[18] As a "demon," Djalioh is the other "within" us. "What in those days," writes Freud, "were thought to be evil spirits to us are base and evil wishes, the derivatives of impulses which have been rejected and repressed. In one respect only do we not subscribe to the explanation of these phenomena current in medieval times; we have abandoned the projection of them into the outer world, attributing their origin instead to the inner life of the patient in whom they manifest themselves."[19]

The way the name *Djalioh* is introduced into the text is enlightening about his nature as creature of the psyche. At the start of the tale, the narrator presents three characters—Paul, Adèle, and her mother Madame de Lansac—when suddenly at the tail end of a paragraph, this strange name jumps out like a jack in a box: "Madame de Lansac left to give some orders for the next day and to close all the doors, to lock all the locks, leaving only Paul and Djalioh" (p. 103).

Appearing so soon after the locking of the locks, this name, in a sense, enters by the keyhole, like the little devils (Diablotins) of the prologue: "Come to me dreams of a poor fool! Come one and all, my good friends the Diablotins. . . . Come one and all, children of my brain, give me for a moment one of your follies, one of your strange laughs. . . . You will arrive by my keyhole."[20]

To the questions already asked, let me add one last one: by eliminating this young, diabolical, crazy, excessive Flaubert for the sake of a more civilized Flaubert, are we not, in effect, exorcising some of our very own literary demons? In the name of a certain civilized image that we have of literature, we refuse its savage and impure manifestations.

The Fossilized Romantic

"I am an old raving romantic," Flaubert tells Sainte-Beuve and the critics of the future. We all know that Djalioh, like Madame Bovary, is Flaubert himself. But the didactic simplification of the Romantic disciplined by realism persists till the end. It must be said that not only was Flaubert always a Romantic, as everyone knows, but also that he was *never* a naïve Romantic, a dyed-in-the-wool Romantic.

Flaubert was Romantic to the end, but prematurely, precociously, he belonged to that species of Romantics which was rotten from the start, perhaps even the most radical among the Romantics, gnawed at by irony to such a degree that their Romanticism begins at a point beyond Romanticism itself. Like Lautréamont, and thirty years before him, Flaubert felt, beginning with *Quidquid volueris*, that Romanticism was not viable, that "literature" was no longer viable; their works are at the same time the death and the funereal celebration of literature in its last glorious form. Disappointment, regret, and derisive laughter are already there, from the start and forever.

The kinship between the young Flaubert and Lautréamont becomes apparent in the reaction of the critics. What has been said about *Quidquid volueris* is what has been said for a long time about *Les Chants de Maldoror*: that it is exaggerated ("I exaggerated a little," Ducasse admits with false modesty in a letter), insane, in bad taste, spottily successful, ends badly, too much like oratory, melodramatic, unbelievable, and so on.

The parallel can be extended even further. Lautréamont went from the *roman noir* to the *platitudes* of the *Poésies*. Flaubert also begins with the *roman noir* and ends up with *Bouvard et Pécuchet*.[21] In the interval, however, he was the author of masterpieces. Imagine for a moment that we bypassed this great interlude and we read Flaubert like Lautréamont, detecting in his work the sudden change, the replacement of the wild Romantic by the caricaturist implicated in *bêtise*, without the possibility of assimilation and without the indication of a resolution to the literary crisis or the general crisis.

Quidquid volueris and *Bouvard et Pécuchet*, when thought of as the two key chronological points in Flaubert's work, are not assimilable on the level of plot or on the level of style: they are unbelievable stories, enunciated in an uncertain tone for the listener, who does not know how to hear them. These two works do not permit us to speak *reasonably* of them, except if we regard the first as a rough outline and the second as a long shot. The first is too much (hyperbole), the second is too little (platitude); nothing can be said about them if we remain attached to traditional literary categories, because the first will bog down our discourse in its pathetic eloquence, and the last, as Flaubert hoped, will lead us into the quicksand of generalized *bêtise*. This is exactly like *Les Chants de Maldoror* and the *Poésies*. What Flaubert and Lautréamont are saying is this: "Since it is insane to be Djalioh / Maldoror, I will be "sane" and "scientific" like M. Homais or the school manuals." Evidently, however, Bouvard and Pécuchet, like Ducasse in *Poésies*, finally prove to be the subverters of reason and science. Ineducable, in short.

The narrator's discourse in *Quidquid volueris*, like Count Lautréamont's, already shows the traces of the wound from which literature suffers, through the introduction of self-criticism and differences in level of the enunciation:

. . . the moon, through the tall elms, shown limpid and calm across their interconnecting branches. Again the moon! Of course, she must necessarily play a big role, it is the sine qua non of any gloomy work, like the rattling of teeth and bristling of hair; but, anyway, that day there was a moon. Why take her away from me, my poor moon? Oh! my moon, I love you! You shine well on the steep roof of the château, of the lake you make a wide belt of silver, and in your pale glimmer each drop of rainwater that falls, I say each drop, suspended from the edge of a rose leaf, seems a pearl on a beautiful woman's breast. This is old enough! But let's stop there and come back to the subject at hand. [22]

In the same way as Lautréamont, young Flaubert subverts his own romantic style; he lets himself slip into comparisons and shows that the word *like* can engender an automatic and infinite discourse: "His soul took to what was beautiful and sublime, like ivy to debris, flowers to springtime, the tomb to the corpse, and unhappiness to people" (p. 105). [23]

The Romantic is assassinated by the most exacerbated of the Romantics, on the level of the story (*récit*), and on the level of discourse (*discours*). The character of Djalioh dies at the end of the story, and his internal discourse, of an inspired lyricism, is definitively recuperated by the discourse of the grocers who comment on the action on the last page of the tale. The grocers' discourse prevails over that of the ape-man, just as that of Homais is to prevail over that of Emma, at the end of *Madame Bovary*. Is not Homais the perfect example of a Homo sapiens, he who believes in evolution and progress? "Fabricando fiat faber, age quod agis," cites Homais. [24]

Djalioh disappears, but in Flaubert's later works the traces of this murder remain visible. While M. Paul continues his social life and the fresh young Adèle is transformed into stinking carrion, Djalioh is assigned a special fate: he is, in a certain sense, immortalized: "Oh! He is superb, varnished, polished, well groomed, magnificent, since, as you know, the zoological society took possession of him and has made him into a fine skeleton" (p. 113).

Like Djalioh, the Romantic will remain fossilized in the archeological strata of the Flaubert domain. The Goncourts understood it well, when they said to their friend: "He's a man with something that's been killed underneath." "With me nothing has been erased," Flaubert himself confirmed in a letter to Louise Colet. Djalioh's skeleton has its symbolic counterpart in the stuffed parrot which Flaubert kept on his table. They are the two trophies of this suicidal hunt, lyricism and eloquence reduced to the condition of fetishes.

The ape and the parrot are complementary: the one appears human but is without a voice, the other has the voice without the appearance. They are both exotic, both Brazilian (the parrot is from the Amazon) and, as such, they commemorate the loss of a paradise where the heart spoke its true language.[25]

In the process of repression, the corpse does not disappear: "As for the memory of Rodolphe, it had descended to the very bottom of her heart, and there it remained, more solemn and immobile than a king's mummy in a crypt" (p. 647). All one has to do, in this extract from *Madame Bovary*, is replace Rodolphe with Djalioh, and Emma with Flaubert to give *Quidquid volueris* its proper place in the monument that is Flaubert's oeuvre.

Flaubert keeps on killing Djalioh, and the paradox is the same as that which produced *Maldoror-Poésies*. What his age offered him as the antidote to madness, as the alternative to delirium, was *bêtise*. And, with Flaubert's pen, *bêtise* itself goes mad, the remedy becomes poison, and his submission to the grocers' discourse becomes the sharpest form of revolt: Romanticism is triumphant and agonizing in its own denial and derision.

A great author's early works are not only the beginning and the source; since, if there is such a thing as stylistic progress, writing (*l'écriture*) knows no progress, it is nothing but change spiraling around the same. The ape-man is not only the idiot who will be surpassed by the masterful writer; Romanticism is not merely a movement that is supplanted by another; barbarism, clichés, *bêtise* are not the others of literature, but integrate its very matter; the Other is not the only beast, and we cannot rid ourselves of it unless we abstain from desire.

Writing feeds on the dead zones of individuality and on the debris of that superb mummy, literature.

[Translated by Robert Riger]

Notes

1. René Descharmes, *Flaubert: Sa Vie, son caractère et ses idées avant 1857*, (Paris: Librairie des Amateurs, 1909), p. 4. Though outdated in

certain respects, Descharmes's study remains fundamental. By examining Flaubert's juvenilia according to the principles of Lanson and Sainte-Beuve, Descharmes has brought to the fore the fundamental questions of all of Flaubert's works, with a sensibility and a finesse lacking in later clinical analyses of the novelist.

2. All references in the text to the works of Flaubert are to volume 1 of Gustave Flaubert, *Oeuvres complètes*, 2 vols. (Paris: Seuil, L'Intégrale, 1964). [Translations are by the translator.—EDS.]

3. D. L. Demorest, *L'Expression figurée et symbolique dans l'oeuvre de Flaubert* (Paris: Les Presses modernes, 1931), pp. 53–127. On romantic sources, see René Dumesnil, *Gustave Flaubert: L'Homme et l'oeuvre* (Paris: Desclée de Brouwer et Cie., 1932), and Jean Bruneau, *Les Débuts littéraires de Gustave Flaubert (1831–1845)* (Paris: Armand Colin, 1962).

Psychoanalytically, Marthe Robert sees in it, as in the rest of Flaubert's juvenilia, the still fresh obsession with "the primal scene" (*Roman des origines et origines du roman* [Paris: Grasset, 1972]). Sartre considers the first works as "easily decipherable" and *Quidquid volueris* readable, "if rid of the author's hyperbolism," as the admission of the difficulties the young Flaubert had with language (*L'Idiot de la famille—Gustave Flaubert de 1821 à 1857* [Paris: Gallimard, 1971]).

Referentially, Maurice Bardèche observes that "at the end the ape Djalioh does not behave himself" (*L'Oeuvre de Flaubert* [Paris: Les Sept Couleurs, 1974], p. 26).

Stylistically, Jonathan Culler considers this tale as a failure: "The tale exceeds the thematic demands made on it by the narrator. . . . The Flaubertian text, one might say, has discovered excess as a source of power, but the young Flaubert misinterprets this lesson and cannot apply it with success until much later and in a different narrative mode. . . . He cannot consequently speak with any real authority. . . . [It is a question] of the failure of the text to project an experience which might serve as its basis" (*Flaubert: The Uses of Uncertainty* [Ithaca, N.Y.: Cornell University Press, 1974], pp. 40–41).

4. André Leroi-Gourhan, *Le Geste et la parole: Technique et langage*, 2 vols. (Paris: Albin-Michel, 1964), 1:12. Leroi-Gourhan also writes: "The assimilation of the ethnic group to a sort of ideal 'ego' uniting the qualities of the good and the beautiful opposes the tendency to place outside the familiar group monstrous peoples, who fit in their appearance and in their moral the ultimate in evil and ugliness. The same attitude can be seen during the prescientific period in regard to the ape who is the monstrous antipode of civilized man. This adequately explains the murky assimilation of demons,

of unknown peoples, and of apes in the geographic imagery up until the sixteenth century. This attitude is directly transposed in the anthropology of the eighteenth century and gives rise both to the attempted scientific justifications of racist prejudices and to human paleontology" (p. 12).

5. In the tale, Djalioh is indirectly compared to a gargoyle: "He shook and leaned himself up in a saint's nook, empty in large part, only one figure remained, it was grotesque, horrible and scary" (p. 106). Curiously, the first picture, which illustrates the myth of the ape-man in Leroi-Gourhan's book, was taken from a church at Rouen. A caption accompanies it: "Stained-glass window from the church of Saint-Ouen, Rouen, fifteenth century. A demon leaving the body of a possessed woman. Note the appearance of 'a humanlike ape,' the prominent eyebrows, the large nostrils, the muzzle, the griffinlike hands, and the big toe set wide apart. In the left hand the demon holds a long object" (p. 309). Now this object suggests, by its position, the bow of a violin, the instrument which Djalioh plays in one passage of the tale.

6. Jean-Jacques Rousseau, *Discours sur l'origine et les fondements de l'inégalité*, in *Oeuvres complètes*, ed. Jean Starobinski, 4 vols. (Paris: Pléiade, 1964), 3:208.

7. Bruneau, in *Les Débuts littéraires de Gustave Flaubert*, cites one of these commentaries: "In the past few days the curious have gone to the Jardin des Plantes to see a young orangutan which was brought from Sumatra to Paris by Captain Vanaghen. *Orangutan* in Malaysian means 'wild man.' The orangutan, in fact, resembles a man to a frightening degree" (*Revue du Théâtre*, supplement to the 197th installment, 8 [May 1836]: 302). Bruneau continues: "Let us add that Flaubert could have seen orangutans at the Rouen circus. *L'Indiscret* of 9 November 1834, gives a report of the program from the Lalanne Circus where the inconceivable suppleness of the orangutan was admired" (p. 130).

When it comes to the literary antecedents of the ape-man as a character in fiction, one can cite Swift's *A Voyage to the Country of the Houyhnhnms* (1726) and Walter Scott's *Count Robert of Paris* (1831). Bruneau notes the similarities between Flaubert's story and the tale "Le Brick du Gange," by Eugène Chapus, published in *La Revue de Paris*, in September 1831; in it there is an orangutan who rapes and murders a young woman. Also, he says: "*Le Colibri*, of 24 November 1836 (no. 60) contains a short story, unsigned, entitled *Jack en bonne fortune*: it is about the orangutan from the Jardin des Plantes, who is found at the rue de la Harpe with his mistress, a grisette Théresine, 'half drunk from cider and love'" (p. 131).

The subject will be taken up later in the famous "Murders in the Rue

Morgue" by Poe (1841), the source of which is probably Walter Scott's novel. The appearance of all of these fictions since the eighteenth century attests to the fascination exerted by the anthropoid apes described by the travelers and later seen for the first time in the zoos and circuses.

8. Their comments are reminiscent of the remarks of a Frenchman from Rouen in 1509, faced with the Indians brought from Brazil: "They speak with their lips, they have no religion. . . . They do not know what bread, wine, or money are" (in Paul Gaffarel, *Histoire du Brésil français au seizième siècle* [Paris: Maisonneuve, 1878]).

9. Jacques Lacan, "Subversion du sujet et dialectique du désir dans l'inconscient freudien" (1960), in *Écrits* (Paris: Seuil, 1966), p. 797.

10. Jean de la Varende, *Flaubert par lui-même* (Paris: Seuil, 1958).

11. This specular character of the ape is equally emphasized in Walter Scott's novel. Sylvanus, the orangutan, first surprises Count Robert by his uncertain aspect of resemblance / difference to people: "The tremendous creature, so like, yet so very unlike, to the human form" (*Count Robert of Paris*, in *The Waverly Novels* [New York and London: Harper and Brothers, 1880], 29:198).

And the second appearance of the ape is even more significant in this regard. While the philosopher Agelastes is in the middle of giving a long discourse on the subject of evil to Countess Brenhilda, the couple sees Sylvanus's face appear *in a mirror*: "On this glass the philosopher had his eyes naturally fixed, and he was confounded at perceiving a figure glide from behind the shadow of a curtain, and glare at him, with the supposed mien and expression of the Satan of monkish mythology, or a satyr of the heathen age. 'Man!' said Brenhilda, whose attention was attracted by this extraordinary apparition, as it seemed, of the Fiend, 'have thy wicked words, and still more wicked thoughts brought the Devil amongst us?'" (p. 319).

12. Jacques Lacan, "Fonction et champ de la parole et du langage en psychanalyse" (1953), in *Écrits*, p. 319.

13. Two complementary phantasms have always accompanied the speculations about anthropoid apes: that of their extraordinary sexual activity and that of the impregnation of native women by them. Among the monsters described by the first navigators, there were men with monkey's tails who were thought to be the fruit of relations between apes and women. Rousseau cites the translator of the *Histoire générale des voyages*, (Paris: Didot, 1748), who refers to stories by Battel, an English traveler of the late sixteenth, early seventeenth centuries, and by Dapper, a seventeenth-century Dutch doctor and geographer, about orangutans: "The Negroes tell strange stories about this animal. They maintain not only that it rapes women and girls but that it

dares to attack armed men; in a word, there is much evidence that this is the satyr mentioned by the ancients" (p. 210). "This beast, he says, is so similar to a man that it had occurred to several travelers that it could have been produced by a woman and an ape" (p. 209). Starobinski corrects an erroneous note used by Rousseau, and refers to volume 4 of the Didot edition, Paris, 1747: "They say that the males of the species grab women when they are found alone, and caress them to excess" (p. 1371). The question of the crossing of an ape with men was also of scientific interest. In his *Histoire naturelle*, Buffon maintained that "constant reproduction is what constitutes a species"; the individual resulting from a fusion of two different species was sterile. And for the thinkers of the eighteenth century, the very definition of a *monster* implied sterility. This question continued to interest science in the nineteenth century.

14. In 1865, Flaubert would write to the Goncourts, about the Legion of Honor: "We will stick the rays of the star in each others' asses to have some fun" (*Correspondance*).

15. Jacques Lacan, *Télévision* (Paris: Seuil, 1973), p. 53.

16. Similarly, in Walter Scott's novel, Sylvanus is horrified when faced with Count Robert, demonstrating the relativity of the points of view: "At length the creature approached the bed; his hideous eyes were fixed on those of the Count; and, as much surprised at seeing him as Robert was at the meeting, he skipped about fifteen paces backwards at one spring, with a cry of instinctive terror, and then advanced on tiptoe, holding his torch as forward as he could between him and the object of his fears, as if to examine him at the safest possible distance" (*Count Robert of Paris*, p. 199).

17. Jacques Lacan, "La Chose freudienne" (1955), in *Écrits*, p. 428.

18. The attribution of a demonic nature to the ape is attested to by medieval imagery, by the narrative of the travelers of the sixteenth and seventeenth centuries. In all modern fiction where apes appear, from Swift to Poe, this satanic character is recalled; Djalioh does not escape the rule. In Walter Scott's story, a curious association brings us back, by chance(?), to Flaubert's obsessions: "But for the gift of speech, which we cannot suppose any of the family to have attained, we should have believed the satyr seen by St. Anthony in the desert to have belonged to this tribe" (*Count Robert of Paris*, p. 199).

19. Sigmund Freud, "A Neurosis of Demoniacal Possession in the Seventeenth Century," in *Studies in Parapsychology*, ed. Philip Rieff (New York: Collier, 1963), p. 92.

20. Djalioh, who enters the tale "by the keyhole," ends up by committing crimes in an absolutely closed place: "Finally he entered the salon, quietly,

on tiptoes, and once he had entered, he double-locked the door" (p. 112). The main events in the tale are situated in a closed space, separated from the "world," the space of dreams and hallucinations.

21. Let us note that even though *Bouvard et Pécuchet* is Flaubert's last work, he had been working on it since his youth. He spoke of it to Maxime Du Camp in 1843, and Jean Bruneau mentions that the project of the *Dictionnaire des idées reçues* dates from 1845–46. Thus there is no real interval between Romanticism and *platitude*.

22. P. 103. Cf. Lautréamont in *Les Chants de Maldoror:* "In these sorts of stories, where a passion of some nature or other is given, it fears no obstacle to make a place for itself, there is no reason to dilute in a drinking cup the gum-lacquer of four hundred banal pages" (Isidore Ducasse, comte de Lautréamont, *Chants VI*, in *Oeuvres complètes* [Paris: Corti, 1958], p. 352).

23. "All these tombs spread around the cemetery, like the flowers in a field, a comparison which somehow lacks truth . . ." (*Chants I*, ibid., p. 153).

24. Homais, the man (*l'homme*), has as suggestive a name as that of one of his sources, the Abbé Bourgeois, from whom Flaubert borrowed a few of the phrases attributed to the pharmacist (cf. Dumesnil, *Gustave Flaubert*).

25. These two Brazilian animals in Flaubert's work, with all of the symbolism they suggest, are not foreign to the history of Normandy and the city of Rouen. In the sixteenth century, many Normans traveled between France and Brazil. In 1509, Captain Thomas Aubert brought back aboard *La Pensée* Indians and wild animals that were paraded through the streets of Rouen. One Jean d'Ango, a brazilwood merchant, built a castle near Dieppe decorated with bas-reliefs representing the tropical paradise; Indians and exotic animals lived there with the proprietor. His tomb, in the Church of Saint-Jacques at Dieppe, bears a similar bas-relief. In 1550, Henry II and Catherine de Medici participated in a feast at Rouen: here sailors simulated, with the help of a number of Brazilian Indians and animals, a battle between the Tabajaras and Tupinambas. Up through the nineteenth century, there existed a house in Rouen called the Ile du Brésil; its wooden ornaments can still be found at the city's museum of antiquities. In these friezes one can see savages, parrots, and apes (small ones, since Brazil, contrary to Flaubert's fiction, has no orangutans or other great apes). Information about the age-old relations between Brazil and Normandy can be found in Paul Gaffarel, *Histoire du Brésil français*; Ferdinand Denis, *Une Fête brésilienne célébrée à Rouen en 1550* (Paris: Librairie J. Techner, 1851); Affonso Arions de Mello Franco, *O Indio Brasileiro e a Revolucão Francesca* (Rio de Janeiro:

Livraria José Olympio Editora, 1937). It is evident that Flaubert was able to see the traces of this history in Normandy, where the dreams of a tropical paradise and the myth of the noble savage existed well before Rousseau and the Romantics.

Fetishism and Allegory in *Bouvard et Pécuchet*

Charles Bernheimer

Of the numerous structures of substitution that abound in Flaubert's writing, fetishism is surely one of the most evident. What reader has not noticed the way Frédéric focuses on Madame Arnoux's shoes, the hem of her dress, the fur trim of her black velvet coat? These objects of clothing classically fulfill the Freudian description of the origin of the fetish. "The foot or shoe," writes Freud in his 1927 essay, "owes its attraction as a fetish, or part of it, to the circumstance that the inquisitive boy used to peer up the woman's legs toward her genitals. Velvet and fur reproduce—as has long been suspected—the sight of the pubic hair which ought to have revealed the longed-for penis." As is well known, Freud identifies that longed-for penis as "the woman's (mother's) phallus which the little boy once believed in and does not wish to forego" because "if a woman can be castrated then his own penis is in danger." The fetish thus acts as "a token of triumph over the threat of castration and a safeguard against it."[1] Its function is to repair the gap revealed through the discovery of castration, while simultaneously serving as a reminder of the unwelcome truth of that revelation. It may be considered the emblem for a perversion of Eros, the symbol for a refusal to accept difference whose symbolic role is precisely to enable such acceptance on a provisional basis. But the intense fear of castration persists.

From the point of view of D. W. Winnicott, the fetish is a transitional object whose mediating function in the facilitation of reality-acceptance has been drastically reduced in favor of its function as a symbol of union.[2] Fetishism is a kind of desperate effort to salvage the narcissistic theory of sexual sameness just when it is about to be revealed as a fiction. The fetishist has *seen* the evidence of sexual difference, but he denies his anxiety-producing perception by finding a substitute for the desired organ. This substitute is chosen on a metonymic model of physical proximity, but the object thus approached is actually a fantasy (the mother's penis). The metonymic structure of reference to presence is used by the fetishist to mask his discovery of absence. This duplicity, Freud observes, saves the fetishist from becoming a homosexual since, in his psychical reality, the woman still has the attribute necessary to be sexually attractive.

These theoretical considerations seem particularly relevant to *L'Éducation sentimentale*, given Madame Arnoux's role as a mother figure. Frédéric's fetishistic response to her represents both a denial of his mother's difference—the fetish in this sense symbolizes sexual sameness—and a provisional acceptance of that difference: insofar as it is detached and independent, the fetish can be manipulated as he pleases (like the gloves and handkerchief Madame Arnoux gives him). But the detachable quality of the fetish, its role, in Freud's terms, as a permanent memorial to the horror of castration, leaves it vulnerable to alienation from the fetishizing subject. The auction of the Arnoux household's possessions dramatically stages this kind of alienation. Frédéric watches as articles of Madame Arnoux's clothing are examined by potential buyers who pass them from hand to hand. His mournful awareness of her loss causes him to think of his erstwhile fetishes as relics. "After that they sold her dresses, then one of her hats from which a broken feather hung limply [surely not a gratuitous detail], then her furs, then three pairs of shoes; and the distribution of these relics, which vaguely recalled the shape of her limbs, seemed an atrocity to Frédéric, as if he had witnessed crows tearing her corpse to pieces."[3] Here it becomes evident that the operation of the fetish-relic is closely linked to the maintenance of an image of bodily integrity, be the body that of the mother or of the self. Indeed, as Frédéric witnesses the sacred objects being sold, he feels "a deathly torpor, a sense of disintegration." The return of the fetish to its social role in an economic exchange divorces it from its reassuring connection to the phallic mother, illusory image of unity and continuity, and places it in an impersonal system of changing valorizations.

There is, however, a certain category of fetish of which the subject can less easily be dispossessed and whose use in social exchange in no way subverts its function in the phantasmal arena. These fetishes are linguistic; they are the codes of social discourse, discourse systematized into self-contained ideological structures. Such codes belong to what Jean Baudrillard, interpreting Marx's conception of the fetish, has called the fetishism of the signifier. "In fetishism," he writes, "it is the passion of the code that expresses itself. Regulating and subordinating at once objects and subjects, this passion gives them both over to abstract manipulation. . . . The actual fetishism of the object attaches itself to the object-sign emptied of its substance and of its history, reduced to being the mark of a difference and the résumé of a whole system of differences."[4] In their last encounter, Frédéric and Madame Arnoux together celebrate their loyalty to just such a codified fetish, a popularized version of the literary ideal of Platonic love. This code allows Frédéric to reconstitute Madame Arnoux as a whole being, but one that is entirely abstract, an artificial creature of ready-made phrases. Here we are reminded of the etymology of the word *fetish* from the Latin *facticius*, made by art, which developed in Portuguese and Spanish into words designating, precisely, the work of imitation through signs. Frédéric does still refer to a more explicitly bodily fetish when, observing the point of Marie's *bottine* protruding a little from under her dress, he declares, "The sight of your foot disturbs me" (p. 161). But by the very act of articulating his disturbance Frédéric removes it from the silent dimension of subjective feeling and makes it part of a shared code of sublimating discourse. The code is a defense against the reality of perception: the shocking sight of Marie's white hair, and behind that, of the mother's castration. To escape from "the dread of incest," Frédéric turns Madame Arnoux into nothing more than a name, a name subject to infinite repetition within a code of romantic idealization. "For me," he tells her, "all the delights of flesh and spirit were contained in your name, which I repeated to myself, trying to kiss it with my lips. I imagined nothing beyond your name" (p. 161).

Now, I want to argue that Bouvard and Pécuchet are also contained, "flesh and spirit," in their names, with "nothing beyond." Indeed, their "flesh and spirit" is constituted, dissolved, and reconstituted on what I believe to be an essentially fetishistic model. However, Flaubert's use of that model in *Bouvard et Pécuchet* dissociates the psychoanalytic structure of fetishism from its psychical origins and gives it autonomy apart from any identifiable subject. The clerks' successive fetishes are the codes of signification proposed by the society and by the library. Not surprisingly, one of the first of these to operate in the text is the code defining the signs of sexual difference. The encounter of Bouvard and Pécuchet is explicitly placed in the great Romantic tradition of the *coup de foudre*.[5] Angular Pécuchet, still virgin at forty-seven, afraid of draughts and spices, deferential toward religion, prudish, plays the female role, while rotund Bouvard, bon vivant, liberal, pipe-smoking, ribald, atheistic, has the male lead. Sexual identities thus appear more metaphorical than physical, more a product of society's conventional attitudes than of anatomical destiny. The very conventionality of these attitudes, however, undercuts the distinctions they maintain. The mutual attraction of Bouvard and Pécuchet is not based on the one's appreciating the strong femininity or masculinity of the other. Rather, it is based on their sharing the same artificial set of clichéd opinions and received ideas, within which are included certain views about male-female difference. Thus even though Pécuchet is a shy virgin and Bouvard a lusty widower, they agree that women are "frivolous, bad-tempered, and stubborn" and go on to make the well-balanced observation that "despite that [women] were often better than men; at other times they were worse" and to conclude that "in short, it was better to live without them" (p. 53). So the reader's response to Pécuchet's sensibility as feminine enters into a network of commonplace definitions of women that makes any conclusion about the nature of sexual difference seem as arbitrary as the clerks' decision to do without the so-called opposite sex.

In a probing article, Claudine Gothot-Mersch studies the various scenarios for the novel in order to determine whether Flaubert conceived of his characters consistently in terms of a romantic couple.[6] She finds many notations that point in this direction, such as: "The lovers look at each other," or "They cherish each other. The marriage is made." But other textual indications suggest that Flaubert did not bother to maintain the coherence of those clichéd codes that he provisionally used to construct character. Gothot-Mersch observes that Bouvard is more sentimental than Pécuchet (in regard to Gorju and the children) and that he cries more easily (at the time of the fire, in front of the broken chest, confronted with the decaying carcass). Moreover, in one of the scenarios for the penultimate chapter, Flaubert wrote: "Pécuchet took responsibility for Victor. Bouvard, gentler, more feminine, for Victorine." Indeed, there is a certain *flottement du sens* perceptible in these contradictory suggestions as to sex roles, but the meaning of that *flottement* is clear: it points precisely to the arbitrariness of all received ideas about gender. (Are women really more sentimental than men? Do they cry more easily?)

However, the plot itself suggests that there may be pragmatic wisdom in the clerks' apparently groundless decision to avoid women. The presence of actual women entails disease (Pécuchet's fate with Mélie) or financial loss (Bouvard's experience with Madame Bordin) and confirms the clerks in their initial resolve ("No more women, okay? Let's live without them!" [p. 272]). It would appear that the clerks can maintain a certain fluid indeterminacy of gender identity only by retreating from the physical realities of sexual difference. With Pécuchet as symbolic woman, love can flourish, for sexual difference is not a bodily fact, but the arbitrary product of a shared social code.

Subsequently, the clerks replace the code of clichés that initially served to cement their friendship (and which included the mainspring of the plot: "What a good time we could have in the country!" [p. 52]) with a succession of books. Each of these books contains a specialized vocabulary, a hermeneutic code, that they adopt and cathect with erotic energy. The function they expect the book to perform is fetishistic in that its role is to signify and systematize difference precisely by denying the *reality* of difference. The book should, in other words, perform analogously to the code that allowed their romance to flourish at the outset.

Ideally, the clerks want all signification to be translatable into substitute signs within a hermeneutic totality. Thus they are never more happy than on the few occasions when they manage to become both subjects and objects of the code they currently favor. For instance, Pécuchet, during pauses in his gardening, studies his manual while imitating the pose of the gardener pictured on its frontispiece. "This resemblance," we are told, "even flattered him very much. It raised the author in his esteem" (p. 47). Having adopted the technical vocabulary of gardening ("They talked incessantly about sap and cambium, paling, fracture, thinning of buds" [p. 96]), carefully numbered each of his saplings to coincide with his list of their names, and dressed himself in the characteristic costume of the profession, Pécuchet regards himself as fully integrated into the code of signs elaborated in his technical manual. He even seems to consider himself the original model of what he is in fact imitating, as if his sense of origin were a function of his being able to read himself as a sign belonging to a systematic code.

That the translation of a problematic physical reality into purely linguistic formulations has something to do with fetishism is suggested by the case Freud cites in the second paragraph of his essay on fetishism. In this curious case, the phrase from the patient's mother tongue, English, *a glance at the nose*, had been transformed in German into a *Glanz auf der Nase*, that is, "a shine on the nose," and this special brilliance had been exalted into a fetishistic condition. As Guy Rosolato has pointed out, the word that is omitted from Freud's account of this extraordinary case, although it cannot help be heard in the interplay of *glance* and *Glanz*, is the Latin word for penis, *glans*.[7] Rosolato observes that the occulted Latin word acts in Freud's text as a kind of universal signifier, untranslatable itself while it supports and gives meaning to the process of translation between the English and German homophones. Thus the text's *exemplary* denial of the Latin word *glans*, of the word that explicitly evokes the fantasy of the mother's penis, is the equivalent of the fetishist's denial of the difference between the sexes. The absence of *glans*, where the real meaning lies, promotes the movement of translation between languages, while it retains the hidden fantasy of the ultimate inclusion of all semantic differences in one universal language.

Now it is precisely this fantasy that seems to me to determine the structure of Bouvard and Pécuchet's existence. They are constantly attempting to find the rule that will enable them to translate specialized languages either into material reality or into other specialized languages. Were the clerks psychologically plausible characters, one might argue that their fetishistic devotion to books prevents their relationship from becoming overtly homosexual. But the whole psychological framework of analysis collapses as soon as we realize that the clerks' model for continuity and sameness exists much less in the order of biological life than it does in that of bibliography. The fetishist's fantasy of a universal sexual organ is displaced in the clerks' case by a fantasy of a universal library. Whereas the explicitly erotic fetish refers metonymically to sexual uniformity, the book as fetish refers metonymically to what Baudrillard calls "the systematicity of signs."[8] The erotic fantasy that sustains the clerks' enterprises is the conception of a fully interpreted and intelligible world that would dissolve all difference between nature and culture by assimilating both into a uniform code of signification. Such a fantasy resembles Borges's Library of Babel, which "includes all verbal structures, all variations permitted by the twenty-five orthographical symbols, but not a single example of absolute nonsense."[9] The universal library is like the mother's *glans*. It allows for the meaningful determination of differences only by abstracting the signifier from the signified. As maintained in the face of experience, the fantasy of the mother's penis signifies castration, but the signifier, the fetish itself, restores the threatened sense of continuity by a kind of reflexive mirroring, the *glance* reflected back by the shiny *Glanz*.

It is this kind of reflexiveness, or translatability, that the clerks expect each of their bookish codes to be able to produce, as if by contagious magic. Indeed, the ideological fetishism of the signifier is the late capitalistic version of the primitive belief in the magic of names and the omnipotence of thoughts. As Freud points out, the survival of such beliefs in modern man is symptomatic of obsessional neurosis.[10] The obsessive separates himself defensively from the world by retreating into systems and categories whereby a threatening reality is represented and ordered. That this reality is defined most specifically as the difference between the sexes is made clear from Freud's case histories of both the Rat-man and the Wolf-man. The compulsive defends against the fearful implications of sexual difference by considering difference the product of an intellectual act, by making it a purely structural function.

No object of interpretation has significance for the clerks unless it refers as a part to the maternal totality of meaning, unless it serves to bridge the gaps of temporal experience and reconstitute the illusion of sameness and continuity. But the clerks' fetishes repeatedly fail to perform their desired homogenizing function. Even the phallus as universal symbol proves inadequate to the task (remember the moment when "for Bouvard and Pécuchet everything became a phallus" [p. 180]). Unlike Frédéric and Madame Arnoux, they find no code to signify the union of "flesh and spirit." Nature's manner of transforming itself in time remains totally alien to the linguistic code of changes invented to translate natural phenomena into cultural signification. The clerks' study of geology, for instance, convinces them that "everything decays, crumbles, changes form. Creation is put together in a fluctuating and transient manner" (p. 159). Later in the novel when they take on speculative disciplines such as aesthetics, philosophy, and religion, these purely cultural creations seem just as resistant to translation into a single differential code as had the uncertain fluctuations of nature. Thus, having studied the major philosophers, Bouvard concludes: "The proofs of God's existence given by Descartes, Kant, and Leibniz are not the same and mutually cancel each other out" (pp. 308–9).

Instead of achieving translation, integration, and ultimate sameness, the clerks' activities result in the revelation of unbridgeable difference and the proliferation of ruins. Their discovery of semantic arbitrariness, irreducible heterogeneity, and temporal flux in every field of knowledge they explore signals the collapse of the fetishistic mechanism that determines their existence. Yet the clerks do not respond to this collapse with the castration anxiety the psychoanalytic model for their conduct would lead one to expect. They are occasionally discouraged by their failures, but most often they move on without regret to the next supposedly authoritative code. This apparent advance is not progressive, however. The clerks make no instructive connections between their various failures. Each remains isolated, and their very lives seem to reflect this fragmented and discontinuous structure. It is as if their subjectivities were recreated with each new code they fetishize and existed only as long as the unifying function of that code remained in force. They have no psychological history, no past lives that permeate the present. Admittedly, we are given the barest outlines of Bouvard's and Pécuchet's biographies, but these supposedly lived pasts play no significant role in the present of the narrative and could just as well be the reductive digests of two books they have read. Thus for the reader their existence as coherent psychological subjects is as problematic as is the coherence of any one of the hermeneutic codes they adopt. Their fetishism seems to have an almost entirely structural function in the text, as the vehicle of the desire for structure.

The results of the clerks' obsession with structure are nowhere more brilliantly displayed than in their ornamental garden. This is how the garden appears to the clerks' astonished guests when, after dinner, the curtains are drawn apart:

In the twilight it was something quite frightening. The rock, like a mountain, occupied the lawn, the tomb formed a cube in the middle of the spinach, the Venetian bridge a circumflex accent over the kidney beans— and the cabin beyond made a large black smudge, for they had burned its roof to make it more poetic. The yews, trimmed into the shapes of stags or armchairs, stretched one after the other as far as the blasted tree, which extended diagonally from the arbor to the bower, where love apples hung like stalactites. A sunflower here and there displayed its yellow disc. The Chinese pagoda, painted red, looked like a lighthouse on the mound. The peacocks' beaks, caught by the sun, sent sparks of light back and forth, and behind the fence, cleared of its boards, the completely flat countryside closed the horizon. [Pp. 106–7]

This surreal landscape collects in one space objects belonging to at least two disparate conceptions of what constitutes a garden. On the one hand are some familiar components of a vegetable garden: spinach, kidney beans, love apples (tomatoes), to which one could perhaps link the sunflower. On the other hand are the widely divergent elements belonging to the clerks' fetishizing interpretation of the symbolic code for ornamental gardens found in Pierre Boitard's book *L'Architecte des jardins* (1852). These are the rock, tomb, Venetian bridge, burnt cabin, blasted tree, and Chinese pagoda. The first series of elements has a coherence we recognize from our experience of vegetable gardens; the second series is an entirely incoherent mixture born of the clerks' response to the arbitrary symbolic equivalences invented by Boitard.

The juxtaposition of these two systems, the one homogeneous, the other heterogeneous, gives rise to a third system of images, which are the metaphoric transformations of elements from the first two: mountain, cube, circumflex accent, large black smudge, stalactites, disc, lighthouse. These metaphors apparently reflect the impressions of the clerks' guests who are viewing the garden for the first time. The paragraph is introduced by the sentence "The curtains parted and the garden appeared" (p. 106) and followed by a single-sentence paragraph, "The astonishment of their guests filled Bouvard and Pécuchet with true delight" (p. 107). However, we may well wonder how any of the guests could have known that the turned-up tin hat on red stilts was meant to be a pagoda, that what was described earlier as "a quadrilateral of black plaster, six feet high, resembling a dog kennel" (p. 101) was indeed a tomb, that the bridge was Venetian, or that the black smudge had once been a cabin. Observing this, one might conclude that the metaphors belong to the narrator, who is putting himself momentarily in the place of the clerks' guests and condensing their collective response to the scene into his own terms. Yet his terms are intended to explain the guests' astonishment, so the origin of the series of metaphors vacillates and ultimately remains undecidable.

The metaphoric images themselves, however, have just as much presence in the paragraph as do the images of perceptible objects. They do not serve to unify the scene in relation to a perceiving subject, but appear as separate entities in a kind of unstable collage. In fact, by the end of the passage the reader's confident assumption that perception determines reality has effectively been destroyed. Does anyone actually *see* a Chinese pagoda or the beaks of peacocks? The various elements come to seem equally derealized in a landscape that juxtaposes some of the components of a traditional still life to the geometric forms of abstract art (cube, circumflex accent, black splotch, yellow disc). Finally, all of the nouns in the paragraph, be they "spinach" (actual garden vegetable) "stags" (shape given to yew trees), "stalactites" (appearance of love apples, already a figurative description for tomatoes), or "lighthouse" (metaphor for the "chinese pagoda," itself an obscure symbolic construction), are absorbed into the sparkling play of reflections between the peacocks' beaks (cones made of an unspecified substance) and ultimately flattened out on the plane of the horizon.

If the clerks initially experience a kind of erotic *jouissance* at the response of their guests to their fantastic exhibit, it is because they imagine that the guests have been able to read the garden's meaning and that they are all united in a shared enjoyment of the victory of ideology over nature. Moments later, however, they find that the code has not been understood after all: "The tomb was not understood, nor the burned cabin, nor the ruined wall" (p. 107). And the guests even permit themselves various critical remarks, based on their own ideological viewpoints, about what they find lacking or excessive. But whereas the clerks fail to absorb difference into universal signification, another kind of absorption takes place through the agency of Flaubert's style. Indeed, the process of equalization and leveling that occurs in the description of the garden perfectly fulfills Roman Jakobson's description of the poetic function: the metaphoric principle of equivalence has been projected onto the metonymic axis of succession. [11] The clerks are agents of metaphoric structurality: their desire is to translate the world into representational codes bound within a hermeneutic totality. Their defeat comes as this ideal is projected onto the metonymic axis of temporal succession, or, in Jakobson's phrase, as "similarity is superinduced upon contiguity." [12]

The effect of such projection, as Joel Fineman has brilliantly argued, is essentially allegorical. [13] The allegorical quest, in Fineman's view, is motivated formally by the desire to recuperate the fracture in some original hermeneutic totality caused by the inevitable metonymic component of any metaphoric structure. Flaubert makes this quest seem particularly futile in that the clerks' fetishism suggests the purely phantasmatic nature of the very notion of totality. Metonymy for them is a figure for bonding structure to a lost origin, the perfect systematicity of all signs; it is not a figure for temporal succession, but one for regressive nostalgia. Opposed to this desire is the conception of metonymy embodied in Flaubert's style. His writing conveys temporality as the repetitive accumulation in space of isolated fragments and disjunctive pieces, the creation, one could say, of ever more gaps. "Allegories," says Walter Benjamin in a memorable formulation, "are, in the realm of thoughts, what ruins are in the realm of things."[14]

Spread out on the metonymic axis, signs in *Bouvard et Pécuchet* seem to become part of a *danse macabre* celebrating their emancipation from the maternal context of the library, or any other unifying context, and their subjection to materiality and death. Indeed, this movement of deconstruction and designification may be understood quite precisely in psychoanalytic terms as a function of the death instinct, whose aim, Freud declared, "is to undo connections and so to destroy things."[15] The death instinct works to diminish tensions to a zero point, to a point where all significant differences are reduced to their common denominator in inorganic matter.[16]

Flaubert's technique of flattening out onto a single plane discrete images isolated from their normal context is a manifestation of this mode of reduction, one that is typical of allegorical practice. Angus Fletcher remarks: "An allegorical world gives us objects all lined up, as it were, on the frontal plane of a mosaic, each with its 'true,' unchanging size and shape. . . . Allegory has an idealizing consistency of thematic content because, in spite of the visual absurdity of much allegorical imagery, the relations between ideas are under strong logical control."[17] Flaubert's logical control could not be stronger. But the ideal his logic is serving, the truth of the images he presents in the discontinuous, surrealistic surface of his text, does not fill the gaps between unrelated images with redeeming meaning. Rather, it insists on those gaps as being themselves the revelation of the final truth. It is one of the most radical aspects of Walter Benjamin's theory of allegory that he considers this insistence, whereby "allegory goes away empty handed,"[18] as determining what is most specific to the allegorical universe.

The clerks' obsession with structure, and with its loss, gives them the unnatural Faustian energy, the antisocial tendencies, and the quasi-scientific curiosity about the order of things that Fletcher associates with the allegorical hero. Their lives, however, are subject to the destructuring violence that flattens them out as effectively as the elements of their garden are equalized in the reflections of the peacocks' beaks. These reflections thus perform a function directly opposed to those functions I discussed earlier between *Glanz* and *glance*. The fetish, I noted, permits the decoding of the significant difference between homophones and the meaningful translation between languages. In contrast, Flaubert's style foregrounds words in their essential untranslatability as things. In allegory, comments Benjamin, "word, syllable, and sound are emancipated from any context of traditional meaning and are flaunted as objects."[19] This objectification makes translation impossible, while it creates a pervasive sense of substitutability, any word seeming to be of equal value to the next, as if their relation to reality were as arbitrary as the assignation of proper names. That arbitrariness defines the radical difference that, in allegory, separates a creation at once "fluctuating and transient" from its signification, indeed even from its proper nomination.

The possibility of such nominal dissociation is suggested in the opening scene of the novel when each clerk reads the other's name in the hat he has just removed and placed by his side on the bench. The proper referent for the name is indicated by the metonymic proximity of hat and person and on the basis of the social convention through which you signify ownership by inscribing your name. But there is, of course, no necessary link between the names and the individuals who have just removed (their?) hats. Either man might have borrowed his headpiece, perhaps from a friend who had been given the hat by someone else, who in turn might conceivably have written his father-in-law's name in it as a mnemonic device. In any case, by the end of the novel the clerks have repeatedly experienced the arbitrariness of names—their failure to demonstrate possession or signify origin. At that point they decide to treat any name, be it found in a hat, museum, or library, as mere language subject to copy.

According to Flaubert's plan for the conclusion to the second volume, their last act would have been to reproduce the rough draft of a letter, found by chance amidst masses of discarded writing, in which the clerks themselves are designated as "inoffensive imbeciles" (p. 443). The clerks ask themselves what to do with it and decide: "No reflections! Let's copy it! The page must fill up, 'the monument' must be completed—equality of everything, of the good and the bad, the beautiful and the ugly, the insignificant and the characteristic. Only phenomena are true" (p. 443). From fetishists of the signifier, the clerks have become memorialists of the signifier's demise. First among the differences that are canceled out through the activity of transcription is the code that established their own sexual difference. In one of the scenarios, Flaubert noted at the end of the novel: "In the joy of copying and the community of passion they become the same man and . . . resemble each other physically."[20] This collapse of physical difference reflects the collapse of nominal specificity that makes the clerks' names appear in the *copie* as just two syllabic combinations (with the same etymological meaning: *bos* = *pecus*) among countless others—Taranis, Pacchioni, Borelli, Clodowig, Fécamp, Cambrian, Gabrielle de Vergy, Agamemnon, Mont Faunes, Foureau, Béchet, Buffon, Becquerel, Bouvard, Marescot, Marmontel, Marianne—so many names out of a mad hatter's hat, signifying nothing.

Or perhaps they do signify something, in the manner in which a relic signifies the death of a whole being and by its presence, albeit as a fragment, even a repulsive one, assures against the reality of our own death. Indeed, the relic plays the same role in relation to the death instinct that the fetish does in relation to Eros. What is denied by the fetish is the reality of castration; what is denied by the relic is the reality of the putrefying corpse.[21] Yet the relic also participates in the uncanny power of death's otherness, just as the fetish gains its efficacy from that female otherness that it serves at once to forget and to re-member. Thus the clerks' monument is not only a pyramid in which the epistemological claims of the library are laid to rest. The

monument is actually made up of rests, fragments that have survived
the destructive process, whose survival suggests the possibility of
mastering death. This is why " 'the monument' must be completed."
It may be an ironic monument (hence the quotation marks between
which Flaubert places the word) in that it is composed of bits and
pieces of the dead. But as monument it has a chance to hold firm
and erect through time. Its creation, like that of the fetish, is a
symptom of obsessional neurosis. The monument brings structure
back into the chaos of fragments. (We need only think of the
clerks'—and Flaubert's—numerous *classements*). In terms of this return of structure, the *copie* represents that moment of *Umschwung*, of
turnabout, that Benjamin describes when allegory "denies the void in
which it is represented [and] faithlessly leaps forward to the idea of
resurrection."[22] Flaubert's leap is much less extravagant: he imagines
that a monument to death can survive the death it memorializes.

Notes

Since this essay was written, the book has been published from which
most of it is taken: *Flaubert and Kafka: Studies in Psychopoetic Structure*
(New Haven, Conn.: Yale University Press, 1982). My chapter there on
Bouvard et Pécuchet provides a much fuller reading of the novel than I am
able to give here, but the book only suggests in passing the possibility of the
kind of allegorical interpretation I have attempted in this article.

1. Sigmund Freud, "Fetishism," in *Sexuality and the Psychology of Love*,
ed. Philip Rieff (New York: Collier, 1963), pp. 215–17.

2. See D. W. Winnicott, *Playing and Reality* (London: Pelican Books,
1974), especially chap. 1 "Transitional Objects and Transitional Phenomena."

3. Gustave Flaubert, *L'Éducation sentimentale*, in *Oeuvres complètes*, 2
vols. (Paris: Seuil, 1964), 2:158. Subsequent references in my text are to this
edition. All translations from the French are my own.

4. Jean Baudrillard, "Fétichisme et idéologie: La Réduction sémiolo-
gique," *Nouvelle Revue de psychanalyse*, no. 2 (Fall 1970), entitled *Objects
du fétichisme*, pp. 216–17.

5. Flaubert, *Bouvard et Pécuchet*, ed. Claudine Gothot-Mersch (Paris:
Gallimard, 1979), p. 59. Subsequent references in my text are to this edi-

tion, the most accurate currently available. The text of the Seuil L'Intégrale edition is not reliable.

6. Claudine Gothot-Mersch, *"Bouvard et Pécuchet:* Sur la genèse des personnages,"* in *Flaubert à l'oeuvre* (Paris: Flammarion, 1980).

7. Guy Rosolato, "Le Fétichisme dont se dérobe l'objet," *Nouvelle Revue de psychanalyse,* no. 2 (Fall 1970), pp. 31–39.

8. Baudrillard, "Fétichisme et idéologie," p. 217.

9. Jorge Luis Borges, *Labyrinths: Selected Stories and Other Writings,* ed. Donald A. Yates and James E. Irby (New York: New Directions, 1964), p. 57.

10. See Sigmund Freud, *Totem and Taboo,* trans. James Strachey (New York: Norton, 1950), pp. 86–90.

11. See Roman Jakobson, "Linguistics and Poetics," in *The Structuralists from Marx to Lévi-Strauss,* ed. Richard and Fernande De George (New York: Anchor Books, 1972), p. 95.

12. Ibid., p. 111.

13. Joel Fineman, "The Structure of Allegorical Desire," in *Allegory and Representation: Selected Papers From the English Institute, 1979–80,* ed. Stephen Greenblatt (Baltimore, Md.: Johns Hopkins University Press, 1981), pp. 26–60.

14. Walter Benjamin, *The Origin of German Tragic Drama,* trans. John Osborne (London: New Left Books, 1977), p. 178.

15. Sigmund Freud, *An Outline of Psychoanalysis,* trans. James Strachey (New York: Norton, 1949), p. 5.

16. Eugenio Donato has suggested that Flaubert conceived of the force that defeats the clerks' desire on a model analogous to the second law of thermodynamics. This law states that energy goes from a differentiated to an undifferentiated state. Time is understood as moving toward an abolition of differences through a slow but inexorable process of corruption and decay. Such a conception bears an evident similarity to the Freudian death instinct, which works to reduce tensions and return the differentiated organism to an inanimate state. See Eugenio Donato, "The Museum's Furnace: Notes toward a Contextual Reading of *Bouvard and Pécuchet,"* in *Textual Strategies: Perspectives in Post-Structuralist Criticism,* ed. Josué Harari (Ithaca, N.Y.: Cornell University Press, 1979), pp. 213–38.

17. Angus Fletcher, *Allegory: The Theory of a Symbolic Mode* (Ithaca, N.Y.: Cornell University Press, 1964), pp. 104–5.

18. Benjamin, *The Origin of German Tragic Drama,* p. 233. Benjamin's theory of allegory is far too complex for me to summarize here. The characteristics he considers specific to the allegorical universe are "the secret,

privileged knowledge, the arbitrary rule in the realm of dead objects, the presumptive infinity of the loss of hope" (p. 232). I discuss Benjamin's ideas at greater length in the first part of my chapter on *The Castle* in *Flaubert and Kafka*.

19. Benjamin, *The Origin of German Tragic Drama*, p. 207.

20. Quoted by Gothot-Mersch, *"Bouvard et Pécuchet,"* p. 151.

21. Pierre Fédida makes this point in his article "La Relique et le travail du deuil," *Nouvelle Revue de psychanalyse*, no. 2 (Fall 1970): "The relic, which in itself is a ridiculous and repulsive remnant, puts the corpse and its putrefaction outside the sphere of representation" (p. 252).

22. Benjamin, *The Origin of German Tragic Drama*, p. 233.

Flaubert's Presuppositions

Intertextuality in fiction is the key to the novel's significance. The significance system consists in the relationship between the writer's idiolect and the sociolect, which latter belongs to both reader and writer. Only the writer knows the idiolect's sign system thoroughly. It is up to the reader to evaluate, categorize, and interpret this sign system by detecting its references to the sociolect, by listening to the *voix de l'autre* ("voice of the other") or sorting out the *texte de l'autre* ("text of the other"), or *le discours social* ("social discourse"), in Claude Duchet's phrase, and this through, and in spite of, the idiolect's interferences.[1] In short, the reader is able to interpret the text only by way of the intertext. To my mind, the real problem is understanding what makes interpretation mandatory rather than a matter of free choice. A related problem is to find out how the reader manages to pinpoint the locus of the intertext: even if he does not accomplish this, something within the text drives him on to track down and make out the shape of the missing piece of the puzzle.

The answer, the factor that guides the reader and dictates his interpretation, seems to me to be presupposition,[2] that is to say, the implicit and requisite preceding conditions of an explicit statement. In the novel specifically, presuppositions have explicit corollaries on the surface of the text—metonymies. These figures refer to sign complexes that they substitute for and repress, as it were, pushing them back into intertextual latency.

A quotation, for instance, may seem merely to presuppose the text it is culled from. In fact, however, it presupposes a particular use of the quotation, a context-bound quoting behavior. The quotation therefore derives the significance it has in the novel from an interpretant, halfway between the quoted text and the quoting text. This interpretant is encoded in the sociolect.

There is such a quotation in the opening scene of *Madame Bovary*. You will recall that young Charles Bovary's awkwardness has set off riotous hilarity among his new classmates. Confused and rattled, he yet cannot bring himself to part with his complicated headgear.

> "What are you looking for?" asked the master.
> "My c-c-c-cap," said the new boy shyly, . . .
> "Five hundred verses for all the class!" shouted in a furious voice, stopped, like the *Quos ego*, a fresh outburst.[3]

In *Quos ego* we recognize—or at least Flaubert's contemporaries recognized—a phrase from Vergil's *Aeneid*. The allusion is to the scene where the Winds—children of Aeolus—throw the sea into turmoil and threaten to sink the Trojan ships; Neptune rises from the briny deeps and puts an end to their mischief with these two words alone—he does not even have to complete the menacing command. *Quos ego*, just two personal pronouns: *Quos*, "those who(m)," and *ego*, "I." Presumably, those who dare to stir up my waters, them (*quos*) will I (*ego*) punish or destroy. The merest beginning of the sentence is enough to scare off the Winds. A famous example of iron-handed dominion, but above all a famous quote because it exemplifies the ultimate in rhetorical efficacy, concision triumphant, and a figure called *reticence* or *aposiopesis*. The speaker breaks off in mid-sentence: this both conveys his supposed excitement and annihilates his hearers by hinting that what he was about to declare is too overpowering to put into words. Vergil's phrase has served imitators from Boileau and Racine down to Flaubert and beyond. The nineteenth-century Larousse, however, calls attention only to the many parodies of Neptune's two-word blast, and concludes:

The *quos ego* of Neptune is the expression of supreme dissatisfaction on the part of a superior.[4]

Here, quite obviously, the quotation fits the context. Obeying typographical rules, the Latin is quoted in italics. In his provocative paper on Flaubert's manipulations of italics, Duchet seems to think this particular quote, at least, merely conforms to usage: says he, it reflects the mentality of a sort of elementary school elite, calling as it does upon the schoolboy's store of classical learning (p. 153). But Duchet also points out that although there may be nothing here to modify any character delineation or alter its meaning, such passages do indicate that there is present in the text what has already been spoken in and by the sociolect: "an extra-diegetic reference, an *horstexte* of the text, the already-there, the already-spoken of the novel's social world" (p. 151). If, on the other hand, the characters *are* contaminated here by the quotation from the sociolect, they are made to look like the reality of the reality-reflection that is the sociolect, to look like a product of the sociolect. What I should like to add is that the mechanisms of the text are more complex than those of a mere literary allusion and that they extend far beyond the passages underscored by italics.

First of all, the text here seems to do no more than quote Vergil. If that were all there was to it, the presupposition would be the same as in Vergil—a threat so dread it works without having to be fully pronounced. We should have a parody, a spoofing translation of a classroom scene into epic code. It would have to be interpreted as Flaubert's own joke, and diversely evaluated: an idle jest, perhaps, perhaps a heavy-handed one. This would only confirm the disquiet of those readers who think this introduction does not quite fit the novel, that it is a sort of weakening, a sudden show of vulnerability in an objective author who wishes to remain invisible but is betrayed by a moving memory from his own childhood rather than his hero's.

But what is quoted here is the quotation of a quotation, another text that includes the Vergil quotation as one of its own constituents.

And within this other text the Vergil quotation is already one of the text's stereotyped components, a component whose meaning is governed, not by the Vergilian meaning, but by the quotation's role in a new representation. The quotation is thus not a sign standing for pedantry. It is already part and parcel of a stereotyped portrait of the schoolteacher as figure of fun. In the collection of satiric vignettes, *Les Français peints par eux-mêmes* (published with Gavarni and Henri Monnier illustrations in 1840), there is one *monographie* on *Le maître d'études* where the harried teacher's uniform formulas are signs of the social outcast's sole claim to superiority: his status of classroom tyrant.[5] The *monographie's* words seem to have dictated Flaubert's passage:

God knows what prodigious quantity of imitations of the famous *quos ego* he performed calling to order *the first person* who talks . . . and he stops, sure of its effect; or equally, *a hundred lines* and he does not name the one he means to warn, so that thanks to this adroit reticence each student sees the formidable hundred lines of verse suspended above his head.[6]

Note *reticence*, the very name of the trope supremely exemplified ever since Quintilian by *quos ego* (Quintilian, *De institutione oratoria* 9.2.54). The description of the teacher and his suspense strategy are both derived from the definition of the trope. Nothing could be clearer than that the system determining both descriptive and narrative sequences is discursive, verbal, rather than referential. Thus Flaubert's quotation is quoting, not Vergil, but the descriptive system of the word *teacher*, one of whose components is borrowed from Vergil. Further, this system is not just a fragment of discourse, a prefabricated text: it is composed of elements already marked. In our particular case they are already comical, so that the reader reads into Flaubert an embedded semiotic system. Whence a different interpretation. *Quos ego* is not a questionable joke of Flaubert's, but a faithful rendition of a kind of score well established in language, a score whose accuracy as representation is therefore guaranteed by the sociolect. Far from being *hors d'oeuvre*, the scene is an overture, for this score actualizes a structure that is to inform significance of the novel again and again throughout its length.

Significance flows from the defeat of Neptune himself, defeat of his all-powerful trope by the weakest of adversaries, by the innocent bumblebee of a boy, a well-meaning kid named Charles. The boy is turned thereby into the epitome of the spoiler, of the square peg in the round hole. And the farcical clincher here is the tyrant's overthrow by this hapless David of the classroom: the teacher has to mop his brow—gesture of the harassed boss undone by the naïvest underdog in so many low comedies, of the big cat of animated cartoons undone by a puny mouse.

What the quotation presupposes is an intertext of a norm. What it entails is a sequence of variations on Charles's perennial contradiction: innocence and destructiveness, the sequence in which the future Charles is to bungle the surgery that was to establish his fame, irritate his wife most acutely whenever he tries hardest to please her, at his every step produce the reverse of what he intends—the misery of well-intentioned negativity.

The italics merely point to words whose presuppositions enable the reader to make the connection between text and intertext. But these italics are by no means necessary for the presupposition to be perceived or for the connection to be made: at most they are a deixis of interpretation, somewhat akin to the *points d'ironie* ("irony marks") that Balzac aspired to introduce into the typographical arsenal. But irony is only a special intertextual case. More generally, metonymy, as I have suggested, is the connecting link between novel and intertext: the instant the reader grasps the fact that the metonym is a fragment, a fraction therefore presupposing a whole, metonymy becomes a reference to the complex to which it owes its meaning, that is, a descriptive system either available to our linguistic competence or actualized within another text.

Let us verify this by the system most central to *Madame Bovary*, the representation(s) of the adulteress. This representation might be studied as a theme. The thematic approach, however, cannot tell us why a given actualization of a theme is effective and convincing. Presupposition offers an explanation, since it is by presupposing that a verbal sequence compels the reader to compare text and intertext. Presupposition creates a logical need for gap-filling. The intertext that responds to this need actualizes the semes of a kernel word, first in the shape of a sentence, then as a system of representations.

Everything in the system organized around this verbal nucleus derives from the single matrix sentence. Instead of trying to hypothesize the matrix, I will apply this moral pronouncement of Proudhon (entered under *adultère* in the first volume of Larousse, published in 1866, nine years after the novel): "Adultery is a crime which in itself contains all others." No phrasing could be apter for generating the descriptive system in question here; the whole novel can be shown to derive from that system. It is significant that one initial nudge should set in motion the entire causal concatenation, from one single transgression on through all species of disorders, to the final ineluctable retribution. That one lone transgression should suffice demonstrates the power of one lone taboo: no woman shall be free. The weakness of her sex makes it necessary that she be held in connubial bondage: once unshackled, the wife must and will fall prey to the evil temptations her nature makes her incapable of resisting. There is no incident in the long chain of events that is not contained in the very kernel of the system. Once again, I shall quote from *Les Français peints par eux-mêmes*, this time from a piece "La femme adultère" (1841). The essay offers what looks like an exhaustive catalog of all possible choices the adulteress may make in the course of her shady career. The author is one Hippolyte Lucas, a forgettable writer whose very anonymity seems to make him the voice of the sociolect:

> Adultery! . . . a word which is rarely pronounced, even these days, when the thing is so widespread, and one that is even taken as a sign of ill-breeding, but that we may be allowed to use. This word, the despair of worldly people, ought to gratify etymologists. No expression better conveys its idea. Adultery comes from a Latin verb that signifies *alter*, and nothing in fact more alters things and feelings. [*Les Français*, 3:265]

Nothing could be clearer: one word's ultimate presupposition, its etymology, entails the whole fictional text. Our spokesman for society expatiates: "Once started down this tortuous path, a woman cannot stop herself" (3:267). A further rule must be observed if the system's well-oiled wheels and cogs are to get going: the deduction of entailment from presupposition must be exemplary. Opposition or distance between the two poles of this diegesis must therefore always tend towards a maximum polarization: hence the *monographie*'s insistence that the first fatal step leads inevitably to the last fatal leap. These inseparable and complementary poles thus set the limits of the fictional space extending from an imaginary or metaphorical transgression (wicked thoughts nurtured by immoral and forbidden readings) to the most definitive of all actual or literal transgressions—the one that drags the heroine out of existence, and out of the text, simultaneously putting an end to what can be lived or to what can be told in words. The adulteress either commits suicide or sinks into prostitution. As for the first metaphorical step, I might call it fictional without any play on words, since the errant wife is stepping out of bounds when she secretly indulges in the reading of scandalous novels and in a daydreaming identification with the women who slink about the never-neverland of wish-fulfillment. This peculiar susceptibility to the printed word is perhaps more generally assumed to be an attribute of woman, rather than just adulteress: throughout the Romantic era, a woman is one who reads novels as a substitute for active living; she regresses into moral and legal minority the moment she marries. I hardly need point out that *Madame Bovary* is a fiction about the dangers of fiction.

A second presupposition of *adulteress* is a negative husband: he must be a good man, good as a human being (otherwise, if he were bad, his badness would mitigate his victimization by the wife); but he must be a frustrating mate: "The blame for adultery lies . . . with the imbecility of husbands" (3:265). *Imbécillité* here may be taken in extreme cases in its strong primary acceptation. What is implied, then, is that the husband is sexually inadequate. This failure unleashes the female predispositions that are as much a presupposition of the word *woman* as is her vulnerability to reading: *Woman, thy name is Lasciviousness*. If the husband plays an aging David to her young Abishag, or an Abelard to her Heloise, as our essayist puts it metaphorically, then the husbandless bride will "cut the Gordian knot with Alexander's sword" (3:269). The full weight of implicitness charging these images with innuendo, the pent-up power packed into the presupposition, is palpable. Now I realize that this version of the frustrating male is not the one Flaubert selected. Charles does have what it takes to keep his female satisfied, if only she would give him a chance. But the point is that so strong is the presupposition of woman's natural lubricity, *any* frustration at all will set it off. The more general ill consequence entailed by the husband's presupposed deficiency is *ennui*. Boredom, we know; and its other face—the vision of escape—*is* the solution Flaubert chose.

The result is the detailed and suspense-laden actualization of this essential seme of woman: her unbridled sexuality. Witness the *monographie* ticking off the stages in the progress of the disease, from *femme sensible* (one lover) to *femme galante* (more than one). Ill repute forces the victim "to go hide her shame in some great city where for lack of any natural support she ends by lowering herself to the condition of a kept woman [*une femme entretenue*]" (more than one lover, plus financial backing) (3:267). And then the grand finale: "unless suicide triumphs over prostitution."[7]

The intensifying drive of the salacity sequence best testifies to the generative power of presupposition: the steps traced in the *monographie* prefigure Emma's descent into hell. First, a sense of shame, or of anxiety: in Emma's case, the silent witness of the drafts, and in the printed version, the dismal sounds that scare her, following her first tryst with Rodolphe. Then the rapid development in Emma of a brazen, Machiavellian (the *monographie*'s very word [3:265]) gift for dissembling: she weaves all sorts of lies and pretexts for getting off to Rouen. And finally, the lurid apotheosis:

This divinity of the household will be transformed into a disheveled bacchante, while her husband consumes his days and nights in long work so that she can have a decent existence; she will give herself over to the prodigal joys of the courtesan. [3:266]

I will not labor the point by quoting the scene where our Yonville Messalina disrobes in a rage of sexual frenzy, with her girdle-laces whistling like serpents—a revealingly "mad" hyperbole. What proves the existence of a model, a paradigm, is the sexual rewrite of the extreme unction scene, where the dying Emma kisses the image of Christ in an unambiguous climax—a translation into sexual code of the ultimate pathological consequences flowing from the initial given. Similarly, another sick end product of intertextual presupposition, Balzac's old miser Grandet on his deathbed grabbing the golden crucifix, translates into *greed* code the accelerating-fall structure.

I cannot emphasize enough how powerful the logic of entailments is, how necessary the complete unfolding of the sequence of tragic aftereffects following upon the adulteress's transgression. So necessary, indeed, that the rejected alternative, the prostitution ending, refuses to go away altogether. It hovers about, but with the suspense of the choice rejected, the temptation spurned. Hence a partial reheroization of the fallen heroine. I am thinking of how Emma calls to the *notaire* for help, and of the ambiguous last interview with Binet (a scene without ambiguity when read by a witness like Madame Tuvache).[8] Better still, some readers are so alive to the lure of the more melodramatic outcome that they improve on Flaubert: the *Madame Bovary* entry in Larousse's *Grand dictionnaire* (1867) cannot resist playing out the alternative unactualized by the novel. The suicide is appropriate, but it makes the denouement too physical, that is, "too true to realism," realism being misunderstood as a preference for material description exclusive of moral considerations. The dictionary goes on to offer a rewrite of the denouement:

Instead of poison, shame was necessary. Madame Bovary . . . ought to have dragged out the rest of her days working the banal corner of some disreputable block.[9]

Thus do the entailment paradigms operate to contaminate the entire text they produce. Consequently, the text does not come to a finish until after every component of the descriptive and narrative complex has been affected. So with the final result of the alteration implicit in the word *adultery*, or in its etymology (again, when I say "etymology," I am referring to a meaning to be found elsewhere, a semantic key to the text, retrievable in the intertext of the kernel word's origin, an interpretation of discourse to be provided by the intertext of another language). Adulteration presupposes the presence of a purity to be destroyed. The purity topically ascribed to the married woman, her sanctity as a mother, this purity is that of the family of which she is the priestess. By her act, then, she destroys what in her keeping was holiest, the children. Sometimes she gets herself an abortion "happy . . . if the womb that bears them does not become their tomb"; but if she lets them live, she ignores them: "The same indifference, the same neglect rules over all" (*Les Fran-*

çais, 3:266), and the unfortunate progeny are handed over to the grudging care of a nurse. Which scenario, as we know, Emma Bovary follows to the letter.

This need for the derivation to be exhaustive in order to be exemplary, this need for the text not to stop until the last consequences have been drawn, only this need can satisfactorily explain why a novel ostensibly about Emma Bovary should go on long after she is dead and buried, and go on, not to relieve those she has wronged, but to extinguish them.[10] Charles and her daughter are not secondary characters; they are her corollaries, the victims crime presupposes, the spoilable objects an exemplary corruption demands. This is the satisfactory explanation, because it rests upon the generative power of the entailment; the ending must be complementary or corollary to the beginning.

The text's saturation by the enthymemelike descriptive system, the text's paranoia, we might say, is the narrative aspect of the presupposition's semiotic process. At the descriptive level the process results in a uniform marking of such words in the text as are also words of the system: this marking reflects their value, their symbolism, for instance, within the system. A change does occur, however; within the system these words are metonymic of the kernel lexeme, of the presupposing lexeme. In the text, on the contrary, they are free of the grammatical constraints imposed upon them by the system and free of their kernel-lexeme metonymy: they become its metaphors. Take the celebrated *fiacre*, for example. This hackney coach is not of Flaubert's invention; it is a prop borrowed from the adulteress system: honesty in a wife presupposes she has no secrets from her husband, and so she is at liberty to use his carriage and horses as she pleases. Infidelity calls for secrecy and requires a cabman who does not know her. Our *monographie* pictures "the carriage with blinds drawn" carrying her to her clandestine rendezvous. This *fiacre* cancels out the meaning of the family conveyance and posits intrigue; in fact it is so well established as a metonym of wifely treason that when Balzac's virtuous Mme Jules takes a hackney in *Ferragus*, she is at once convicted of infidelity in the eyes of an observer. The use of the *fiacre* in Flaubert is certainly much more serious or more to the point: to transform a vehicle *to* sin into a vehicle *of* sin is to go way beyond the sociolect. As far as literary scandal is concerned, the scene we are bound to imagine going on inside fully explains why *La Revue de Paris* dropped the episode from the serial publication of the novel.[11] But what I contend is that it might not have occurred to Flaubert to use a hansom cab as a kind of *maison du berger* of illicit love, had it not been for the preliminary marking of *fiacre* as a metonym of adultery. Above all, this marking protects the reader against the temptation to question the verisimilitude of the whole protracted encounter: as a vehicle it may not be very practical for committing the act in; as a word it extends the adultery isotopy on into the descriptive code. As a word *fiacre* translates into urban discourse, into the discourse of an urban setting ("It's done in Paris," says Léon, more aptly than he may intend), into the rustic metaphor for dalliance that riding into the woods with Rodolphe constitutes. *Aller se promener au bois* ("take a ride in the woods") and *prendre le fiacre* ("take the cab") are for a woman cliché metaphors for having an affair.

Now, what I have just said about markings and metaphorical transfers applies as well to symbols: we feel, for instance, that there is more to certain key episodes than meets the eye; but linear reading does not yield a satisfactory meaning. We fail to grasp their symbolic significance unless we make a detour through the intertext. Presuppositions then lead us on to the correct interpretation.

During Emma's death agony, a blind beggar appears: a case in point. Critics all agree he is symbolic, but they do not agree of what: fate, damnation, hell, or, quite simply, reality.[12] For anyone in Emma's predicament, they are synonymous anyway. The particular significance of the beggar's song is more opaque:

Often the heat of a summer's day
Makes a young girl dream her heart away.

Emma raised herself like a galvanized corpse, her hair streaming, her eyes fixed, staring.

To gather up all the new-cut stalks
Of wheat left by the scythe's cold swing,
Nanette bends over as she walks
Toward the furrows from where they spring.

"The blind man!" she cried.

And Emma began to laugh, an atrocious, frantic, desperate laugh, thinking she saw the hideous face of the poor wretch loom out of the eternal darkness like a menace.

The wind blew very hard that day
It blew her petticoat away.

A final spasm threw her back upon the mattress. They all drew near. She had ceased to exist. [P. 238]

Years ago D. L. Demorest (in *L'Expression figurée dans l'oeuvre de Flaubert* [Geneva: Slatkine reprints, 1931], pp. 466–69) suggested that the song symbolizes, word by word, step by step, the course of Emma's life and demise. He did not say just how. I propose to read it as a metaphor of Emma's degradation: a sexual one and therefore most apt. The position of the short-skirted girl is explicit: prone, hence revealing, a commonplace of voyeurism. The tricks of the wind are also explicit; they expose the girl's flesh, play the role of sexual aggressor—an ironic image and one with many salacious variants in folksongs about catching girls in the bushes or rolling them in the hay. Now the obscenity of the gesture presupposes that a skirt is not for lifting, while the skirt presupposes the woman. The decent woman is one whose skirt is unliftable; in skirt code, sexuality is skirt-lifting, and the metonym for a loose woman is a liftable skirt, all points well exemplified in French *gauloiserie*.

Now recollect that the first time Emma hears the song, it is quoted:

Often the warmth of a summer day
Makes a young girl dream her heart away.

And all the rest was about birds and sunshine and green leaves. [P. 193]

An incomplete quotation, a summary far from accurate, a misleading paraphrase of the complete text. But that was before the fall, before the first lover, before the fatal first misstep. Now we know the real text, the literal truth. Emma knows, she laughs bitterly, and dies. My interpretation: there are two readings of a song symbolizing Emma in her own eyes (and inviting the reader to see her as she sees herself). The first, the innocent reading, is Emma fantasizing,

Emma wallowing in the idealized love affairs detailed for her in silly *romans pour dames*. The second reading, postlapsarian, a metatext of the prostitution denouement, gives us sex despoiled of its sublimations, a stark depiction of the heroine as slut: in brief, the coarse carnality no longer hidden behind the veil of self-delusion, or if you prefer, a *roman réaliste*. Any possible reservations about my *skirt* presuppositions would surely give way if I could produce a virtuous *unliftability* intertext presupposed by the sinful liftability. Well, I can. Better still, my proof comes equipped with the kind of stylistic features that demonstrate that no reader can help noticing its import and that the writer, or first reader, was well aware of the potentialities of the *text versus intertext* polarization. My evidence is the phrase "jupe insoulevable" ("unliftable skirt"): *insoulevable* is one of Flaubert's rare coinages, if not his only one—and he would not have departed from the sociolect's accepted lexicon without good reason. What is more, the phrase occurs in a passage of *L'Éducation sentimentale* that stands in direct semiotic opposition to our death scene: the meeting between Frédéric and Madame Arnoux in the country. Here is his best opportunity to bed her at last, but the lady's chastity remains impregnable:

This dress, blending with the shadows, seemed huge to him, infinite, unliftable; and precisely because of that his desire redoubled.[13]

Then Madame Arnoux reminds him she is another man's wife. Curtain. I could not have dreamed up a neater symmetry (*soulevable / insoulevable*), nor could I have dreamed up a more perfect moral correspondence: metonymy for the wife who resists temptation to unfaithfulness: "a dress huge . . . unliftable"; metonymy for the wife who falls: "a petticoat blown away."

This on metonymy brings me back to my opening remarks. Significance, that is, the text seen as one signifying unit (as opposed to meaning, where such units are infratextual—lexical or phrastic), significance depends upon the presuppositions contained in certain words. These words are metonymic (they function *like* metonyms: for example, they are quotations; or they *are* metonyms). The role of metonymy in the novel is well recognized as far as its diegetic and descriptive functions are concerned: metonymies transform *topoi* into a narrative, and metonymies are the raw material of mimesis, especially of realism.

We still have to find out how metonymy is able to turn into metaphor or symbol—an apparent paradox. The answer, I suggest, is to differentiate semantic and semiotic, meaning and significance. In the linearity of the text, in the verbal sequence, metonymy remains metonymic: that is its meaning. Its significance, contrariwise, shows itself in the intertextual reference: metonymy becomes the substitute for the intertext, thus assuming the symbolic function.

Notes

1. Claude Duchet, "Discours social et texte italique dans *Madame Bovary*" in *Langages de Flaubert*, ed. Michael Issacharoff (Paris: Minard, 1976), pp. 143–63; cf. Duchet's "Signifiance et in-signifiance: Le Discours italique dans *Madame Bovary*" in *La Production du sens chez Flaubert*, ed. Claudine Gothot-Mersch (Paris: Union Générale d'Éditions, 1975), pp. 358–78.

2. See Jonathan Culler, "Presupposition and Intertextuality," *Modern Language Notes* 91 (1976): 1380–96; Marc Angenot, "Présupposé, topos, idéologème," *Etudes françaises* 13, nos. 1–2 (1977): 11–34; Michael Riffaterre, "La Trace de l'intertexte," *La Pensée* 215 (1980): 4–18.

3. *Madame Bovary*, ed. and trans. Paul de Man (New York: Norton, 1965), p. 3. Translations of *Madame Bovary* are from this edition and will be referred to in the text by page number. Other translations are my own. Vergil *Aeneid* 1.135 is quoted; on the structure of quotation, see Antoine Compagnon, *La Seconde Main* (Paris: Seuil, 1979), pp. 49–92.

4. Pierre Larousse, *Grand Dictionnaire universel du dix-neuvième siècle*, s.v. "*quos ego*," vol. 13 [1875].

5. *Monographie* was the French nineteenth-century literary genre also known as *physiologie*; see Fritz Nies, *Genres mineurs: Texte zur Theorie und Geschichte nichtkanonischer Literatur* (Munich: Wilhelm Fink, 1978), pp. 111–12.

6. Eugène Nyon, "Le Maître d'école," in *Les Français peints par eux-mêmes*, preface by Jules Janin, 8 vols. (Paris, L. Curmer, 1840), 1:339. The collection includes pieces by Balzac, Théophile Gautier, Charles Nodier, and others reprinted from various periodicals.

7. In Eugène Sue's *La Famille Jouffroy* (1854), a noble countess, first

unfaithful, at the last a common drunken whore murdered in a brothel, exemplifies the alternative solution. Emma may have been spared simply because Flaubert preferred to maintain the provincial setting. Cf. Mlle Leroyer de Chantepie, Flaubert's epistolary confidant, who, despite her feminism, writes of Emma: "She must either become a courtesan or die" (26 February 1857, in Flaubert, *Correspondance*, 2 vols., ed. J. Bruneau [Paris: Pléiade, 1973], 2:686).

8. *Madame Bovary*, p. 223 ("'Women like that ought to be whipped,' said Madame Tuvache").

9. Cf. Alfred August Cuvillier-Fleury's review of the novel, quoted in René Dumesnil's edition of *Madame Bovary*, 2 vols. (Paris: Belles-Lettres, 1945), 1:clxvi.

10. Critics have suggested that the novel goes on because it actually focuses on Homais and the triumph of mediocrity (e.g., Victor Brombert, *The Novels of Flaubert* [Princeton, N.J.: Princeton University Press, 1966], pp. 89–90; R. J. Sherrington, *Three Novels of Flaubert* [Oxford: Oxford University Press, Clarendon Press, 1970], p. 143).

11. See the references to the episode during the Flaubert trial: Dumesnil, ed., *Madame Bovary*, 2:219, 250.

12. See P. M. Wetherill, "Madame Bovary's Blind Man: Symbolism in Flaubert," *Romanic Review* 61 (1970): 35–42; and, completed by M. Aprile, "L'Aveugle et sa signification dans *Madame Bovary*," *Revue d'Histoire littéraire de la France* 76 (1976): 385–92.

13. *L'Éducation sentimentale* in *Oeuvres complètes*, 2 vols. (Paris: Seuil, 1964), 2:80.

Demotivation in *Hérodias*

Gérard Genette

What I have to say about *Hérodias* is contained in a few words which will surprise no one, or perhaps in a single word, which risks shocking Flaubert scholars and perhaps also, since it is another risk, pleasing the adherents of that typically American specialization, "deconstructionist" criticism. This word I will keep as the best for last; he who has ears to hear, let him hear. But this little, or this nothing which I have to say, must, if I dare this paradox, be replaced in its "theoretical" context (note well the quotation marks), which is a body of knowledge, the ensemble of a small work I have undertaken on that which I call "hypertextuality." Because *Hérodias* is not only a text, it is also, like many other literary works, a hypertext.

By hypertext, I understand, briefly, a text which derives from another (or several other) text(s)—which I baptize, obviously, hypotext(s)—by way of imitation and / or of transformation. These two operations, which one finds in all the other arts, particularly painting and music, are not the only ones capable of deriving one text from another, but they are—I affirm it after mature reflection, the laborious development of which I will spare you—the only ones which nourish hypertextual activity. Commentary is another one of these, which nourishes another type of hypertextuality, or textual transcendence of the text, which I prefer to baptize, for obvious reasons, *metatextuality*. I will restrict myself for the moment to hypertextuality, which is therefore only, if one may say so, a convenient term to designate the literary products (works) of imitation and transformation. This, basically, does not call for any demonstration, because it is in sum nothing but a pure and simple definition.

The canonical type of imitative derivation is the pastiche, where (to simplify matters) an author imitates the style of another in a functional and predominantly playful register: the pastiche of Flaubert by Proust furnishes a good example of this. In the satirical register, imitation becomes that which current usage rather regrettably calls *parody* and which I prefer to call *charge* (caricature). In the serious register, it ordinarily invests its efforts in *forgery*, apocryphal or not: see the cyclical epics or the sequels of the Middle Ages.

Transformative, or transformational, derivation may also invest itself in a playful register: these are the various forms of *parody* in the strict sense of the term; in the satirical register it is *travesty*, burlesque or otherwise; in the serious register (more or less serious, of course; the boundaries between registers are not at all airtight): this is what I propose to call, in accordance with one of the possibilities of common usage, *adaptation*. Like Goethe's *Faust* or Joyce's *Ulysses*, *Hérodias* is an adaptation, that is to say, a serious transformation, which does not aim essentially, or predominantly, at either amusement or mockery, but rather at a new presentation, and perhaps a new interpretation, of an anterior text—you know which one, and I will return to it.

Contrary to the five other classes of hypertextuality, adaptation is an extremely complex and extremely diverse practice, which includes a very great number of types and of varieties. To order this diversity a bit, I propose to subdivide it, even if provisionally, into two large types. First, I propose the type of adaptations which are in principle purely formal and which do not aim essentially at a semantic or thematic transformation. Summary and translation are, I think, two good examples of these operations which are in principle innocuous or innocent, which I propose to baptize *transcriptions*. In opposition to them I propose the type of *transpositions*, where transformation has for its goal, explicitly or manifestly, a sometimes voluntarily abusive or unfaithful interpretation of the original text: for example, Joyce's *Ulysses*, previously cited, or in a manner perhaps even more striking, Michel Tournier's *Friday*, which is an anti–*Robinson Crusoe*.

Although it may seem surprising, I think one must, at least at first, rank *Hérodias* among the simple transcriptions. The reason for this may perhaps appear clearer if I refine my classification a bit. Among many other forms of transcription I do not wish to enumerate because they do not further concern us here, I would like to call your attention for a moment to two opposed hypertextual practices, each as widespread as the other, even though the second enjoys a very superior literary status and prestige. These two practices are *reduction* and *augmentation*. To illustrate reduction, I will mention only the summary, already remarked on, which we all know and practice, even though there are many other ways, less synthetic and more brutal, to reduce a text, if only that which consists of amputating at the right place: this too happens every day. For augmentation, I will distinguish essentially three procedures, of which the third is hardly anything but a synthesis of the two others. The first consists of adding to the material of the hypotext an invented or imported supplement, which contributes to padding it out. Of this type of operation, I will cite a single but multiple example: that of the successive adaptations, in the Neoclassical era, of Sophocles' *Oedipus Rex*. This prestigious work was, according to the classical canons, judged incapable of sustaining the five acts of a regular tragedy. It was necessary therefore to extend it—and I propose to baptize this type of practice precisely *extension*. An example of extension is the introduction of a new character, invented or borrowed from other areas of the fable. Corneille had recourse to Theseus, who comes to court a daughter of Jocasta whom Oedipus wished to marry someone else, from which arise several dramatic confrontations. Voltaire introduces Philoctetes, former lover of Jocasta who comes, at the death of Laius, to try his luck a second time and fatally to clash with Oedipus. These two extensions proceed evidently by borrowing, and thus by *contamination*, as one used to say about the Latin comedies. Still on the same subject, it is once again a contamination which furnishes Cocteau with the first act of *The Infernal Machine*, where the ghost of Laius appears on the ramparts of Thebes to try to denounce his murderer—needless to specify to you the source of this borrowing.

The second procedure of augmentation is in principle purely stylistic: it consists of swelling the hypotext by a sort of verbal dilation to which essentially expansive figures such as description, comparison, enumeration, dialogue, and so forth contribute. The canonical example of what I will therefore call *expansion* is the *Fables* of La Fontaine, the brilliant accomplishment of a rhetorical practice current during the Neoclassical period, which consisted of dilating these exemplarily concise hypotexts, which one might say had only been written to provoke this type of exercise: Aesop's *Fables*, of course.

The third procedure combines the two others, and it is for this that I was reserving the most traditional and the most valorizing term: it is *amplification*, which one might define as augmentation generalized and on all fronts. I have already studied a characteristic example of this procedure, Saint-Amant's *Moses Saved* (*Moyse sauvé*).[1] One finds there several lines of the biblical text, devoted to the exposure of Moses on the Nile, taking on the dimensions and the character of an epic, by way of expansion (Saint-Amant imagines and recounts in detail all the circumstances and all the peripeteias to which this brief adventure is susceptible), and by way of extension: Saint-Amant reattaches to this episode the whole of the life and the mission of Moses, plus that of Joseph, plus that of Jacob, plus several others which group around him all the destiny, past and future, of the Jewish people. To remain in the biblical context which will also be that of *Hérodias*, I want to discuss briefly the monumental novel by Thomas Mann, *Joseph and His Brothers*, which amplifies by some sixteen hundred pages a story told in the Bible in twenty-six pages, which would be, if you permit me a rather materialist evaluation, a yield of sixty to one. Thomas Mann proceeds here at the same time by extension, since all of the first volume is devoted to the adventures of Jacob, the father of Joseph, which annexes an entire generation; and by expansion, since the career of Joseph becomes for Mann the pretext for a vast psychological, historical, religious, and philosophical novel. One of the means of the expansion will particularly hold our attention, namely that to which the title of this essay makes allusion a bit heavily, and which I call, by a term borrowed from the Russian formalists, *motivation.*

Like many archaic texts, if I dare so call them, the biblical text is here, as Thomas Mann himself emphasizes, greatly laconic, and more specifically greatly discreet (or indifferent) as to the incentives for or psychological motivation of the actions reported. For example—and this example is rather well known—Joseph, in Egypt, finds himself exposed to the advances of his master's wife, Madame Potiphar, who tells him quite simply, as you know, "Lie with me." As you also know, Joseph would have nothing to do with her. In both cases, the Bible shows us the two courses of action without explaining them. Why Madame Potiphar covets Joseph, why Joseph does not respond to her desire—these two interesting *studies of motivation* remain the responsibility of the reader, whose contribution is most often restricted, I suppose, to an expeditious commentary inspired by a slightly summary Freudian influence, along the lines of: "It's their problem." Thomas Mann makes this double "problem" his own, and treats it in detail, and in a parallel fashion, in the savory *remake* of *The Red and the Black* which is (almost to its denouement) *Joseph in Egypt*, where nothing is concealed regarding the multiple excuses, preparations, stages, and progress of the fatal passion of Madame Potiphar, nor regarding the no less multiple motives (seven in all, neither more nor less) of the chastity of the young steward. I will say no more of it, not wanting to spoil for you the reading or rereading of this masterpiece. Let us retain of this detour only the occurrence of motivation in its purest state, when a hypertext sets itself the task (among others) of imagining and furnishing the reader with the motives for behavior that a hypotext was content to tell in a completely exterior and, so to speak, behaviorist manner. This example well shows, I suppose, that the practice of amplification is not as innocuous as it is supposed to be, and as I at first claimed that it was: it stands to reason that this supplement of motives already entails a thematic intervention and at least an interpretation of the hypotext.

One can also envision a more complex case: that of a hypotext which indeed furnishes the network of motivations necessary to justify the behavior that it recounts, and of a hypertext that rejects these original motivations and substitutes new ones for them. I analyze this practice, *à la manière liégeoise*, as composed firstly of a *demotivation*, or suppression of the original motivation, and secondly of a *remotivation*, or addition of a new motivation, and I baptize the whole, to be brief, *transmotivation*. The illustrations of this practice are legion in the immense corpus of serious transformation, and I would even say, for better and for worse, that they are its *soul*. To bring us closer again to our hypertext of reference, of which I have not lost sight, I will borrow an example from the history of modern adaptations of the biblical episode of the beheading of John the Baptist, of which *Hérodias* is only one case among others.

But I must first characterize from this point of view the biblical hypotext, which consists, I remind you, of the two texts, here very similar, of Matthew 14 and Mark 6, which I will with this step compile in a sort of model synthetic hypotext. Contrary to the story of Joseph and Madame Potiphar, that of the execution of John the Baptist is complete and endowed with all necessary motivations: because of his rigid moral standards, John had condemned the marriage of Antipas and his sister-in-law; Herodias therefore wished him dead, but Herod, knowing him esteemed of the people and esteeming him himself, did not dare to have him executed and contented himself with keeping him in prison; in order to force his hand, Herodias uses his fascination for Salome, who dances before him at his birthday feast; seduced, Antipas accords to Salome whatever she might care to ask; Herodias suggests to her daughter that she ask for the head of John, which Herod, bound by his promise, cannot refuse her.

This narrative, as we see, does not call for any supplementary motivation. One can, on the other hand, find its motivation suspect, or without interest for our modern sensibility, and therefore submit it to a work of transmotivation. This is what, for example, Oscar Wilde does in his *Salomé*, where the heroine has Iokanaan decapitated, not at the instigation of her mother, but on her own account, because she loves him and he has spurned her. This idea comes perhaps from Heine, who in *Atta Troll* attributes the same incentive to Herodias herself, adding this commentary as a generalizing motivation: "Otherwise the desire of the woman would be inexplicable. Does a woman demand the head of a man she doesn't love?"

With regard to this extremely common, if not vulgar, temptation, to substitute an incentive of passion for a political incentive, and of course, starting from the same hypotext, it remains for us to characterize briefly the position adopted by Flaubert.

But I find that I have forgotten to put *Hérodias* in its place in my classification of adaptations. According to what I said about it just a moment ago, it must follow that *Hérodias* is, with regard to the biblical narrative, an *amplification*. In order roughly to justify this classification, I will restrict myself to pointing out that Flaubert's text is something like fifty times longer than its hypotext, and that this criterion is sufficient for me. But I do not wish to represent myself as even more schematic than I may be; and, therefore, I will add this extremely summary nuance: in regard to its hypotext, *Hérodias*, it seems to me, originates in a double effort in two movements, which are, moreover, familiar to Flaubert: first movement, amplification; second movement, reduction. I speak here in terms of genesis, and subject to the authority of geneticists.

I said that the biblical narrative here did not call for any supplementary motivation, and Flaubert no more than anyone else needed to furnish it with one, except to explain the original motivations themselves by a general political and religious tableau of the Roman Orient under the reign of Tiberius, which one might describe as a sort of hypermotivation, or motivation of the second degree. The essential principle of its amplification is therefore, as for *Salammbô* or *The Temptation of Saint Anthony*, descriptive, dramatic, and historic expansion: thence the considerable documentary dossier we know of—all the knowledge of the era about the Jewish religion and its sects, Roman colonization, the resistance movements, court intrigues—which could nourish a three-hundred-page novel, detailing in a luminous and exhaustive manner all the interrelationships of passions, interests, ambitions, and machinations that culminate in this decapitated head on a charger. The drafts of this novel show that Flaubert conceived and almost wrote it by successive bits. Then, no doubt as laboriously, he undertakes to *unwrite* it by dint of erasures, ellipses, allusive formulas, replies wrested from their context, far-fetched details shining in the enigmatic and fuliginous disorder of a narrative that more than one reader, even if informed of the story, would judge, like the good Sarcey, "too much for me." Or, like Jules Lemaître: "An excessive effort makes itself felt in this brevity: the characters and the actions are not sufficiently explained; there is too much laconism in this Asiatic glitter."[2] These two reactions among others manifest well, I think, the effect produced upon the average "super-reader" by this double movement of amplification and auto-reduction: that which (with the exception of the laconic glitter of the biblical text) was limpid in twenty lines of Mark or Matthew becomes for once obscure in thirty pages of Flaubert. But that obscurity, if it must be (re)stated, is precisely the art of the later Flaubert.

With these few remarks, I certainly do not claim to exhaust, or even to broach the analysis of this tale, even on the subject of hypertextual transformation. The poetician ought here to have effaced himself before the critic, which for various reasons I will refrain from doing. I would only like to call your attention to the choice made by Flaubert to focus his narrative, almost constantly and in spite of its title, not on the informed, active, and instigating character of Hérodias, but on the passive and manipulated character, Antipas, on him whose point of view least opens our horizons and enlightens us the least about the "cause of effects." A decisive effect of this counterfocusing—as one says in the theater, *contre-emploi* (I do not say *transfocalization*, as I might, because in this instance the hyponarrative was, as one might expect, "omniscient," which means: unfocalized)—is to treat in a quite elliptical manner the essential link in the chain of events, the knowledge of the order given by Hérodias to Salomé to lay claim to the head of Jokanaan. Let me remind you of the text: Salomé has just danced, Antipas is ready to grant her the recompense of her choice. "She did not speak. They looked at one another. There was a snapping of fingers in the balcony. She went up there, came down again, and lisping a little, said with a childish air: 'I want you to give me, in a dish, the head . . .' She had forgotten the name, but went on again, smiling: 'The head of Jokanaan!'"[3]

The reader obviously must pay much attention, and needs much sagacity, in order to infer from this chain of events that Salomé went up to the balcony in order to receive her mother's orders. The reader also, and perhaps above all, needs this guideline, or if you prefer, this key to the Flaubertian text which is, for us, the biblical narrative. I am not sure that a reader, even a shrewd one, could decipher the Flaubertian text without the aid of this grid, which at any rate we all possess before taking it up. It would be necessary, to be completely rigorous, to construct an experiment à la Condillac where one shuts up a child at birth in an artificial environment in order to see how it will react—here, in order to obtain an *uninformed* reader of *Hérodias*.

I spoke just now of deciphering, but this term itself is evidently a petitio principii. The truth is that we—as informed readers—project onto the text of *Hérodias* an interpretation—a chain of motivations—with which the biblical text furnishes us in advance. Taken in itself, I would say that the text of *Hérodias* is subtly but effectively *demotivated* by this ellipsis of the decisive link in the chain of motivations. The uninformed reader would ultimately find herself or himself, and with just cause, in the same situation as Antipas, who is led to sacrifice Jokanaan without exactly knowing why or how. To this extent, therefore, the work of Flaubert may here be defined as an effort, conscious or not—let us say, as an *effect of demotivation*. A most rare effect, of which I scarcely know another example, so much does it go against the current of the ideological propensity natural to serious transformation, which is animated rather by the desire to motivate the unmotivated, or to transmotivate the motivated.

This effect of demotivation is extremely trifling, I admit, and passes generally unperceived as a result of the prejudicial influence of the hypotext. But it is so exceptional that it deserves to be pointed out, and even, as I have just done here, to be emphasized. It contributes to that which must indeed be called Flaubert's deconstruction of the biblical narrative, which becomes here, in the immortal words of Shakespeare, "a tale told by an idiot, full of sound and fury." The idiot of the family, to be sure. I will not attempt to avert the full impact of this epithet by saying that the idiot here knows extremely well what he is doing, and does it on purpose, because I am not sure. I would more willingly believe that Flaubertian writing in its last stage, and by dint of erasures, produces such effects of dislocation and obfuscation without the author having truly perceived and calculated them. We are here, as in the last canvasses of Frans Hals or the last scores of Beethoven, at that limit where art escapes the artist and progresses of its own accord, a little bit further perhaps than the artist might himself have wanted to go. We are thus under the sign of that which Proust called the *involuntary*, for him the sign of authenticity and the gauge of success.

But I imagine what Flaubert would have thought of such praise, and I will stop here, not without returning to the word foretold at the outset. It is an adjective, and you have surely guessed and pronounced it before me—and moreover the contemporary archireader, as we have seen, had pronounced it in his own (and depreciative) manner: *Hérodias* is *unreadable*.

[Translated by Marlena Corcoran]

Notes

This article may well pass as the "desiccated embryo" of a work which has since appeared as *Palimpsestes: La Littérature au second degré* (Paris: Seuil, 1982). The reader will kindly excuse the schematic character here and, for greater subtlety, may wish to consult its final state.

1. See my "L'Univers réversible," in *Figures I* (Paris: Seuil, 1966), pp. 9–20.
2. Jules Lemaître, *Les Contemporains: Études et portraits littéraires*, 8 vols., (Paris: Boivin et Cie., 1923), 8:112.
3. Gustave Flaubert, *Three Tales*, trans. Robert Baldick (Harmondsworth: Penguin Books, 1975), p. 122.

A Bibliography of 1980–81 Conference Proceedings

Nouvelles recherches sur "Bouvard et Pécuchet" de Flaubert: Flaubert et le comble de l'art. Proceedings of the Colloquium held at the Collège de France on 22 – 23 March 1980. Paris: SEDES, 1981. Includes articles by Michel Crouzet, Françoise Gaillard, Claudine Gothot-Mersch, John Greene, Anne Herschberg-Perrot, Jean-Pierre Moussaron, and Jean-Luc Seylaz.

Flaubert. Revue d'Histoire littéraire de la France 4/5 (July-October 1981). An international colloquium organized by the Société d'Histoire littéraire de la France for the Flaubert centenary, held in Paris on 28 – 29 November 1980. Includes articles by Benjamin Bart, Jeanne Bem, Frank Bowman, Victor Brombert, Jean Bruneau, Claude Burgelin, Raymonde Debray-Genette, Jacques Derrida, Alison Fairlie, Claudine Gothot-Mersch, Bernard Masson, Claude Mouchard, and Jacques Neefs.

Gustave Flaubert. Proceedings of the "Journée Flaubert," University of Fribourg, 1980. Fribourg: Éditions Universitaires, 1981. Includes articles by Stefano Agosti, Michel Chaillou, Melaine Dubey, Hans-Jost Frey, Bernard Pingaud, Jean-Luc Seylaz, Patricia Thompson.

Histoire et langage dans "L'Education sentimentale" de Flaubert. Proceedings of the Colloquium of the Société des Études romantiques. Paris:

SEDES, 1981. Includes articles by Maurice Agulhon, Philippe Berthier, Maria-Amalia Cajaeiro-Roggero, Pierre Cogny, Michel Crouzet, Anne Herschberg-Pierrot, Pierre Larthomas, Bernard Masson, Jacques Neefs, and Alan Raitt.

Flaubert: La dimension du texte. Papers presented at the International Centenary Congress organized in May 1980 by the French Cultural Services and the Department of French of the University of Manchester, England. Edited by P. M. Wetherill. Manchester: Manchester University Press, 1982. Includes articles by Mieke Bal, Graham Daniels, Raymonde Debray-Genette, Claudine Gothot-Mersch, André Green, Jacques Neefs, Alan Raitt, P. M. Wetherill, and David Williams.

Flaubert: La femme, la ville. "Journée d'études" organized by the University of Paris – X on 26 November 1980. Edited by Marie-Claire Bancquart. Paris: Presses Universitaires de France, 1983. Includes articles by Michel Crouzet, Jacques-Louis Douchin, Alison Fairlie, Geneviève Idt, Bernard Masson, Alain Michel, Michel Raimond, and Naomi Schor.

Flaubert im Orient: Genese einer Aesthetik der Avantgarde. Proceedings of the Colloquium held at the University of Bielefeld, West Germany, 4 – 9 May 1981. Edited by André Stoll. Frankfurt am Main: Suhrkamp, 1984. Includes articles by Jeanne Bem, Pierre Marc Di Biasi, Monika Bosse, Frank Paul Bowman, Jean Bruneau, Françoise Gaillard, Anne Green, Hans Holländer, Jacques Leenhardt, Margaret Lowe, Arthur Mitzmann, Jacques Neefs, Claude Reichler, Naomi Schor, Gerhard Schröder, André Stoll, and Richard Terdiman.

Flaubert: Proceedings of the Wisconsin Symposium of October 1980. Special Issue of *Nineteenth Century French Studies* 12 (Spring, 1984). Includes articles by Benjamin Bart, Victor Brombert, Jean Bruneau, Claude Duchet, Graham Falconer, Claudine Gothot-Mersch, and Dennis Porter.

Notes on the Contributors

CHARLES BERNHEIMER teaches English and Comparative Literature at the State University of New York, Buffalo. Professor Bernheimer has recently published *Flaubert and Kafka: Studies in Psychopoetic Structure* (New Haven, Conn.: Yale University Press, 1982). He is currently working on a comparative study of the role of prostitution in the nineteenth-century novelistic imagination.

VICTOR BROMBERT, Henry Putnam University Professor of Romance and Comparative Literature at Princeton University, is the author of, among other books, *The Novels of Flaubert: A Study in Themes and Techniques* (Princeton, N.J.: Princeton University Press, 1966). He has just completed a study entitled *Victor Hugo and the Visionary Novel.*

JONATHAN CULLER is Professor of English and Comparative Literature at Cornell University. His numerous books include *Flaubert: The Uses of Uncertainty* (Ithaca, N.Y.: Cornell University Press, 1974), and the recent *On Deconstruction* (Ithaca, N.Y.: Cornell University Press, 1982).

RAYMONDE DEBRAY-GENETTE is Professor of French, University of Paris at Saint-Denis (Paris VIII), and Director of the Centre d'Histoire et d'Analyse des Manuscrits modernes. Professor Debray-Genette has edited two collections of essays on Flaubert, *Flaubert—Miroir de la critique* (Paris: Didier, 1970), and *Flaubert à l'oeuvre* (Paris: Flammarion, 1980).

EUGENIO DONATO was until his recent untimely death Professor of French and Comparative Literature, University of California at Irvine. He was the author of several seminal articles on Flaubert, notably, "The Museum's Furnace: Notes Toward a Contextual Reading of *Bouvard et Pécuchet*," in *Textual Strategies: Perspectives in Post-Structuralist Criticism*, ed. Josué V. Harari (Ithaca, N.Y.: Cornell University Press, 1979).

SHOSHANA FELMAN teaches French at Yale University. Among Professor Felman's books are *La Folie et la chose littéraire* (Paris: Seuil, 1978), which includes an essay about Flaubert, and *Le Scandale du corps parlant: Don Juan avec Austin; ou, La Séduction en deux langues* (Paris: Seuil, 1980). Both books are forthcoming from Cornell University Press. Professor Felman is currently working on a book entitled *Psychoanalysis in Contemporary Culture: Jacques Lacan and the Adventure of Insight*.

FRANÇOISE GAILLARD, a Professor of French at the University of Paris at Jussieu (Paris VII), has written extensively on nineteenth-century French literature and contemporary French thought.

GÉRARD GENETTE is Directeur d'Études at the École des hautes Études en Sciences sociales. Professor Genette, cofounding editor of *Poétique* and author of some of the most influential works of contemporary French poetics, recently published *Palimpsestes: La Littérature au second degré* (Paris: Seuil, 1982).

FREDRIC JAMESON teaches French at Yale University. Coeditor of the journal *Social Text*, Professor Jameson is the author of several books, including *The Political Unconscious: Narrative as a Socially Symbolic Act* (Ithaca, N.Y.: Cornell University Press, 1982).

LEYLA PERRONE-MOISÉS teaches French at the University of Sao Paulo. Her most recent books are *Fernando Pessoa—Aquém do eu, além do outro* and *Roland Barthes—O saber com sabor*.

DENNIS PORTER, Professor of French and Chairman of the Department of French and Italian at the University of Massachusetts, is the author of *The Pursuit of Crime: Art and Ideology in Detective Fiction* (New Haven, Conn.: Yale University Press, 1981). Professor Porter is currently preparing a comparative study of travel literature.

MICHAEL RIFFATERRE is University Professor at Columbia University. Editor of *Romanic Review*, author of numerous books and articles, Professor Riffaterre's forthcoming books include: *Text Production* (New York: Columbia University Press), *Typology of Intertextuality* (Bloomington: Indiana University Press), and *Troloppe* (New York: Methuen).

THE EDITORS. Naomi Schor teaches French at Brown University. She is the author of *Zola's Crowd* (Baltimore: Johns Hopkins University Press, 1978) and *Breaking the Chain: Women, Realism, and the French Novel* (New York: Columbia University Press, forthcoming). She is currently preparing a book on the history of the detail as aesthetic category. Henry F. Majewski is Professor of French Studies at Brown University. He is the author of *The Preromantic Imagination of L. S. Mercier* (Atlantic Highlands, N.J.: Humanities Press, 1971). He has just completed a book entitled *Representations of Creativity in French Romantic Writing: From Paradigm to Parody.*

THE TRANSLATORS. Brian Massumi, Rachel Bowlby, and Richard Russell are all graduate students in the Yale University French Department. Elizabeth Aubé, Marlena Corcoran, and Nancy Jones are graduate students at Brown University, in the departments of French, English, and Comparative Literature, respectively. Susan Huston is Assistant Professor of French at Amherst College. Robert Riger, who obtained his B.A. at Brown University, works for the Book-of-the-Month Club in New York City.

Index

Abraham, Nicholas, and Torok, Maria, 36, 37, 41–43; *L'Écorce et le noyau*, 35

Actants, 78

Adaptation, 193

Aesop, *Fables*, 195

Aestheticism, 133

Aesthetics, 77, 103, 167; Flaubert's, xii, 38, 140; of formalism, 101; principles of, 30; and religion, 80; and sadism, 81; in *Trois Contes*, 13

Allegory, xiii, 6–7, 17, 25; Benjamin's theory of, 171–72, 174, 175–76n18; and fetishism, 160–76

Allen, Woody, xiv, 10, 11; *Side Effects*, 10; "The Kugelmass Episode," 10–11

Alterity: deferred, 145–50; elimination of, 144. See also Other; Otherness

Amplification, 195, 196; and auto-reduction, 199; *Hérodias* as, 198

Aphasia, 145, 147; literary, 149

Archireader, 201. *See also* Super-reader

Arinos de Mello Franco, Alfonso, *O Indio Brasileiro e a Revolucâo Francesca*, 158n25

Assimilation, 144, 154–55n4

Augmentation, 194–95

Austin, J. L., xii–xiii

Balzac, Honoré de, xi, 90, 181, 184, 186; *Ferragus*, 186; *Sarrasine*, 126

Banfield, Ann, 14

Bardèche, Maurice, *L'Oeuvre de Flaubert*, 154n3

Barth, John, "The Literature of Replenishment," x–xi

Barthes, Roland, xiii, xiv, 5, 9, 83, 86, 87, 88–89, 92, 93, 116, 117, 118, 120, 124, 126, 130, 131, 132, 134–35; "Diderot, Brecht, Eisenstein," *Image-Music-Text*, 137n8; "l'effet de réel," 5, 78, 110, 121; *The Pleasure of the Text*, 117, 124, 130, 132; *S/Z*, 126

Baudelaire, Charles, 113; *Ecrits intimes*, 114–15n12

Baudrillard, Jean, 162, 166

Beethoven, Ludwig van, 201

Benjamin, Walter, 77, 171, 172; *The Storyteller*, 83

Bergounioux, Pierre, 101

Bergson, Henri, *Le Rire*, 99n5

Bernheimer, Charles, xiii; *Flaubert and Kafka*, 175–76n18

Bêtise, 85–99 passim; Barthes on, 87, 89; dissociation as, 85; fear of force of, 88; formal criticism of, 85–86; formal structure of, 87; generalized, 151; great book of, 93; as ideology, 96; inertia of, 93; as *koïné*, 98; as language, 89; made visible, 122; madness of, 153; origin of, 95; passive aspect of, 88; and reality, 94; and representativity, 97–98; Sartre on, 87; success of, 98; threat of, 88; as unifying, 94; and universalizing, 97

Bible, xiii, 195–97; Adam, 59; Cain, 54; Gospel, 21; John, Book of, 23; Mark 6, 197, 199; Matthew 14, 197, 199; Moses, 195; Old Testament, 24; Prophets, Book of the, 24

Bovarysme, 106–7, 113; Jules de Gaultier's, 3

Brée, Germaine, x

Brombert, Victor, xii, 27

Bruneau, Jean, *Les Débuts littéraires de Gustave Flaubert*, 154n3, 155n7

Buffon, Georges-Louis Leclerc de, *Histoire naturelle*, 156–57n13

Burgelin, Claude, 101

Capitalism, 83; late, 166; pre-, 80, 82, 83

Charge, 193

Chateaubriand, François René de, 80

Closure: impossibility of, 80; phallocentric, 135

Cocteau, Jean, *The Infernal Machine*, 195

Code, 121; babel of, 82–83; Barthes's cultural, 92; of clichés, 164; epic, 179; general French, 89; hermeneutic, 165, 168; linguistic, 167; passion of, 162; play of, 5; of postmodernism, 5; as representational, 170; of romantic idealization, 163; sexual, 184; of signification, 166; skirt, 188; symbolic, 169

Cohn, Dorrit, 14

Condillac, Etienne Bonnot de, 200

Connotation, 83

Conrad, Joseph, 80

Constative: as the obligative, 87; and performative, 15

Contamination, 194

Contradiction, 48–50, 61, 62, 70–71; of black and white, 54, 56; country of, 58; as cultural symptom, 51; destiny of, 54; in Flaubert's correspondence, 105; ironic, 63; Julian child of, 52; Julian text of, 54–55, 60; text as resolution of, 80; unconscious of, 59

Corneille, Pierre, 194

Corpse, 140, 153; Abraham and Torok on, 36–37; absent, 32; Blanchot on, 32–34; and Crypt, 42; De Man on, 35; Alfred Le Poittevin's, 40–41; and relic, 173, 176n21; and representation, 33–34, 41; sister's, 38–39; /Thing, 34–35; and writing, 38

Creuzer, George Fredrich, *Symbolik und Mythologie* (translated as *The Religions of Antiquity* and *Les Religions de l'Antiquité*), 40, 41

Crypt, xiii, 37, 42–44, 153; Flaubert's, 30–45

Culler, Jonathan, xii, xiv, 101, 121; *Flaubert: The Uses of Uncertainty*, 154n3

Darwin, Charles, 143, 144

Debray-Genette, Raymonde, xii, 5, 112

Deconstruction, x, xii, 10, 117, 132, 192; and designification, 171; Flaubert's of biblical narrative, 200

Decontextualization, xiii, 86, 92

Delacroix, Eugène, *La Mort de Sardanapale*, 81

De Man, Paul, 35, 37, 41

Demorest, D. L., 141; *L'Expression figurée dans l'oeuvre de Flaubert*, 188

Demotivation, 197; effect of, 200–201; and ellipsis, 200–201

Denis, Ferdinand, *Une Fête bresilienne célébrée à Rouen en 1550*, 158n25

Derivation, 193

Derrida, Jacques, 35, 42–44; *Fors*, 42, 44; *Of Grammatology*, xiii

Descartes, René, 167

Descharmes, René, 140

Descriptive system, 180; enthymemelike, 186; in *Madame Bovary*, 181–82

Desire, 118, 135–36; edge of, 147; end-oriented forces of, 120; male, 134, 137–38n15; versus need, 146; for structure, 168; *texte de désir*, 118–19, 129, 133–34

Despotism, 81, 82; oriental, 77

Details: far-fetched, 198–99; functional, 110; not gratuitous, 161; insignificant, 6, 7; striking, 32; unwritten physical, 108

Difference, xiii, 128, 170, 171–73, 175n16; denial of, 161, 165, 166; graphic, 137n7; and identity, 79; irreducible, 146; from itself, 63; male, 136; mark of, 161–62; reality of, 165; sexual, 163, 164, 167; systematic code of, xiii; unbridgeable, 167

Discourse, 14, 22, 26, 40, 80, 85, 151, 180, 185; direct, xiii, 14–16, 17, 19–20, 21, 24, 26, 71; dramatic form of, 26; free indirect (I′), xiii, 14, 17, 20–22,

Discourse (*continued*)
24–26, 94, 123; grocer's, 152,
153; hierarchy of, 122; of the
"I", 71–72; indirect, 14, 17; irresponsibility of, 93; of knowledge,
124; level of, 152; opining, 86;
Romantic, 22; sublimating, 162;
social, 18, 20–21, 162, 177; urban, 187
Donato, Eugenio, xiii; "The Museum's Furnace" in *Textual
Strategies*, 175n16
Du Camp, Maxime, 6
Duchet, Claude, 177, 179

Eco, Umberto, 80
Ecriture féminine, 132
Education: scriptural, 139–53
Enlightenment: bourgeois, 82;
Flaubert stereotype, 82
Enunciation, 15, 64, 86, 87, 89,
92, 96, 151; obscuring of,
sources of, 15, 26
Essence, 3–4, 101, 129, 148
Ethnocentrism, 142, 143, 144; and
ethnic hierarchy, 148
Evolutionism, 144–45; and juve-
nilia, xiv, 139–41 and passim
Expansion, 195–96; historic, 198;
narrative, 16–17
Extension, 194–95

Fédida, Pierre, "La Relique et le
travail du deuil," *Nouvelle Revue
de psychanalyse*, 176n21
Felman, Shoshana, xii–xiii, 22; *La
Folie et la chose littéraire*, 12n19
Feminism, xiv–xv, xvi n8, 2, 3–4,
11n7, 116, 134; French, 117,

131; Mlle Leroyer de Chantepie's, 190–91n7
Ferenczi, Sandor, 35
Fetishism: Baudrillard on, 162,
166; Freud on, 160–61, 165;
ideological, 166; and language,
165–67; and lyricism, 152; of the
neck, 127; psychoanalytic structure of, 163; of the signifier, 162;
and voyeurism, 130; Winnicott
on, 161. *See also* Allegory
Feydeau, Ernest, 7, 108
Figuration: dis-, 35; origin of
Flaubert's, 32; and representation, 33; and speculation, 34
Fineman, Joel, 170
Flaubert, Caroline, 37, 39, 40
Flaubert, Gustave:
— *Bouvard et Pécuchet*, xiv, 91,
97, 111, 124, 151, 160–76
passim
— *Dictionnaire des idées reçues*,
84–99 passim; 124
— *L'Education sentimentale*, xiv,
82, 92, 97, 105, 108, 111, 161,
189
— *Hérodias*, xiii, 192–201 passim
— *La Légende de Saint Julien
L'hospitalier*, xiii, 46–75 passim,
102
— *Madame Bovary*, xiv, 1–12 pas-
sim, 102, 106, 109, 111, 116–38
passim, 145, 150, 152, 153,
177–91 passim
— *Salammbô*, 31, 77, 81, 111,
198
— *La Tentation de Saint Antoine*,
39, 41, 77, 107, 112, 122, 198;
Trois Contes, xiii, xiv, 13–29
passim, 76–83 passim

—Oeuvres de jeunesse: *L'Educa-tion sentimentale*, first version, 38, 107, 113; *Mémoires d'un fou*, 106, 139; *Novembre*, 104, 139; *Quidquid volueris*, xiv, 139–59 passim; *Rêve d'enfer*, 139
— *Correspondance*, xiv, 31, 37, 57, 69, 87, 100–115 passim; with Amélie Bosquet, 104; with Louis Bouilhet, 103, 107; with Georges Charpentier, 69; with Gustave Charpentier, 102; with Maxime Du Camp, 39, 40; with Jules Duplan, 103; with Léon Henni-que, 111; with Mlle Leroyer de Chantepie, 103, 191n7; with Princesse Mathilde, 105; with Mme Roger des Genettes, 108; with George Sand, 101, 105; with Hippolyte Taine, 108; with Ivan Turgenev, 114n10
Fletcher, Angus, 171
Forgery, 193
Formalism, 101, 109, 126
France, Anatole, 145
Freud, Sigmund, 2, 36, 53, 60, 82, 131–32, 134, 135, 149, 160–61, 165, 167, 171; "Dangers of Fore-Pleasure," 135; *Three Essays on Sexuality*, 131–32

Gaffard, Paul, *Histoire du Brésil français au XVIème siècle*, 158n25
Gaillard, Françoise, xiii
Gallop, Jane, 137–38n15
Gaultier, Jules de, *Le Bovarysme*, 3
Gautier, Théophile, 144
Genette, Gérard, xiii; *Palimpsestes,*

la littérature au second degré, 201
Gide, André, *Les Faux mon-nayeurs*, 102
Goethe, Johann Wolfgang von, *Faust*, 193
Gothot-Mersch, Claudine, 4, 164
Gueuloir, 128, 141

Hals, Frans, 201
Hassan Ihab, x; "Postmodernism," *New Literary History*, xv–xvi n5
Heath, Stephen, 118
Hegel, Georg Wilhelm Friedrich, 31–32, 34, 43–44
Heidegger, Martin, 43
Heine, Heinrich, *Atta Troll*, 197
Historicism, 26; Flaubert's libidi-nal, 78–83
History, 26, 81, 96–97, 198; classi-cal, 78; executive of, 98; literary, ix; the making of, 84–99; medi-tation of, 83; writer's relationship to, 76
Hjelmslev, Louis, 79
Homer, 104
Hors-texte, 104
Hugo, Victor, *Feuilles d'automne*, 40; *Notre-Dame de Paris*, 148
Hypermotivation, 198
Hypertext, xiii, 196; *Hérodias* as, 192; of reference, 197
Hypertextuality, 192, 193, 194; and transformation, 199
Hypotext, xiii, 194, 196, 200; bibli-cal, 197; definition of, 192

Ideologeme, 80, 81
Ideology, xii, xv, 77, 80, 98, 107; *bêtise* as, 96; and fetishism, 166;

Ideology (*continued*)
of form, 83; and nature, 170; and
structures, 162; in transformation, 200
Idiolect, 20, 98; and sociolect, 177
Imaginary, 80; languages of the, 83;
social, 96
Impressionism, 125
Incorporation, 37; definition of, 36;
and introjection, 35, 42
Interpretant, 178
Intertext, 177, 181, 185, 187,
189–90; locus of, 197; of a
norm, 181; and text, 181, 189
Intertextuality, 24, 177; and exchange, 123; and latency, 178;
and presupposition, 184; and reference, 190
Introjection: Abraham and Torok
on, 37, 42; Ferenczi's definition
of, 35–36; and incorporation,
35, 42; and sister's body, 39
Involuntary, 201
Irony, 47, 49, 52, 59, 62–63, 64,
67, 101, 102, 104, 174, 188;
Barthes on, 5; and intertextuality, 181; Romantics and, 150;
tragic, 66
Isotopy, 85, 187
Italics, 181; Duchet on Flaubert's,
179; irresponsible, 18

Jakobson, Roman, 120, 170
James, Henry, 119
Jameson, Fredric, xiii
Jouissance, 121, 130, 135; erotic,
170; and feminine sexuality,
137–38n15; versus *plaisir*, 118,
122; price of, 131; *texte de*,
117–18, 124, 131, 132
Joyce, James, *Ulysses*, 193–94

Kant, Immanuel, 167
Keats, John, 41
Koïné, 97, 98

Lacan, Jacques, 131, 144, 147, 149
La Fontaine, Jean de, *Fables*, 195
Lagache, Daniel, 36
Lamartine, Alphonse de, 134
Langlois, Ernest, 69
Laplanche, Jean, and Pontalis, J.-
B., 36
Larousse, Pierre, *Grand Diction-
naire*, 179, 182, 185
Lautréamont, Comte de (Isidore
Ducasse), 141, 152; *Les Chants
de Maldoror*, 150–51, 153;
Poésies, 151, 153
Legend, 53, 56–57, 58, 62–63;
birth of, 46, 47; etymological
sense of, 65; of exile, 61; generic
category of, 15; of marked skin,
55; of the Other, 56; property of,
67; source of, 69; and Western
mythology, 59
Leibniz, Gottfried Wilhelm von,
167
Lemaître, Jules, 199
Le Poittevin, Alfred, 37, 40–41
Leroi-Gourhan, André, 142–43; *Le
Geste et la parole: Technique et
langage*, 154n4
Leskov, Nikolai Semenovich, 83
Lévi-Strauss, Claude, 27, 82–83
Lewis, Philip, "The Poststructuralist Condition," *Diacritics*, xv n5
Livy, 26
Lubbock, Percy, *The Craft of Fiction*, 1, 3, 4
Lucas, Hippolyte, "La Femme
adultère," *Les Français peints
par eux-mêmes*, 182, 185–86

Lyotard, Jean-François, *La Condition post-moderne*, xvi n5

Mallarmé, Stéphane, 54, 78; "Hérodiade," 26

Mann, Thomas, *Joseph and His Brothers*, 195; *Joseph in Egypt*, 196

Marginal: revaluation of the, xii, xiii, xiv

Marx, Karl, 162

Meaning, xiii, 1, 5, 7, 47, 63, 110, 113–14, 170; absence of, 78, 80, 85; collapse of, 130; and contradiction, 48; of a country, 59; elusion of, 101; excess of, 78; and intentionality, 101; maternal totality of, 167; production of, xiii; quest for, 80; redeeming, 171; versus significance, 189–90; and silence, 50; stable, 77; ultimate, 35; Vergilian, 180

Metaphor, xiv, 42, 54, 55, 62, 169, 183; for artistic creation, 112; bawdy, 107; and displacement, 32; for Emma's degradation, 188; and icon, 77, 97; Jakobson on, 170; and metonymy, 16–17, 171, 186, 190; musical, 45; of pyramid, 30; rustic, 187; and sexual identities, 163; vegetative, 148; of writing, 56

Meta-récits, 9

Metatext, 189

Metatextuality, 193

Metonymy, xiv, 77, 82, 186; *bras* as, 86; and fetishism, 161, 166, 170; *fiacre* and, 187; Gallop on, 137–38n15; and intertextuality, 181; Jakobson on, 170; and met-

aphor, 16–17, 171, 186, 190; and presupposition, 178, 186; and proximity, 172; and seriality, 78

Mimesis, 101–2, 190; against, xii, 103; and fallacy, 111; impossible, 106; theory of, 111–12

Mirror, 146, 156n11; and reproduction, 110; stupid speech as, 96; stage, 149

Modernism, xii, xiii; as *doxa*, 101; Flaubert as prophet of, 103; and postmodernism, x–xi, xiv–xvi n5, 5, 7, 9

Modernity, x, 100; characteristic of, 105; exemplar of, 104; fashionable, 109; Flaubert's, xi, 104, 114n3

Monet, Claude, 131

Montaigne, Michel de, 38, 39

Motivation, 196–98

Mulvey, Laura, 130

Myth, 23, 25, 28, 74n8; of apeman, 142–43; biblical, 59–60, 79, 80; Christian, 27, 46; consummable, 17; of depth, 109; evangelical, 59–61; Greek-Latin, 46, 59, 178–81; of guilt and innocence, 60; as *mythos*, 16; of noble savage, 158–59n25; as sacred utterance, 27

Naming, 6–7, 12n19; and killing, 59–60

Narcissism, 49, 161

Narratability, 130

Naturalism, 5

Neoclassicism, xi, 194, 195

Nietzsche, Friedrich Wilhelm, 68, 76

Nyon, Eugène, "Le Maître d'éco-

Nyon, Eugène (*continued*)
le," *Les Français peints par eux-
mêmes*, 180

Oedipus, 19, 46, 59, 62
Oracle: and ambiguity, 47–48
Orientalism, 80, 82
Other: essence of, 148; Lacan's,
147; legend of the, 56; relation to
the, 143; story of the, 64; text of
the, 177; vehicle for, 23; voice
of, 63, 177. *See also* Alterity;
Otherness
Otherness, 37, 145–50, 153;
Julian's to himself, 55; woman
and, 173

Parody, 12n19, 104, 179; versus
charge, 193; and postmodernism,
x; and representation, 8, 11
Pastiche, 15, 26, 122, 193
Peirce, Charles Sanders, 89
Perrone-Moisés, Leyla, xiii–xiv
Phonetics, 148; and pleasure,
126–29
Plaisir. See Pleasure
Pleasure, xii, 11; versus *jouissance*,
118, 122; question of, 117–36
passim; renewal of interest in,
116; *texte de plaisir*, xiv,
117–20, 124, 126, 129–31,
134–36
Pluralism, xii
Pollock, Jackson, 131
Pontalis, J.-B., 36
Porter, Denis, xiv
Postmodernism, xiii, xiv, 11, 117,
124, 133; Woody Allen and, xiv,
10; Barthes and, 5, 131; code of,
5; as condition, xv–xvi n5, 9; def-

inition of, x–xi, xv–xvi n5;
Flaubert and, xi–xii; and mod-
ernism, x–xi, xv–xvi n5, 5, 7, 9;
or poststructuralism, x
Poststructuralism, x, xv–xvi n5, 116
Premodernism, xi, xii, 7
Presupposition, 84; and adulteress,
183; and entailment, 182;
Flaubert's, 177–90; mechanisms
of, xv; and semiotic process, 186
Production, modes of, 83
Proudhon, Pierre Joseph, 182
Proust, Marcel, 119, 193, 201

Quintilian, *De institutione oratoria*, 180

Racine, Jean Baptiste, 178
Reader, xiv, 18, 24, 44, 104–5,
112, 123, 125, 131, 149, 168,
169, 185; as active, 10, 117, 132;
Barthes on, 9; -centered criticism, 116; and hypotext,
199–200; male, 135; pleasure of,
117–22, 126, 134; and presupposition, 177, 181; responses of,
27, 102–3, 133–34, 163; responsibility of, 196; super- (archi-),
199, 201; uninformed, 200
Reader-response criticism, 10, 116
Realism, 26, 48, 83, 103, 120,
121, 124, 150, 155, 185, 189;
classical, 122, 125; doctrine of,
108; Flaubertian, 81; French,
117; and mimesis, 190; political,
84; versus realism, 7–8
Reality, effect of, 5, 78, 110, 121
Reduction, 194, 198
Referent, 9, 57, 65, 68, 87, 89,
122, 129, 180; absence of, 87;

common, 91; Derrida on, 43; Jakobson on function of, 120; reader as, 10; and realist narrative, 126; and reality, 85, 92, 102; and repetition, 7; status of, xii; as unseemly, 141

Referentiality: non-, 103, 131; textual self-, 109, 112, 135; undermining of, 12 n19

Relic, 173, 176n21; fetish-, 162

Representation, 8, 11, 14, 16, 82, 96, 125, 129, 132; accuracy of, 180; of the adulteress, 181; Barthes on, 137n8; *bêtise* and, 97–98; bias against, 103; classical realist, 122, 130; codes of, 170; crypt and, 42–43; and figuration, 32–33; frame of, 77; impossibility of, 41; and incorporation, 36–37; languages of, 78; modes of, 83; phallocentric, 131; production of, 67; relation of corpse to origin of, 33–35, 40–41; versus reproduction, 105, 109, 111; Ricardou on, 5–9; of sex, 119; sexist, xiv; space between subject and, 32; spatial, 79; sphere of, 176n21; static ideas of, 76; system of, 181; and text, 132; theatrical, 83, 123; and themes, 8; tyranny of, 135; of utterance, 17

Reproduction, 4, 106, 109; doctrine of, 110, 112; and representation, 105, 109, 111

Reticence (aposiopesis), 20, 27, 178, 180

Ricardou, Jean, 5–6, 7, 10, 109; *Nouveaux problèmes du roman,* 5

Riffaterre, Michael, xiv–xv, 11n7

Rimbaud, Arthur, 78

Robbe-Grillet, Alain, 109

Robert, Marthe, *Roman des origines et origines du roman,* 154n3

Roman noir, 151

Romantic(s), 41, 147, 157–58n25, 183; sympathy for primitives, 144; fossilized, 150–53

Romanticism, xi, 31, 141, 145, 150, 153

Rosolato, Guy, 165

Rousseau, Jean-Jacques, 143, 156–57n13; *Discours sur l'inégalité,* 142, 155n6

Said, Edward, 33, 80

Saint-Amant, Marc Antoine Gérard de, *Moses Saved (Moïse sauvé),* 195

Sainte-Beuve, Charles Augustin, 150

Sarcey, Francisque, 199

Sarraute, Nathalie, xi, 5, 88

Sartre, Jean-Paul, xiii, 87, 88, 101, 104, 114n12; *L'Idiot de la famille,* 154n3

Saussure, Ferdinand de, xiii

Schor, Naomi, 2; "Ecriture, parole, et différence dans *Madame Bovary,*" xvi n8, 2

Scott, Walter, *Count Robert of Paris* in *The Waverly Novels,* 155n7, 156n11, 157n16 and n18

Shakespeare, William, 104, 200

Shanks, J. Piaget, 148

Shelley, Percy, 37; *The Triumph of Life,* 35, 41

Signatory, 58, 65, 66; "I" of, 61, 70–72; narrator-, 67

Signature, 44; Flaubert's, 46–73 passim

Signifier: demise of, 173; detached, 130; excess of, 120; extravagance of a, 122; fetishism of, 162, 173; play of, xiv, 126; reflexiveness of, 166

Signifying practices, 79

Silence, 19, 63, 64, 72; and gap, 49–53; guilty, 18, 58; Julian's, 53; production of, 71; spoken, 101; voice in The, 23

Sociolect, 178, 179, 180, 187, 189; and idiolect, 177; Hippolyte Lucas as voice of, 182

Sophocles, *Oedipus Rex*, 194

Speech, 14, 90, 122, 146; -acts, decontextualization of, xiii; direct and indirect, 123; efficacy of, 96; illocutionary force of, 95; organs of, 128–29, 131; poetic and referential function of, 131; production of, 127

Starobinski, Jean, 157n13

Structuralism, ix–x, xii, xv–xvi n5, 116

Subject: absence of, 5; centrality of, 107, 110; denial of, 106; excess of, 107; fixity of, 4; generative power of, 108; illusion of, 111; insignificance of, 101–2; of *Madame Bovary*, 2–3; paradox of, 111; prestige of, 101; and representation, 132; sameness of, 140; status of, xii, 100–114; unifying, 112

Sublation, 32, 34, 36

Suetonius, 26

Summary, 193

Super-reader, 199. *See also* Archireader

Symbol, 26, 42, 53, 63, 77, 96, 121, 169, 170, 188; of firmness, 86; Hegel on, 31–32; and metonymy, 190; phallus as universal, 167; significance of, 187; taken for sign, 25; of union, 161

Tacitus Cornelius, 26

Textuality: Barthes's theory of, 132; problematics of, 101, 109; pure, 113; self-referential, 112

Theme, 14, 79, 133, 193, 196; of adulteress, 181; and criticism, 112; interpretive, 83; versus meaning, 80; and representation, 8

Thibaudet, Albert, 113

Torok, Maria, 36, 37, 41–43; *L'Écorce et le noyau*, 35

Tournier, Michel, *Friday*, 194

Transcriptions, 193–94

Transformation, 192–94; hypertextual, 199; serious, 200

Transmotivation, 197

Transposition, 194

Travesty, 193

Triptych, 77, 78

Unconscious: political, 83

Undecidability, 89, 101, 169; between distance and proximity, 70; production of, xiii; semantic, 132

Utterance: dead, 89; disorder of in *Trois Contes*, 13–25, 28n1; efficaciousness of, xiii, 16; and stupidity, 92

Vergil, 178–80; *Aeneid*, 178

Victorianism, xi, 130

Voice, 25, 27; in feminine texts,

137n10; of God, 24; versus utterance, 15, 16, 19, 23
Voltaire (Jean-Marie Arouet), 194

Warhol, Andy, 9
Weber, Max, 80
Wilde, Oscar, *Salomé*, 197
Window: blindness and, 67; blood
and, 68; as figure of writing,
67–68; Flaubert as instrument
of, 70; as legend, 65–67; referential, 65, 68; silence of, 64; and
tale, 69–70
Wittvogel, Karl, 77
Woman, 141, 148; attribute of,

183; essential seme of, 184; Félicité as, 82; and male gaze, 130,
137n9; presupposition and,
183–84; as other, 148; stereotypical role of, 51; symbolic, 164
Word, 23, 24, 27
Writing, 44, 103, 132; art of, 71;
Barthes on, 5; and corpses, 38;
mediation of, 106; metaphors of,
55–56, 61–62; nonreferential,
131; rhetorical figure of, 167–68;
un-, 198

Zola, Emile, xi, 4; *L'Assommoir*,
105